3 Properties In 8 Months:
Real Estate Made Simple: How anyone can achieve big results fast

By **Cristian Caponi**

Copyright ©

3 Properties In 8 Months: Real Estate Made Simple: How anyone can achieve big results fast By Cristian Caponi Copyright © 2024 by Cristian Caponi All rights reserved.

Published by Cristian Caponi

ISBN: 9798304553063

First Edition: 9/2024

Cover Design by Cristian Caponi

No part of this book may be reproduced, stored in a retrieval system, or transmitted in any form or by any means without the prior written permission of the author and publisher.

Disclaimer: This book contains no financial advice, you must seek a financial advisor.

Dedication

This book is dedicated to my mother, father, and grandmother, whose love, support, and guidance have been the foundation of my success. Their unwavering love and support is what has gotten me to where I am today.

Acknowledgments

I would like to express my gratitude to everyone who has been part of this journey. Special thanks to my lord and saviour Jesus Christ, my family who believed in my vision, and to all the readers investing in themselves by picking up this book. May this book be a testament to your hunger towards achieving anything you desire in life.

Table Of Contents

1. Table Of Contents
2. Introduction
3. **Chapter 1: Getting Started: Why Property Investment? – PG 9 - 25**
    - Introduction to Property Investment
    - The Concept of Below Market Value (BMV)
    - How to Identify BMV Properties
    - The Role of Negotiation in Securing BMV Deals
    - Leveraging Instant Equity for Further Investments
    - Maximising Rental Returns on BMV Properties
    - Risks and Challenges in BMV Property Investment
4. **Chapter 2: Finding Your First Property – PG 26 - 49**
    - Introduction
    - Understanding Your Investment Goals
    - Researching the Property Market
    - Setting Your Investment Criteria
    - Finding Potential Properties
    - Evaluating Property Value
    - Making an Offer and Negotiating
    - Closing the Deal
    - Case Studies and Examples
5. **Chapter 3: Financing Your Investments – PG 50 - 84**
    - Introduction to Financing in Property Investment
    - Understanding Different Loan Types
    - Assessing Your Borrowing Capacity
    - Structuring Your Loans for Property Investment
    - Creative Financing Strategies for Property Investors
    - Understanding Interest Rates and Loan Repayments
    - The Role of Deposit and Loan-to-Value Ratio
    - Navigating the Mortgage Application Process
    - Refinancing Your Property Investments
    - Managing Debt in Property Investment
    - Tax Considerations in Property Financing
    - Case Studies: Financing Strategies That Worked
6. **Chapter 4: My Journey: From 1st to 3rd Property – PG 85 - 103**
    - Introduction: The Start of My Property Investment Journey
    - The First Property: One-Bedroom Unit
    - The Second Property: Another Unit in a Growing Suburb
    - The Third Property: One-Bedroom Villa
    - Key Strategies That Drove My Success
    - Challenges and Lessons Learned
    - Reflections on the Journey So Far
7. **Chapter 5: Understanding the Market – PG 104 - 133**
    - Introduction to Market Dynamics
    - The Basics of Property Market Cycles
    - Supply and Demand in Property Markets

- Economic Indicators and Their Impact on Property Markets
- Government Policies and Their Influence on Property Markets
- Researching Local Property Markets
- Identifying High-Growth Areas
- The Role of Rental Demand in Property Markets
- How Global Events Influence Local Property Markets
- The Role of Real Estate Agents and Market Analysts
- Staying Informed: Tracking Market Trends and Data

8. **Chapter 6: Making Smart Decisions – PG 134 - 159**
    - Introduction to Smart Decision-Making in Property Investment
    - Setting Clear Investment Goals
    - Risk vs. Reward: Understanding the Trade-offs
    - Due Diligence: Thorough Research Before Buying
    - Analysing Cash Flow and Returns
    - Avoiding Emotional Decision-Making
    - Evaluating Multiple Investment Options
    - The Role of Advisors and Experts
    - Long-Term Thinking: Planning for the Future
    - Reviewing and Refining Your Strategy

9. **Chapter 7: Property Management Tips – PG 160 - 178**
    - Introduction: The Importance of Property Management
    - Finding and Retaining Quality Tenants
    - Setting Rent and Managing Payments
    - Maintaining and Repairing Properties
    - Navigating Legal and Regulatory Compliance
    - Financial Management and Record Keeping
    - Enhancing Tenant Satisfaction
    - Property Management Technology

10. **Chapter 8: Scaling Your Portfolio: The 4th Property and Beyond – PG 179 - 203**
    - Introduction: The Shift to a Growth Mindset
    - Financing Multiple Properties: Overcoming the Challenges
    - Diversifying Your Portfolio: Expanding Across Property Types
    - Risk Management as Your Portfolio Grows
    - Streamlining Property Management for Scale
    - Leveraging Market Opportunities
    - Building a Support Network for Continued Growth
    - Scaling Strategies for Long-Term Success
    - Avoiding Common Pitfalls When Scaling

11. **Final Thoughts and Key Takeaways**

Introduction: Unlocking the Path to Property Wealth

At 18 years old, when most of my peers were focused on navigating the challenges of university life or starting their first jobs, I found myself standing in front of my first investment property. The key to that front door represented more than just access to a physical space; it was the key to a future of financial freedom, security, and opportunities that many only dream of. But let me be clear—this journey didn't happen overnight, and it certainly didn't come without its fair share of challenges and hard lessons learned.

When I first became interested in property investment, I was met with a fair amount of scepticism. After all, what does a teenager know about real estate, let alone about building a property portfolio? The truth is, I didn't have all the answers at first. But what I did have was a hunger to learn, a willingness to take calculated risks, and a vision for what could be possible if I played my cards right.

This book is the result of my experiences, both the successes and the mistakes, as I ventured into the world of property investment. I've structured it to serve as a blueprint—a step-by-step guide that I wish I had when I first started. Whether you're young like me or more seasoned in life, my goal is to show you that it's never too early or too late to start building your wealth through real estate.

Why Property?

You might be asking yourself, why property? What makes real estate a reliable avenue for investment, especially in an era where stocks, cryptocurrencies, and other investment vehicles dominate the headlines? The answer is simple: property is tangible. Unlike stocks or digital currencies, real estate is something you can see, touch, and, most importantly, control. It's a long-term investment that, if managed wisely, can provide consistent income, tax benefits, and the potential for significant appreciation.

Property investment isn't just about buying houses or apartments; it's about understanding the market, recognizing opportunities where others see risks, and making informed decisions that align with your financial goals. It's a blend of art and science, intuition and analysis, patience and decisiveness. And the best part? You don't need a degree in finance or a vast amount of capital to get started. What you need is the right knowledge, a solid strategy, and the courage to take that first step.

My Journey: From Novice to Investor

I started with nothing more than a strong desire to change my financial future and the willingness to work hard for it. At the age of 18, I purchased my first property—a small, modest house that many seasoned investors might have overlooked. It wasn't a mansion or a luxury apartment, but it was mine, and it was the beginning of something much bigger.

With each property I acquired, I gained more experience, learned from my mistakes, and fine-tuned my investment strategy. By the time I had my third property, I began to realise that I was onto something powerful. What I had achieved by 19 was no longer just a dream or a personal milestone; it was a replicable process, a blueprint that others could follow.

What You'll Learn in This Book

In **"3 Properties In 8 Months: Real Estate Made Simple: How anyone can achieve big results fast,"** I'll walk you through the entire process of becoming a successful property investor—from understanding why property is a powerful wealth-building tool to the nuts and bolts of finding, financing, and managing your investments. Here's what you can expect to learn:

1. **Getting Started:** Why property investment is a smart choice and how to prepare yourself mentally and financially for this journey.
2. **Finding Your First Property:** Strategies for identifying the right property, evaluating potential deals, and avoiding common pitfalls that new investors face.
3. **Financing Your Investments:** An in-depth look at various financing options, including mortgages, leveraging existing assets, and creative funding strategies.
4. **My Personal Journey:** Insights and lessons from my experience of acquiring and managing three properties, with an inside look at how I'm preparing for my fourth.
5. **Understanding the Market:** How to analyse real estate markets, recognize trends, and make informed decisions that will maximise your returns.
6. **Making Smart Decisions:** Tips for negotiating deals, managing risk, and ensuring your investments remain profitable over time.
7. **Scaling Your Portfolio:** Practical advice on how to grow your property portfolio sustainably, with a focus on long-term wealth creation.

Why I Wrote This Book

I wrote this book because I believe that financial independence through property investment is achievable for anyone willing to put in the effort. You don't need to come from a wealthy family or have insider knowledge to start building your own empire. All you need is a willingness to learn, a strategic approach, and the determination to act on the opportunities that come your way.

As you read through the chapters, you'll find actionable steps, real-world examples, and the mindset shifts necessary to succeed in property investment. This isn't just a book about buying houses—it's a guide to transforming your financial future.

Whether you're just starting out or looking to refine your investment strategy, **"3 Properties In 8 Months"** is designed to equip you with the knowledge and confidence to take control of your financial destiny. So, let's get started on this journey together. Your path to property wealth begins now.

Chapter 1: Getting Started: Why Property Investment?

Introduction:

At the age of 15, while most teenagers were focused on typical adolescent pursuits—hanging out with friends, playing video games, or stressing over school—I found myself captivated by a book that would alter the course of my life: *Rich Dad Poor Dad* by Robert Kiyosaki. It wasn't the usual teenage fare, but something about the book's message resonated deeply with me. The concepts of financial independence, building wealth through smart investments, and understanding the difference between assets and liabilities opened my eyes to a world of possibilities.

Kiyosaki's book introduced me to the idea that financial success wasn't just about earning a high salary. Instead, it was about making money work for you by accumulating assets—particularly real estate. This idea of leveraging investments for wealth creation intrigued me. It was a different way of thinking, one that emphasised strategic decisions and long-term planning over short-term gratification. From that moment on, I was determined to carve out a future in property investment.

Early Influences and the Sydney Property Market

Growing up in Sydney, one of the most expensive real estate markets in the world, the dream of owning property seemed far-fetched for most people, let alone a teenager with limited resources. Sydney's property market is known for its sky-high prices, driven by strong demand, limited supply, and a booming economy. For many young people, the prospect of entering the property market in Sydney felt like an unattainable goal, a distant dream that could only be realised with significant financial backing from family or years of saving.

However, Kiyosaki's lessons taught me something crucial: success in property investment wasn't solely about having vast amounts of capital. It was about strategic thinking, understanding the market, and most importantly, identifying opportunities where others saw barriers. This mindset shift was empowering. It allowed me to see beyond the immediate challenges and focus on what was possible with the right approach.

As I delved deeper into the world of real estate, I realised that Sydney, despite its daunting prices, wasn't the only market worth considering. Australia is a vast country with diverse property markets, each with its own set of dynamics and opportunities. While Sydney was out of reach for someone just starting, there were other markets that offered better affordability and equally strong potential for growth.

The Decision to Pursue Property Investment

After high school, while many of my peers were preparing to head off to university, I decided to take a different path. The conventional route of higher education, though valuable, didn't appeal to me in the same way property investment did. I knew that if I wanted to succeed in this field, I needed practical experience, not just academic knowledge. So, instead of enrolling in university, I secured a job as a sales associate at a local real estate agency.

This job was more than just a source of income; it was an education in itself. Working in the real estate industry provided me with invaluable insights into how the market operated, the intricacies of property transactions, and the art of negotiation. I learned firsthand how to assess property values, understand market trends, and, most importantly, how to identify a good deal. This on-the-ground experience was crucial in building the foundation for my future investments.

But more than anything, my job allowed me to build a network within the industry. I met seasoned investors, real estate agents, property managers, and others who had been in the business for years. These connections proved invaluable, offering advice, mentorship, and sometimes even opportunities that wouldn't have been available to the general public.

First Steps into the Property Market

With my newfound knowledge and experience, I was eager to make my first property investment. However, I quickly realised that Sydney's real estate market, despite my passion and determination, was still beyond my reach. The high entry costs meant that any investment in Sydney would require a significant amount of capital, something I hadn't yet accumulated. But rather than letting this discourage me, I saw it as an opportunity to look elsewhere.

I began researching other property markets across Australia, focusing on areas with high growth potential but lower entry costs. After months of analysis, one market stood out: Perth. At the time, Perth was experiencing a property downturn, with prices significantly lower than those in Sydney. However, the fundamentals were strong—affordable housing, growing population, and a recovering economy. It ticked many of the boxes I was looking for: affordability, potential for growth, and a less competitive market environment.

In July of that year, after months of preparation and saving, I made my first purchase: a one-bedroom unit in Fremantle, a suburb of Perth, for $190,000. The property was an off-market deal—something I had learned to value during my time working in real estate. Off-market properties often come with less competition, allowing for better negotiation on price. The unit itself was a bit of a fixer-upper, but I saw this as an advantage rather than a drawback. With some cosmetic renovations, I could increase its value and rental appeal without spending a fortune.

The process of purchasing my first property was both exhilarating and nerve-wracking. There were moments of doubt—wondering if I was making the right decision, if I was overextending myself financially, or if the Perth market would take longer to recover than I anticipated. But I trusted the research I had done and the lessons I had learned. Today, that property is valued at $280,000 and rents for $410 per week, a testament to the power of making informed, strategic investments.

Building Momentum: The Second and Third Properties

The success of my first property gave me the confidence and, more importantly, the equity to continue investing. Just three months later, I purchased my second property, another one-bedroom unit in Langford, a suburb of Perth, for $250,000. This property was strategically located in a growth area, and I managed to secure it below market value by acting quickly and negotiating effectively. The value of this property also rose rapidly, and it's now valued at $400,000.

By this point, I had established a pattern: identifying properties in undervalued markets, negotiating to purchase them below market value, and making strategic improvements to increase their rental income and overall value. The success of my first two investments allowed me to build equity quickly, which I could then leverage to finance further purchases.

My third purchase came shortly after, a two-bedroom villa near Bassendean, another suburb of Perth. This time, I used the equity from my second property to finance the purchase. The villa cost $300,000 and, like my previous investments, was in an area with strong growth potential. After purchasing the property, I made minor improvements to increase its rental appeal. Today, it's valued at $375,000 and rents for $480 per week.

In just one year, I had gone from owning nothing to building a portfolio of three positively geared properties. This rapid expansion was made possible by focusing on below-market-value (BMV) properties, allowing me to create instant equity and leverage it for further investments. Each purchase was a step toward financial independence, driven by the principles I had learned from Kiyosaki and refined through my own experiences.

The Importance of Strategy in Property Investment

What I've learned through my journey is that property investment isn't just about buying real estate—it's about strategy. Every decision, from choosing the right market to negotiating the purchase price, to making improvements that add value, is part of a larger plan. My strategy from the beginning was clear: find properties below market value, create equity through smart purchases and improvements, and leverage that equity to continue growing my portfolio.

But beyond the financial gains, there's something deeply satisfying about the process itself. There's a thrill in finding a property with untapped potential, in negotiating a deal that benefits both parties, and in seeing a once-overlooked property transformed into a valuable asset. It's not just about the money—it's about creating something tangible and lasting.

Looking Ahead

As I reflect on my journey so far, I'm excited about what the future holds. My goal isn't just to accumulate wealth for myself, but to share what I've learned with others. I've already started running seminars and workshops for young investors, helping them understand the principles of property investment and how to apply them in today's market. I'm also preparing to start work as a buyer's agent, sourcing properties for others and helping them achieve their own financial goals.

The road ahead will undoubtedly have its challenges, but I'm confident in the path I've chosen. With each property I purchase, I'm building not just my portfolio, but my future—and the future of those I help along the way. The journey into property investment has been incredibly rewarding, and I'm excited to see where it leads next.

The Concept of Below Market Value (BMV) in Property Investment

In the world of property investment, understanding the concept of Below Market Value (BMV) is crucial for anyone looking to maximise their returns and build a successful portfolio. At its core, BMV refers to purchasing a property for less than its current market value. This might sound simple, but the ability to identify and secure BMV properties is a skill that can significantly enhance your investment strategy.

What Does BMV Mean in Property Investment?

BMV in property investment is when a property is bought at a price lower than its appraised or current market value. The market value of a property is typically determined by factors such as location, property condition, comparable sales in the area, and the overall demand in the housing market. However, various situations can lead to a property being sold at a price below its market value.

For example, a homeowner might need to sell quickly due to financial difficulties, a divorce, or relocation for work, and thus may be willing to accept a lower offer to expedite the sale. Alternatively, a property might be listed below market value because it requires renovation or is part of an off-market deal where fewer potential buyers are aware of its availability.

The key to BMV investing lies in being able to recognize these opportunities and act swiftly. For investors, buying BMV properties means you're immediately walking into a deal with built-in equity, setting a strong foundation for future financial gains.

The Benefits of Buying Below Market Value

The advantages of purchasing properties below market value are numerous, making it a highly attractive strategy for both new and seasoned investors. Here are some of the key benefits:

1. **Instant Equity:** One of the most significant advantages of buying BMV is the immediate equity you gain upon purchase. Equity is the difference between the market value of the property and the outstanding mortgage or the price paid. When you purchase a property for less than its market value, you effectively create instant equity. This equity can then be leveraged for various purposes, such as refinancing to extract cash, funding further property purchases, or simply bolstering your financial security.
For example, if you purchase a property valued at $300,000 for $250,000, you've instantly gained $50,000 in equity. This equity not only increases your net worth but also provides a cushion that can protect against market fluctuations. Even if the property's value dips slightly, you're still in a positive equity position, which reduces your financial risk.
2. **Reduced Risk:** Buying BMV properties inherently lowers your investment risk. When you acquire a property at a lower price, you have a larger margin of safety. This means that even if the market experiences a downturn, your investment is better insulated against potential losses. The lower purchase price also means that your mortgage and other associated costs are reduced, further decreasing the financial burden.
Moreover, properties bought below market value tend to have a higher rental yield relative to their purchase price, making them more resilient during economic downturns. The combination of lower upfront costs and higher potential returns makes BMV properties a safer investment, especially in volatile markets.
3. **Enhanced Returns:** The potential for enhanced returns is another compelling reason to pursue BMV properties. Since you're buying at a discount, the property's value only needs to rise to its actual market value for you to realise a profit. Any appreciation beyond that point represents pure gain. This can significantly boost your return on investment (ROI), particularly if you choose to sell the property in the future or use it as collateral for further investments.

Additionally, the higher rental yields typically associated with BMV properties contribute to a stronger cash flow. This positive cash flow can then be reinvested into other properties or used to pay down debt more quickly, accelerating your path to financial independence.

Case Study: A BMV Property Purchase and Its Impact on My Portfolio

To illustrate the power of BMV investing, let's delve into a real-life example from my own experience.

A few years ago, I came across a one-bedroom unit in Fremantle, Perth, that was listed for $190,000. After conducting thorough research, I determined that similar properties in the area were valued at around $240,000. The unit was being sold off-market by an owner who needed to liquidate their assets quickly due to personal circumstances. Recognizing this as a prime BMV opportunity, I moved swiftly to secure the property.

The property required some cosmetic renovations, but nothing that would break the bank. I invested a modest amount in improving the unit, focusing on enhancing its appeal to potential tenants. The renovations included updating the kitchen, repainting the walls, and installing new flooring. These improvements increased the property's rental appeal and allowed me to command a higher rent.

Immediately upon purchase, I had gained $50,000 in equity, purely based on the difference between the purchase price and the property's market value. This instant equity played a crucial role in my next steps as a property investor. A few months later, I was able to refinance the property, tapping into the equity to fund the deposit for my next investment—a second unit in Langford, Perth.

The Langford property followed a similar pattern. I purchased it for $250,000 in an area where comparable properties were selling for around $300,000. Once again, I focused on making targeted improvements that would enhance its value. This second BMV purchase allowed me to build equity quickly, which I then leveraged to acquire a third property.

The impact of these BMV purchases on my portfolio was profound. By consistently buying below market value, I was able to expand my portfolio rapidly while minimising financial risk. Each new purchase generated positive cash flow, which further fueled my investment strategy. In less than a year, I had built a portfolio of three properties, each contributing to my overall financial growth.

How to Identify BMV Properties

Identifying Below Market Value (BMV) properties is a critical skill for any successful property investor. The ability to source these deals can significantly enhance your returns, reduce investment risks, and accelerate portfolio growth. However, finding BMV properties requires a strategic approach, careful evaluation, and a keen understanding of the market. This section explores effective strategies for sourcing BMV deals, how to evaluate a property's true market value versus its asking price, and a step-by-step guide to identifying a BMV property.

Strategies for Sourcing BMV Deals

To identify BMV properties, investors need to explore various avenues. Here are some of the most effective strategies:

1. **Auctions:** Property auctions are a popular hunting ground for BMV deals. Properties sold at auction are often priced lower due to various circumstances, such as repossessions, estate sales, or properties that have failed to sell through traditional methods. Buyers at auctions have the opportunity to purchase properties quickly and, often, below their market value. However, auctions can be competitive, so it's crucial to do your homework and set a strict budget before bidding.
2. **Distressed Sellers:** Properties owned by distressed sellers are another excellent source of BMV deals. Distressed sellers may need to sell their property quickly due to financial difficulties, divorce, relocation, or other pressing life circumstances. These sellers are often more motivated to accept a lower offer to secure a quick sale. Building relationships with real estate agents, who can alert you to these opportunities, is key to sourcing these deals.
3. **Off-Market Opportunities:** Off-market properties are those not publicly advertised for sale, making them a prime opportunity for BMV purchases. These properties might be sold directly by the owner or through discrete channels, such as real estate agents or property sourcing specialists. Off-market deals can often be negotiated more favourably because there is less competition. Networking with local real estate professionals, attending property networking events, and even direct marketing to homeowners can help uncover off-market opportunities.
4. **Property Networks and Wholesalers:** Being part of property investment networks or working with wholesalers can also lead to BMV deals. These professionals often have access to properties before they hit the open market or have direct connections with sellers who are looking to sell quickly. Building relationships within these networks can provide a steady stream of potential BMV properties.

Evaluating a Property's True Market Value vs. Its Asking Price

Once you've identified a potential BMV property, the next step is to evaluate its true market value. Understanding the difference between a property's market value and its asking price is essential to determining whether a deal truly represents BMV.

1. **Comparable Sales (Comps):** The first step in evaluating a property's market value is to look at comparable sales, or "comps," in the area. Comps are recently sold properties that are similar in size, location, and condition to the property you're interested in. By comparing the sale prices of these properties, you can get an accurate estimate of the market value of the property you're considering.
2. **Condition of the Property:** Assessing the condition of the property is also crucial. A property may be priced below market value because it requires significant repairs or renovations. While this can still represent a good deal, you must factor in the cost of these repairs when evaluating the property's true value. In some cases, the cost of repairs can turn a seemingly BMV property into an overvalued one.
3. **Local Market Trends:** Understanding local market trends is another critical aspect of evaluating a property's value. Are property prices in the area rising or falling? What is the demand for rental properties? Local market trends can influence whether a property is truly BMV or if the asking price simply reflects the current market conditions.
4. **Professional Valuation:** Finally, consider getting a professional valuation. A professional valuer will provide a detailed report on the property's market value, taking into account factors such as location, condition, and market trends. This valuation can serve as a solid benchmark for determining whether the asking price is below market value.

Example: Step-by-Step Process of Identifying a BMV Property

Let's walk through a step-by-step example of identifying a BMV property:

1. **Research and Identify Potential Deals:** Start by researching various sources for potential BMV deals. This might involve browsing auction listings, speaking with real estate agents about distressed sellers, or networking to find off-market opportunities.
2. **Conduct Preliminary Analysis:** Once you've identified a potential property, conduct a preliminary analysis. Look at comps in the area to get a rough estimate of the property's market value. Check the property's asking price and compare it to the comps to see if it's priced below market value.
3. **Visit the Property:** Arrange a visit to the property to assess its condition. Take note of any repairs or renovations that may be needed and estimate the costs involved. This step is crucial in determining the true value of the property.
4. **Evaluate Local Market Conditions:** Analyse local market conditions to understand the potential for future appreciation. If the area is experiencing growth or has upcoming infrastructure projects, this could increase the property's value over time.
5. **Negotiate and Make an Offer:** If the property meets your criteria and is priced below market value, start the negotiation process. Use your research and valuation as leverage to secure the property at the best possible price.
6. **Finalise the Purchase:** Once your offer is accepted, complete the necessary legal and financial steps to finalise the purchase. At this point, you'll have secured a BMV property, adding instant equity to your portfolio.

Figures: Comparison of a Property's Market Value vs. Purchase Price in Different Scenarios

Let's consider two scenarios to highlight the impact of BMV:

Scenario 1:

- Market Value: $300,000
- Purchase Price: $270,000
- Immediate Equity: $30,000

Scenario 2:

- Market Value: $300,000
- Purchase Price: $240,000 (due to seller distress)
- Immediate Equity: $60,000

In Scenario 1, you've secured the property 10% below market value, giving you $30,000 in instant equity. In Scenario 2, thanks to a distressed seller, you bought the property at 20% below market value, gaining $60,000 in equity. This additional equity can be leveraged for further investments, showcasing the significant advantage of BMV investing.

The Role of Negotiation in Securing BMV Deals

Negotiation plays a pivotal role in securing Below Market Value (BMV) property deals. It's not just about haggling over price; effective negotiation requires understanding the seller's motivations, building rapport, and employing strategic tactics to arrive at a deal that benefits both parties. Whether you're dealing with distressed sellers, navigating market conditions, or simply trying to get the best possible price, mastering the art of negotiation can significantly enhance your ability to acquire BMV properties.

The Art of Negotiation: How to Negotiate with Sellers to Achieve BMV Deals

Negotiation is as much about psychology as it is about numbers. To negotiate successfully, you must first approach the process with the right mindset. Here are some key principles that can help you negotiate BMV deals effectively:

1. **Preparation is Key:** Before entering into any negotiation, it's crucial to be well-prepared. This means having a thorough understanding of the property's market value, the local real estate market conditions, and the seller's circumstances. The more information you have, the better equipped you will be to make a persuasive case for a lower price. Preparation also includes knowing your limits—decide beforehand the maximum price you are willing to pay and stick to it.
2. **Build Rapport:** Building a positive relationship with the seller can make a significant difference in negotiations. Sellers are more likely to agree to a lower price if they feel they are dealing with someone trustworthy and sincere. Take the time to understand their situation, show empathy, and communicate openly. This rapport can lead to a more amicable negotiation process and better outcomes for both parties.
3. **Start with a Low Offer:** In negotiations, the first offer often sets the tone for the rest of the discussion. Starting with a low offer gives you room to manoeuvre and increases the likelihood of securing a BMV deal. However, your initial offer should be justifiable—back it up with facts, such as comparable property prices, the condition of the property, or recent market trends. This approach can help you anchor the negotiation at a lower price point.
4. **Be Willing to Walk Away:** One of the most powerful tools in negotiation is the ability to walk away. If the seller is unwilling to meet your terms, be prepared to leave the table. This doesn't mean you should be inflexible, but rather that you should not be afraid to reject a deal that doesn't meet your criteria. Often, the willingness to walk away can prompt the seller to reconsider and come back with a more favourable offer.
5. **Use Time to Your Advantage:** Time can be a critical factor in negotiations. If the seller is under pressure to sell quickly, you might be able to secure a lower price by drawing out the negotiation process. Conversely, if you are in a hurry to close the deal, the seller might sense your urgency and hold out for a higher price. Understanding the timing of both parties allows you to strategize effectively and use time as leverage.

Understanding Seller Motivations: Distress, Quick Sales, and Market Conditions

Understanding the motivations behind a seller's decision to sell is crucial in any negotiation. Sellers may have various reasons for wanting to offload a property, and tapping into these motivations can help you secure a better deal. Here are some common seller motivations:

1. **Distress:** Sellers who are in financial distress are often the most motivated to sell quickly, even at a lower price. This might be due to job loss, debt, or other financial difficulties. These sellers are more likely to accept a BMV offer if it means they can resolve their financial issues swiftly. As a buyer, showing empathy and offering a solution that meets their needs can help you secure the deal at a favourable price.
2. **Quick Sales:** Some sellers need to sell quickly due to circumstances such as relocation, divorce, or the need to settle an estate. These sellers may prioritise speed over getting the highest possible price. In such cases, a quick and hassle-free transaction can be more appealing than a prolonged negotiation. Offering a fast closing process can be a powerful negotiating tool.
3. **Market Conditions:** Market conditions can also influence seller motivations. In a buyer's market, where there are more properties for sale than buyers, sellers may be more inclined to accept lower offers to ensure a sale. Conversely, in a seller's market, where demand exceeds supply, sellers may hold out for higher prices. Understanding the current market conditions allows you to tailor your negotiation strategy accordingly.

Example: Successful Negotiation Tactics That Led to a BMV Acquisition

Let's consider a real-life example of a successful negotiation that led to a BMV acquisition:

I once identified a property in Perth that was listed at $320,000, but through my research, I estimated its market value to be closer to $300,000. The property had been on the market for several months with no offers, signalling a motivated seller. During the initial viewing, I learned from the real estate agent that the seller was relocating overseas and needed to sell quickly.

With this information, I started my negotiation with an offer of $270,000, explaining that my offer was based on the property's condition and comparable sales in the area. The seller countered with $300,000. I reiterated my initial concerns, highlighted the long time the property had been on the market, and offered to close the deal within two weeks if we could agree on $280,000.

The seller was initially hesitant but agreed after I emphasised the certainty of a quick sale. By understanding the seller's urgency and negotiating accordingly, I was able to secure the property for $280,000—$40,000 below the asking price and $20,000 below its market value.

Figures: A Breakdown of Negotiation Strategies and Their Impact on Price

To illustrate the impact of negotiation strategies on price, consider the following scenarios:

Scenario 1:

- Asking Price: $350,000
- Initial Offer: $310,000 (low-ball offer)
- Final Purchase Price: $325,000
- Savings: $25,000

Scenario 2:

- Asking Price: $400,000
- Initial Offer: $360,000 (justified with comps)

- Final Purchase Price: $370,000
- Savings: $30,000

Scenario 3:

- Asking Price: $300,000
- Initial Offer: $270,000 (emphasising quick sale)
- Final Purchase Price: $280,000
- Savings: $20,000

In each scenario, different negotiation tactics led to significant savings. Starting with a low offer anchored the negotiation at a lower price, while understanding the seller's motivation allowed for additional leverage in achieving a BMV deal.

Leveraging Instant Equity for Further Investments

One of the most powerful advantages of investing in Below Market Value (BMV) properties is the potential to create and leverage instant equity. Instant equity not only boosts your financial position but also serves as a springboard for further property investments. Understanding how to effectively utilise this equity can significantly accelerate your property portfolio growth. This section explores how instant equity can be harnessed to finance additional property purchases, the concept of refinancing to pull out equity, and provides a case study to illustrate these principles in action.

How Instant Equity Can Be Used to Finance Additional Property Purchases

Instant equity refers to the difference between a property's market value and its purchase price at the time of acquisition. For example, if you buy a property valued at $300,000 for $250,000, you create $50,000 in instant equity. This equity can be strategically used to finance further investments, enhancing your portfolio's growth and increasing your overall wealth. Here's how you can leverage instant equity for additional property purchases:

1. **Reinvestment into New Properties:** The most direct way to use instant equity is by reinvesting it into additional property purchases. By utilising the equity gained from one property, you can potentially fund a deposit or even the full purchase price of a new property. This approach allows you to continuously expand your portfolio without needing substantial new capital.
2. **Building a Portfolio with Minimal Cash:** Leveraging instant equity means you can grow your property portfolio with minimal out-of-pocket expenses. By recycling equity from one investment into another, you effectively use your existing assets to fund new acquisitions. This strategy maximises the return on your initial investments and accelerates portfolio growth.
3. **Improving Cash Flow and Diversifying Investments:** Using equity to acquire additional properties can also improve your cash flow. For example, if your new property generates rental income, this can offset the costs associated with holding multiple properties. Additionally, diversifying your investments across different property types or locations can reduce risk and enhance overall returns.

The Concept of Refinancing: Pulling Out Equity to Fund New Deals

Refinancing is a key strategy for accessing the equity in your property to finance new investments. It involves taking out a new mortgage or restructured loan against a property to release some of the accumulated equity. Here's how refinancing works and how it can be used effectively:

1. **Understanding Refinancing:** Refinancing involves replacing your existing mortgage with a new one, typically with better terms or a larger loan amount. The new mortgage allows you to pull out some of the equity that has built up in the property. For example, if your property's value has increased due to market appreciation or improvements, refinancing enables you to access the increased value.
2. **Steps to Refinance:**
   - **Assess Property Value:** Determine the current market value of your property through a professional appraisal or comparative market analysis.
   - **Calculate Available Equity:** Subtract the remaining mortgage balance from the property's current value to calculate the available equity.
   - **Choose a Lender and Loan Type:** Shop around for lenders offering competitive refinancing rates and terms. Decide whether you want a cash-out refinance (which provides cash for equity) or a rate-and-term refinance (which adjusts your interest rate and loan term without pulling out equity).
   - **Submit an Application:** Provide the necessary documentation to your lender, including details about the property, current mortgage, and your financial situation.
   - **Close the New Loan:** Once approved, close the new mortgage, and the equity is released either as cash or as a reduced loan balance.
3. **Using Refinanced Funds:** Once you've accessed the equity, you can use the funds to finance new property purchases. This could involve covering a deposit, funding a purchase outright, or investing in property renovations to increase its value. The key is to ensure that the new investment offers sufficient returns to justify the refinancing costs and maintain positive cash flow.

Example: Case Study Showing How Equity from One BMV Deal Financed Subsequent Purchases

Let's explore a case study demonstrating how equity from a BMV property can finance further investments:

Initial Purchase:

- **Property A (First BMV Deal):** Purchased for $200,000, valued at $250,000 at the time of purchase.
- **Instant Equity Created:** $50,000

Step 1: Refinancing Property A

- **New Market Value:** $260,000 (after improvements and market appreciation)
- **Outstanding Mortgage Balance:** $180,000
- **Available Equity:** $260,000 - $180,000 = $80,000
- **Refinanced Loan Amount:** $200,000 (new mortgage with a $20,000 cash-out)

- **Cash-Out Funds:** $20,000

Step 2: Purchase of Property B

- **Property B (Second Purchase):** Found a new BMV opportunity for $220,000, market value $270,000
- **Deposit Needed:** $22,000 (10% of purchase price)
- **Funds from Refinancing Property A:** $20,000 used for deposit
- **Additional Funds Needed:** $2,000 (covered from personal savings)

Step 3: Refinancing Property B

- **New Market Value:** $280,000 (after a few months of holding and market increase)
- **Outstanding Mortgage Balance:** $200,000
- **Available Equity:** $280,000 - $200,000 = $80,000
- **Refinanced Loan Amount:** $230,000 (new mortgage with a $30,000 cash-out)
- **Cash-Out Funds:** $30,000

Step 4: Purchase of Property C

- **Property C (Third Purchase):** Purchased for $250,000, market value $300,000
- **Deposit Needed:** $25,000 (10% of purchase price)
- **Funds from Refinancing Property B:** $30,000 used for deposit

By leveraging the instant equity from Property A and Property B, you were able to purchase Properties B and C without significant new capital outlay. This approach not only accelerated the growth of your portfolio but also maximised the returns from your initial investments.

Figures: Flowchart of Using Instant Equity to Build a Property Portfolio

Here's a simplified flowchart illustrating the process of using instant equity to build a property portfolio:

1. **Purchase Property A**
    - **Purchase Price:** $200,000
    - **Market Value:** $250,000
    - **Instant Equity Created:** $50,000
2. **Refinance Property A**
    - **New Market Value:** $260,000
    - **Available Equity:** $80,000
    - **Cash-Out Funds:** $20,000
3. **Purchase Property B**
    - **Purchase Price:** $220,000
    - **Deposit Needed:** $22,000
    - **Funds from Refinancing Property A:** $20,000
    - **Additional Funds Needed:** $2,000
4. **Refinance Property B**
    - **New Market Value:** $280,000
    - **Available Equity:** $80,000

        - **Cash-Out Funds:** $30,000
5. **Purchase Property C**
    - **Purchase Price:** $250,000
    - **Deposit Needed:** $25,000
    - **Funds from Refinancing Property B:** $30,000

Maximising Rental Returns on BMV Properties

Securing a Below Market Value (BMV) property is a smart move for building equity, but ensuring these properties also provide strong rental yields is crucial for maximising your investment returns. Effective strategies for enhancing rental income involve both careful property selection and targeted renovations. This section explores how to ensure BMV properties deliver strong rental yields, the role of renovations and upgrades in boosting rental income, and provides a case study to illustrate these principles in action.

How to Ensure BMV Properties Also Offer Strong Rental Yields

When investing in BMV properties, it's essential to focus on rental yields to ensure the property generates positive cash flow. Here are key strategies for maximising rental returns:

1. **Choose High-Demand Areas:** Selecting properties in high-demand rental markets is foundational to securing strong rental yields. Look for locations with low vacancy rates, growing populations, and strong employment opportunities. Properties near amenities such as public transportation, schools, and shopping centres often attract higher rents and more reliable tenants.
2. **Analyse Rental Demand:** Conduct thorough market research to understand rental demand in the area. This includes reviewing local rental listings, vacancy rates, and average rental prices. Properties in areas with increasing rental demand are more likely to achieve higher rental yields. Pay attention to trends such as new infrastructure projects or major employers moving into the area, as these can drive up rental demand.
3. **Target Properties with Potential for Rent Increases:** Identify properties where you can add value through renovations or upgrades. Such improvements can justify higher rental rates and attract more tenants. Features like modern kitchens, updated bathrooms, and energy-efficient appliances can make a property more appealing and allow you to command a premium rent.
4. **Set Competitive Rent Prices:** Ensure your rental pricing is competitive within the local market. Overpricing can lead to prolonged vacancies, while underpricing may reduce potential returns. Use comparable rental properties as a benchmark to set your rent at a level that maximises returns while remaining attractive to potential tenants.
5. **Professional Property Management:** Consider hiring a property management company to handle tenant screening, rent collection, and maintenance. A professional management team can help ensure that your property is well-maintained, reduce vacancy rates, and handle tenant issues efficiently, contributing to stable rental income.

Renovations and Upgrades: Enhancing Value and Rental Income

Renovations and upgrades are key to increasing both the value and rental income of BMV properties. Here's how to approach this:

1. **Prioritise High-Impact Upgrades:** Focus on renovations that offer the highest return on investment. Kitchen and bathroom upgrades are often the most impactful, as they significantly enhance the property's appeal and functionality. Modernising these areas can attract higher rents and increase the property's overall value.
2. **Enhance Curb Appeal:** The exterior of the property creates the first impression, so investing in curb appeal can make a significant difference. Simple improvements such as landscaping, painting, and repairing any visible issues can enhance the property's attractiveness and justify higher rental rates.
3. **Improve Energy Efficiency:** Upgrades that improve energy efficiency, such as installing new windows, insulation, or energy-efficient appliances, can reduce utility costs for tenants and make the property more appealing. Energy-efficient properties are often in high demand, and tenants are willing to pay a premium for lower ongoing expenses.
4. **Add Modern Amenities:** Incorporating modern amenities such as high-speed internet connections, smart home technology, or in-unit laundry can enhance the property's rental appeal. These features often attract higher rents and can make your property stand out in a competitive rental market.
5. **Regular Maintenance:** Keeping the property in good condition through regular maintenance is essential for maintaining rental income. Address minor repairs promptly and perform routine inspections to ensure the property remains attractive to tenants and operates efficiently.

Example: Case Study of a BMV Property Transformed into a High-Yield Rental

To illustrate the impact of strategic renovations on rental yields, consider the following case study:

Initial Purchase:

- **Property:** A one-bedroom apartment in a high-demand suburb purchased for $180,000, valued at $230,000.
- **Initial Rental Income:** $300 per week.
- **Initial Rental Yield:** (Weekly Rent x 52) / Purchase Price = ($300 x 52) / $180,000 = 0.087 or 8.7%

Renovations and Upgrades:

1. **Kitchen Renovation:** Replaced outdated appliances, installed new countertops, and added modern cabinetry.
2. **Bathroom Upgrade:** Updated fixtures, re-tiled the floor, and installed a new vanity.
3. **Curb Appeal:** Painted the exterior, added new landscaping, and repaired visible damage.
4. **Energy Efficiency:** Installed new double-glazed windows and energy-efficient lighting.

Post-Renovation Results:

- **Updated Rental Income:** $400 per week.
- **Updated Rental Yield:** (Weekly Rent x 52) / Purchase Price = ($400 x 52) / $180,000 = 0.117 or 11.7%
- **Value After Renovations:** $250,000 (increased due to improvements).

Figures: Rental Yield Calculations Before and After Upgrades

Before Renovations:

- **Purchase Price:** $180,000
- **Weekly Rent:** $300
- **Annual Rental Income:** $15,600
- **Rental Yield:** (Annual Rental Income / Purchase Price) x 100 = ($15,600 / $180,000) x 100 = 8.7%

After Renovations:

- **Purchase Price:** $180,000 (unchanged)
- **Weekly Rent:** $400
- **Annual Rental Income:** $20,800
- **Rental Yield:** (Annual Rental Income / Purchase Price) x 100 = ($20,800 / $180,000) x 100 = 11.7%

The renovations not only increased the property's market value but also significantly improved the rental yield. By investing in high-impact upgrades, the property's rental income increased by $100 per week, and the rental yield rose by 3 percentage points. This demonstrates how strategic renovations can enhance both rental income and overall investment returns.

Risks and Challenges in BMV Property Investment

Investing in Below Market Value (BMV) properties can be a lucrative strategy for building wealth and expanding your property portfolio. However, like any investment, it comes with its own set of risks and challenges. Understanding these potential pitfalls and implementing strategies to mitigate them is crucial for protecting your investment and ensuring long-term success. This section explores common risks associated with BMV property investments, how to manage these risks, and provides a real-world example of a challenging BMV deal, along with lessons learned.

Potential Pitfalls of BMV Deals

1. **Hidden Costs:** One of the significant risks in BMV property investment is encountering hidden costs that were not apparent at the time of purchase. These can include unforeseen repairs, maintenance issues, or additional expenses related to property management. For instance, a seemingly great deal on a BMV property may come with structural problems or outdated systems that require costly upgrades. Additionally, properties purchased below market value might have legal or compliance issues that could lead to expensive resolutions.
2. **Overestimating Value:** It's essential to accurately assess a property's value before purchasing, but there is a risk of overestimating its potential. Investors may rely on optimistic appraisals or market projections that do not materialise. Overestimating the value of a property can lead to misguided investment decisions, such as paying too much for renovations or miscalculating potential rental yields. This misjudgment can impact the overall profitability of the investment and create financial strain.
3. **Market Fluctuations:** The property market is inherently volatile, and fluctuations can significantly affect the value of BMV properties. Economic downturns, changes in interest rates, or shifts in local market conditions can reduce property values and rental income

potential. Investing in BMV properties in rapidly changing markets can expose investors to higher risks, especially if the market trends shift unfavourably after the purchase.

How to Mitigate Risks and Protect Your Investment

1. **Conduct Thorough Due Diligence:** Perform comprehensive research before purchasing a BMV property. This includes obtaining a professional property inspection to identify potential issues and assessing the local property market to understand trends and values. Due diligence helps uncover hidden costs and ensures that you make informed decisions based on accurate information.
2. **Budget for Contingencies:** Allocate a contingency fund in your budget to cover unexpected costs. Having a reserve fund helps you manage unforeseen expenses such as repairs, maintenance, or legal issues without jeopardising your investment. Aim to set aside a percentage of the property's purchase price as a buffer for potential surprises.
3. **Accurate Valuation and Appraisal:** Engage a reputable property appraiser to get an accurate valuation of the property. Ensure that the appraisal takes into account the property's current condition and potential for future value appreciation. Cross-check the appraised value with comparable properties in the area to avoid overestimating the property's worth.
4. **Market Research and Analysis:** Stay informed about the local property market and economic conditions. Monitor market trends, interest rates, and local developments that could impact property values and rental demand. Understanding the market dynamics helps you make strategic decisions and mitigate risks associated with market fluctuations.
5. **Legal and Compliance Checks:** Verify that the property complies with local regulations and zoning laws. Conduct a title search to ensure there are no legal encumbrances or disputes associated with the property. Consulting with a legal professional can help you navigate any potential legal issues and ensure that your investment is protected.

Example: A BMV Deal That Didn't Go as Planned and Lessons Learned

Case Study: Property Purchase in a Declining Market

Initial Purchase:

- **Property:** A two-bedroom house purchased for $250,000, valued at $300,000.
- **Renovation Budget:** $30,000
- **Expected Rental Income:** $450 per week
- **Initial Analysis:** Market data indicated a rising trend in property values, and the property seemed to offer a significant discount.

Challenges Faced:

1. **Unexpected Renovation Costs:** During renovations, significant structural issues were discovered that were not identified in the initial inspection. The cost of repairs escalated to $60,000, far exceeding the initial budget. These unexpected expenses strained the investment and delayed the project completion.
2. **Market Decline:** Shortly after purchasing the property, the local property market experienced a downturn due to economic conditions and an oversupply of new developments. Property values fell, and rental demand weakened, leading to lower rental income than anticipated.

3. **Overestimated Rental Income:** The rental market did not support the projected rental income, and the actual rent achieved was $400 per week, below expectations. This reduction in rental income impacted the property's cash flow and profitability.

Lessons Learned:

1. **Importance of a Detailed Inspection:** Ensure that property inspections are thorough and include structural assessments to avoid surprises during renovations. Engaging specialised inspectors for critical areas can help uncover potential issues before purchase.
2. **Realistic Market Projections:** Rely on conservative market projections and consider potential market fluctuations in your investment analysis. Avoid overly optimistic assumptions and base decisions on a range of possible outcomes.
3. **Flexible Budgeting:** Allocate a larger contingency fund for renovations and unexpected costs. A flexible budget allows you to handle unforeseen issues without compromising the investment's viability.
4. **Monitoring Market Trends:** Regularly review market conditions and adjust your investment strategy as needed. Stay informed about economic indicators and local developments that could impact property values and rental demand.

Final Thoughts on the Long-Term Benefits of BMV Property Investment

Despite the risks and challenges associated with BMV property investment, the long-term benefits can be substantial. Successful BMV investments offer significant equity gains, strong rental yields, and the potential for portfolio expansion. By understanding and managing risks, conducting thorough due diligence, and applying effective strategies, investors can maximise the advantages of BMV deals and build a successful property portfolio.

While not without its pitfalls, the strategy of investing in BMV properties remains a powerful tool for wealth creation when approached with careful planning and risk management. The lessons learned from challenging deals contribute to a more informed and resilient investment approach, ultimately enhancing the potential for long-term success in the property market.

Chapter 2: Finding Your First Property

Introduction:

Finding your first property is a significant milestone in your property investment journey. It's more than just a transaction; it's the foundation upon which you'll build your future investments and financial success. The right first property can set you on a path to achieving your investment goals, while a poor choice can lead to missed opportunities and financial strain. Understanding the importance of selecting the right property and the steps involved in the process is crucial for any aspiring investor.

Importance of Finding the Right First Property

Setting the Foundation for Your Property Investment Journey: Your first property is not just the beginning of your investment portfolio; it's the cornerstone of your entire investment strategy. Choosing the right property can provide you with the initial capital and experience needed to expand your portfolio and achieve long-term financial goals. This first purchase often serves as a learning experience that will guide your future decisions, helping you understand the market, property values, and investment dynamics.

A well-chosen property can offer immediate benefits such as positive cash flow, which allows you to reinvest in additional properties. It can also provide the potential for capital growth, increasing the value of your investment over time. Conversely, a poor choice may lead to financial difficulties and hinder your ability to invest further. Therefore, taking the time to carefully select your first property is essential for setting a strong foundation for future success.

How the First Property Impacts Your Future Investments: The impact of your first property extends beyond its immediate financial performance. It influences your ability to secure financing for future investments, build equity, and achieve your broader investment objectives. For example, a successful first property investment can help you build a strong credit history, demonstrate your capability as an investor, and enhance your reputation with lenders and real estate professionals.

Furthermore, the experience gained from managing your first property—whether it involves handling tenant issues, overseeing renovations, or dealing with market fluctuations—will be invaluable as you expand your portfolio. This initial property can provide insights into what works and what doesn't, enabling you to make more informed decisions and avoid common pitfalls in future investments.

Overview of Key Steps

Researching the Market: The first step in finding the right property is conducting thorough market research. Understanding the property market's current state, trends, and future outlook is essential for making informed decisions. Research involves analysing various factors such as location, market demand, economic conditions, and property values.

You'll need to assess different areas and neighbourhoods to identify locations with strong growth potential. This includes looking at factors like employment opportunities, population growth, infrastructure developments, and local amenities. Tools such as online property portals, market reports, and local real estate agents can provide valuable insights and data to help you make well-informed choices.

Setting Investment Criteria: Once you have a solid understanding of the market, the next step is to define your investment criteria. This involves determining what type of property aligns with your investment goals and budget. Key criteria to consider include location, property type, price range, and desired features.

Setting clear criteria helps narrow down your options and focus on properties that meet your specific needs and objectives. For example, if your goal is to achieve high rental yields, you might prioritise properties in areas with strong rental demand and high rental income potential. On the other hand, if you're seeking capital growth, you might focus on emerging neighbourhoods with the potential for significant value appreciation.

Evaluating Potential Properties: With your criteria in place, you can begin evaluating potential properties. This step involves assessing each property's suitability based on your investment criteria. Key aspects to consider include the property's condition, location, rental potential, and overall value.

Conducting property inspections and obtaining professional appraisals can help you gauge the property's true value and identify any potential issues. Additionally, comparing properties within the same area can provide a benchmark for understanding whether a property is priced competitively. Evaluating factors such as recent sales data, rental income, and the property's condition will help you make an informed decision and avoid overpaying.

Making an Offer and Closing the Deal: Once you've identified a property that meets your criteria, the next step is to make an offer and negotiate the terms of the purchase. This involves determining a fair offer price based on your research and appraisal findings, and negotiating with the seller to reach an agreement.

After agreeing on the terms, the closing process begins. This includes finalising the purchase agreement, conducting due diligence, and coordinating with legal and financial professionals to complete the transaction. It's important to ensure that all aspects of the deal are thoroughly reviewed and that you're aware of any additional costs or obligations

associated with the purchase. Closing the deal successfully involves careful planning and attention to detail to ensure that the transaction proceeds smoothly and without complications.

Understanding Your Investment Goals

Short-Term vs. Long-Term Goals:

When embarking on a property investment journey, it's crucial to define your objectives clearly. Understanding whether your goals are short-term or long-term will shape your investment strategy and decision-making process.

- Short-Term Goals: Short-term goals typically focus on achieving quick returns or immediate financial benefits. For example, you might aim to acquire a property that can be quickly renovated and sold for a profit, or one that generates immediate rental income. Short-term goals are often driven by specific financial targets or deadlines, such as saving for a down payment on a future property or achieving a particular return on investment within a few years.

Investments targeting short-term gains often involve more active management and may require you to take calculated risks. The success of such investments depends on market conditions and the ability to execute plans efficiently.

- Long-Term Goals: Long-term goals are centred around building wealth and financial security over an extended period. These goals might include creating a steady stream of rental income, accumulating properties to retire comfortably, or achieving significant capital appreciation over several years. Long-term investments typically focus on properties that offer stable rental income and the potential for value growth over time.

With long-term investments, you are generally less concerned with short-term market fluctuations and more focused on the overall performance of your property portfolio. This approach requires patience and a strategic mindset to maximise returns over time.

Cash Flow vs. Capital Growth:

When setting investment goals, you need to decide between prioritising cash flow or capital growth. Each approach has its advantages and aligns with different investment strategies.

- Cash Flow: Cash flow refers to the net income generated from a property after deducting all expenses, including mortgage payments, maintenance, and property management fees. Properties that offer strong cash flow provide regular income, which can be reinvested or used to cover other expenses. This approach is particularly appealing if you seek steady income and want to build a portfolio of properties that provide financial stability.

  Properties that offer high rental yields relative to their purchase price are ideal for cash flow-focused investors. The key is to find properties in high-demand rental areas with stable or growing rental rates.

- Capital Growth: Capital growth focuses on the increase in a property's value over time. Investors seeking capital growth aim to acquire properties in locations with strong potential for future appreciation. This strategy often involves purchasing properties at a lower price and holding them until their value increases significantly.

  Capital growth investments may not generate substantial immediate income but can lead to significant wealth accumulation in the long run. This approach is suitable for those looking to build equity and benefit from property value appreciation over several years.

Assessing Your Financial Situation

Budgeting and Financing Options:

Before purchasing your first property, it's essential to assess your financial situation thoroughly. Proper budgeting and understanding financing options are key to making a sound investment decision.

- Budgeting: Start by establishing a realistic budget for your property purchase. Consider not only the purchase price but also additional costs such as stamp duty, legal fees, inspection costs, and potential renovation expenses. A detailed budget helps you avoid financial strain and ensures that you have sufficient funds for both the purchase and ongoing property management.

  Create a financial plan that accounts for your income, expenses, and savings goals. This will

help you determine how much you can afford to invest and what type of property fits within your budget.
- Financing Options: Explore various financing options to determine what works best for your situation. Options include traditional mortgages, interest-only loans, and investment loans. Each financing method has different terms and conditions, so it's important to compare rates and choose the one that aligns with your investment strategy.
Additionally, consider consulting with a mortgage broker or financial advisor to get professional advice on the best financing options available to you.

Understanding Borrowing Capacity and Pre-Approval:

- Borrowing Capacity: Your borrowing capacity is the maximum amount you can borrow based on your financial situation, including income, debts, and other financial obligations. Lenders assess your borrowing capacity to determine how much they are willing to lend you. Understanding your borrowing capacity helps you set realistic expectations and avoid properties that are beyond your financial reach.
Factors influencing your borrowing capacity include your credit score, employment status, and existing debts. Lenders will also consider your ability to service the loan, including mortgage repayments and property expenses.
- Pre-Approval: Obtaining pre-approval for a mortgage involves having a lender assess your financial situation and provide an estimate of how much they are willing to lend you. Pre-approval is a crucial step in the property buying process, as it gives you a clear idea of your budget and strengthens your position when making an offer on a property.
With pre-approval, you can act quickly when you find a suitable property, as it demonstrates to sellers that you are a serious buyer. It also helps you avoid delays and potential complications during the buying process.

Choosing Your Investment Strategy

Buy and Hold:

The buy-and-hold strategy involves purchasing a property and holding onto it for an extended period, benefiting from rental income and potential capital growth. This approach is suitable for investors seeking steady income and long-term appreciation.

- Advantages: Provides ongoing rental income and potential for property value increase. Suitable for investors aiming for long-term wealth building.
- Considerations: Requires property management and patience, as returns are realised over time.

Fix and Flip:

The fix-and-flip strategy involves buying a property in need of renovation, improving it, and selling it for a profit. This approach is ideal for investors looking to achieve quick returns through property enhancement.

- Advantages: Potential for significant profit in a short time frame. Allows investors to leverage renovation skills or work with contractors.

- Considerations: Involves renovation costs, market timing, and the risk of overestimating the property's post-renovation value.

Rent-to-Own:

The rent-to-own strategy involves renting a property with an option to purchase it later. This approach benefits both landlords and tenants, providing a pathway for tenants to eventually become property owners while offering investors a steady rental income.

- Advantages: Provides rental income with the potential for future sale. Attracts tenants who are motivated to maintain the property.
- Considerations: Requires careful structuring of the lease agreement and may involve longer investment horizons.

Researching the Property Market

Researching the property market is a crucial step in any successful property investment journey. It involves understanding local market dynamics, identifying high-growth areas, analysing trends, and leveraging tools and resources to make informed decisions. This section will guide you through the key aspects of market research that can significantly impact your investment outcomes.

Analysing Local Property Markets

Key Indicators to Look For:

When researching local property markets, certain key indicators can provide valuable insights into the potential for growth and profitability. Understanding these factors will help you identify areas with strong investment prospects.

- Population Growth: Population growth is a vital indicator of a healthy property market. Areas experiencing significant population increases often see higher demand for housing, which can lead to property price appreciation and increased rental yields. Look for regions with ongoing or planned infrastructure developments, such as new transport links or commercial centres, which are likely to attract more residents.
  A growing population not only drives demand but also stimulates local economies, creating more jobs and increasing disposable income, further fueling the property market. Areas with strong population growth often experience a rise in property values over time.
- Employment Rates: Employment rates and job opportunities are closely linked to property market performance. Areas with low unemployment and a diverse range of industries tend to have more stable property markets. When people have secure jobs, they are more likely to buy or rent properties, driving demand.
  Pay attention to regions with growing industries or large employers, as these can attract workers and create a steady demand for housing. Additionally, consider the quality and type of employment available, as high-paying jobs can support higher property prices and rental rates.
- Infrastructure Development: Infrastructure developments, such as new roads, public transport, schools, and hospitals, can significantly enhance the appeal of an area. These developments often lead to increased demand for housing, as they improve accessibility and quality of life. Keep an eye on government plans for infrastructure projects, as they can signal potential

growth areas.
For example, a new train line or highway can make a previously inaccessible suburb more desirable, leading to a surge in property prices. Areas near major infrastructure projects often see an influx of buyers and investors looking to capitalise on future growth.
- Economic Indicators: Broader economic indicators, such as GDP growth, interest rates, and inflation, also play a crucial role in property markets. A strong economy generally supports property price growth, while rising interest rates can affect borrowing costs and, consequently, property demand. Stay informed about the overall economic environment, as it can impact your investment strategy.

Identifying High-Growth Areas:

Once you understand the key indicators, the next step is identifying high-growth areas—locations where property values are likely to rise in the coming years.

- Emerging Suburbs: Emerging suburbs are areas that are just beginning to experience growth but have not yet fully developed. These suburbs often offer more affordable property prices compared to established areas, making them attractive to investors looking for capital growth. Look for signs of gentrification, such as new cafes, shops, and cultural attractions, as these often indicate an area on the rise.
Investing in emerging suburbs can be highly profitable, as early entry allows you to benefit from significant price appreciation as the area develops. However, it requires careful research to ensure the area has genuine growth potential.
- Urban Regeneration Projects: Urban regeneration projects involve revitalising older, declining neighbourhoods through investment in infrastructure, housing, and community facilities. These projects can dramatically improve the desirability of an area, leading to increased property values. Consider investing in areas targeted for regeneration, as they can offer substantial returns over time.
Governments and local councils often provide information about planned regeneration projects, so keeping informed about these initiatives can help you identify promising investment opportunities.
- Proximity to Amenities: Properties located near essential amenities such as schools, shopping centres, public transport, and recreational facilities tend to attract higher demand. When researching potential investment areas, consider the availability and quality of these amenities, as they can significantly impact property values and rental yields.
Properties in well-connected neighbourhoods with access to good schools and shopping areas are often more resilient to market fluctuations, making them a safer investment choice.

Understanding Market Trends

Historical Price Trends:

Analysing historical price trends gives you a sense of how property values have changed over time in a particular area. By examining past performance, you can identify patterns of growth, stability, or decline, which can inform your investment decisions.

- Long-Term Trends: Long-term trends provide insight into an area's overall growth trajectory. Look for areas with consistent price growth over several years, as these are likely to continue performing well. Avoid areas with volatile price movements, as they may indicate instability or underlying issues.

Long-term price data can be obtained from property databases, local councils, and real estate agencies. Analysing this data helps you assess the risk and potential reward of investing in a particular area.

- Recent Performance: While long-term trends are important, recent performance also matters. A sudden increase in property prices may indicate a boom, but it could also be a sign of a market bubble. Conversely, areas with a recent price dip might offer buying opportunities if the fundamentals remain strong. Consider the reasons behind recent price movements to make informed decisions.

For example, a recent dip in prices due to temporary economic factors might present a good buying opportunity if the area's long-term prospects are still positive.

Current Market Conditions and Future Predictions:

Understanding current market conditions is essential for timing your investments correctly. Market conditions can vary significantly between regions, so it's important to stay informed about the specific areas you're interested in.

- Supply and Demand: The balance between supply and demand is a critical factor in property markets. High demand coupled with limited supply typically leads to price increases, while an oversupply of properties can drive prices down. Keep an eye on new developments, zoning changes, and housing approval rates, as these can affect the supply of properties in an area. In a seller's market, where demand exceeds supply, properties sell quickly, and prices rise. In a buyer's market, where supply exceeds demand, you may find more negotiation power and opportunities to purchase properties below market value.
- Economic and Political Factors: Economic and political factors, such as interest rate changes, government housing policies, and tax incentives, can also impact market conditions. For example, a decrease in interest rates may lead to increased borrowing and property demand, while new housing policies can affect investor sentiment.

Stay informed about these factors through financial news, government announcements, and expert analysis. Understanding the broader economic and political landscape helps you anticipate market shifts and adjust your strategy accordingly.

Tools and Resources

Online Property Portals:

Online property portals are an invaluable resource for researching the property market. Websites such as Realestate.com.au, Domain, and Zillow provide access to a wealth of information, including property listings, historical price data, and market trends.

- Property Listings: Use online portals to browse property listings in your target areas. Pay attention to asking prices, property features, and time on the market, as these can provide insights into local demand and pricing trends. You can also set up alerts to notify you of new listings that match your criteria.
- Market Insights: Many property portals offer market insights, such as median property prices, rental yields, and suburb profiles. These tools help you compare different areas and identify those with the most potential for growth.

Local Real Estate Agents and Market Reports:

Local real estate agents are often a valuable source of information about the property market. They have firsthand knowledge of market conditions, buyer behaviour, and upcoming developments.

- Agent Insights: Engage with local real estate agents to gain insights into specific areas. They can provide information about recent sales, buyer preferences, and market trends. Agents can also offer advice on which areas are likely to see future growth based on their experience and local knowledge.
- Market Reports: Real estate agencies often publish market reports that analyse trends and provide forecasts for specific regions. These reports can help you understand the factors driving the market and make informed decisions. Regularly reviewing market reports keeps you up to date with the latest developments.

Property Investment Forums and Groups:

Property investment forums and groups provide a platform for investors to share experiences, strategies, and insights. Participating in these communities allows you to learn from others and stay informed about market trends and investment opportunities.

- Networking: Joining property investment groups, both online and in person, can help you build a network of like-minded investors. Networking provides access to a wealth of knowledge, including tips on finding deals, avoiding pitfalls, and maximising returns.
- Real-World Experiences: Forums and groups often feature real-world case studies and discussions about specific investment strategies. Engaging with these discussions allows you to learn from others' experiences and apply their lessons to your own investments.

Setting Your Investment Criteria

Setting clear investment criteria is essential to ensuring that your property purchases align with your financial goals and investment strategy. Your criteria should encompass location, property type, price range, and desired features, allowing you to quickly identify suitable properties while filtering out those that don't meet your needs. In this section, we will delve into the key aspects of setting investment criteria to guide your property search effectively.

Location Criteria

The location of your investment property is perhaps the most critical factor in determining its long-term value and rental potential. Here's what to consider when setting your location criteria:

Proximity to Amenities, Schools, and Transport:

When selecting a location, proximity to essential amenities plays a significant role in attracting tenants and ensuring property value appreciation. Properties close to amenities such as shopping centres, parks, and recreational facilities are often in higher demand, leading to better rental yields and quicker resale opportunities.

- Schools: Proximity to quality schools is particularly important for attracting families, who often prioritise education when choosing a place to live. Properties near well-regarded schools

tend to hold their value and can command higher rents, making them a solid investment choice.
- Transport Links: Easy access to public transport is another key factor, especially in urban areas where commuting is common. Properties near train stations, bus stops, or major roadways are more appealing to tenants and buyers alike, as they offer convenience and reduce travel time. Additionally, planned transport infrastructure developments can significantly boost the value of nearby properties.

Neighborhood Analysis:

Understanding the neighbourhood where you're considering investing is crucial for assessing the potential risks and rewards. Conduct a thorough analysis of the following aspects:

- Crime Rates: Low crime rates are a strong indicator of a safe and desirable neighbourhood, which is essential for attracting tenants and ensuring the long-term stability of your investment. Research local crime statistics to avoid areas with high crime rates, which can negatively impact property values and rental demand.
- Community Vibe: The overall community vibe, including factors like cleanliness, noise levels, and the presence of community activities, can influence the attractiveness of a neighbourhood. Areas with a strong sense of community, well-maintained public spaces, and active neighbourhood associations often experience steady demand and property value growth.
- Demographics: Understanding the demographics of a neighbourhood can help you tailor your investment strategy. For example, areas popular with young professionals might be better suited for apartment investments, while family-oriented neighbourhoods might be ideal for single-family homes.

Property Type

The type of property you invest in should align with your investment goals and the demand in the area. Here's a breakdown of the main property types and their implications:

Single-Family Homes vs. Multi-Family Units:

- Single-Family Homes: Single-family homes are standalone properties designed for one family. They are often located in suburban areas and appeal to families seeking stability and privacy. These properties tend to be easier to manage since you're dealing with only one tenant. However, they might offer lower rental yields compared to multi-family units due to the single rental income stream.
- Multi-Family Units: Multi-family units, such as duplexes or apartment buildings, consist of multiple separate living spaces within one property. These properties can generate multiple rental incomes, potentially leading to higher overall yields. However, managing multi-family units can be more complex, requiring more effort in terms of maintenance, tenant relations, and property management.

Apartments vs. Houses:

- Apartments: Apartments, particularly in urban areas, are often more affordable than houses and can offer higher rental yields, especially in high-demand locations. However, they may

come with additional costs such as strata fees, and their value can be more volatile due to the supply and demand dynamics of the apartment market.
- Houses: Houses generally offer more land, which can appreciate over time, potentially providing greater capital growth. They are also more versatile in terms of renovation and expansion opportunities. However, houses tend to be more expensive to purchase and maintain, and the rental yields might be lower compared to apartments.

Price Range and Budget

Setting a realistic price range is essential to ensure that your investment is financially sustainable. Consider the following when determining your budget:

How to Set a Realistic Price Range:

- Budgeting for the Purchase: Begin by assessing your available funds, including savings, potential loans, and any other sources of financing. Calculate how much you can comfortably afford to spend on a property without overstretching your finances. Your price range should allow for a buffer to accommodate unexpected expenses or changes in market conditions.
- Considering Financing Options: Evaluate your borrowing capacity by consulting with a mortgage broker or lender to understand how much you can borrow. Pre-approval for a mortgage gives you a clear idea of your purchasing power and can strengthen your position when making offers.
- Market Comparison: Compare prices of similar properties in your target areas to determine what is realistically achievable within your budget. Be sure to consider the condition and features of the properties to ensure you're comparing like for like.

Considering Additional Costs:

In addition to the purchase price, it's important to factor in the following additional costs associated with buying a property:

- Stamp Duty: Stamp duty is a significant upfront cost that varies depending on the property price and location. Be sure to include this in your budget, as it can add a substantial amount to the overall cost of purchasing a property.
- Inspection Fees: Property inspections, including building and pest inspections, are essential to uncover any hidden issues that could affect the property's value or require costly repairs. These fees should be factored into your budget.
- Legal Fees: Conveyancing and legal fees are incurred during the property transfer process. These fees cover the cost of having a solicitor or conveyancer handle the legal aspects of your purchase, including contract review and title searches.
- Renovation Costs: If you're purchasing a property that requires renovations or upgrades, it's crucial to budget for these costs. A detailed renovation plan and cost estimate will help you avoid overspending and ensure the project is financially viable.

Desired Features and Condition

When setting your investment criteria, it's important to distinguish between must-have and nice-to-have features. Additionally, the condition of the property plays a significant role in your investment decision.

Must-Have vs. Nice-to-Have Features:

- Must-Have Features: Must-have features are non-negotiable attributes that align with your investment strategy and target tenant market. These might include proximity to public transport, a certain number of bedrooms or bathrooms, or off-street parking. Prioritise properties that meet these essential criteria to ensure they attract and retain tenants.
- Nice-to-Have Features: Nice-to-have features are desirable but not essential. These could include luxury finishes, additional living spaces, or a large backyard. While these features can enhance the appeal of a property and potentially increase rental income or resale value, they should not be the primary focus of your search.

Assessing Property Condition:

The condition of the property will influence both its immediate livability and the amount of work required before it can be rented out or resold.

- Move-In Ready: Move-in ready properties require minimal work and can be rented out or occupied immediately. These properties are ideal for investors who want to start generating income quickly without incurring additional renovation costs. However, they may come at a higher purchase price.
- Fixer-Uppers: Fixer-uppers are properties that require renovations or repairs before they can be rented or sold. While they often come at a lower purchase price, the cost and effort of renovations must be carefully considered. For investors with experience in renovations or access to reliable contractors, fixer-uppers can offer substantial value creation opportunities.
- Potential for Value-Add: Consider properties with potential for value-adding improvements, such as the ability to subdivide, extend, or upgrade. These opportunities can significantly increase the property's value and rental income, providing a strong return on investment.

Finding Potential Properties

Finding the right property is a crucial step in your investment journey. It requires a strategic approach, utilising both online resources and traditional methods to identify opportunities that align with your investment criteria. This section will explore how to effectively use property portals, work with real estate agents, explore off-market opportunities, and conduct thorough property inspections.

Using Property Portals

Property portals like Realestate.com.au and Domain have revolutionised the way investors search for properties. These platforms provide a comprehensive database of available properties, along with tools to help you refine your search based on your specific investment criteria.

How to Effectively Use Websites Like Realestate.com.au and Domain:

1. Search Filters: Start by setting specific search filters that align with your investment criteria. These filters can include location, price range, property type, and the number of bedrooms and bathrooms. Refine your search by selecting additional criteria such as land size, property condition, and proximity to amenities. This ensures that you only see properties that match your criteria, saving you time and effort.

2. Advanced Search Options: Use advanced search options to further narrow down your results. For example, you can search for properties listed as "price reduced" or "motivated seller," which might indicate a potential below-market-value opportunity. Some portals also allow you to search for properties by keyword, enabling you to target specific features such as "renovated," "off-market," or "auction."
3. Setting Up Alerts and Filters for Specific Criteria: Property portals allow you to set up email alerts based on your search criteria. This feature is invaluable for staying updated on new listings that meet your requirements. You can set alerts for specific locations, price ranges, and property types, ensuring that you're the first to know when a suitable property hits the market. Regularly review and adjust your filters to stay aligned with any changes in your investment strategy.
4. Saved Searches: Many property portals allow you to save your searches, making it easy to revisit and modify them as needed. This is particularly useful if you're monitoring multiple areas or property types. Regularly check your saved searches to stay updated on market trends and pricing in your target areas.

Working with Real Estate Agents

Real estate agents can be valuable partners in your property search, offering access to listings, market insights, and negotiation expertise. Choosing the right agent and understanding what to expect from their services can significantly enhance your property search process.

How to Choose the Right Agent:

1. Experience and Expertise: Look for agents with a strong track record in the area and property type you're interested in. An experienced agent will have in-depth knowledge of local market trends, property values, and potential investment opportunities. They can also provide valuable advice on the best areas to invest in based on your goals.
2. Reputation and Reviews: Research the agent's reputation by reading online reviews, asking for references, and seeking recommendations from other investors. A reputable agent should have positive testimonials from past clients and a history of successful transactions.
3. Communication and Availability: Choose an agent who is responsive, communicative, and willing to work with your schedule. An agent who understands your investment goals and communicates effectively can help you quickly identify and secure suitable properties.

What to Expect from Agent Services:

1. Market Knowledge: A good agent will provide you with detailed market analysis, including recent sales data, price trends, and information on upcoming developments in your target area. This insight helps you make informed decisions and avoid overpaying for a property.
2. Property Access: Agents can provide access to properties that may not be listed on public portals, including off-market deals and upcoming listings. They can also arrange private viewings and provide detailed property reports.
3. Negotiation Support: Experienced agents are skilled negotiators who can help you secure a property at the best possible price. They can provide advice on making offers, counteroffers, and navigating bidding wars, ensuring that you don't overextend your budget.

Exploring Off-Market Opportunities

Off-market properties are not publicly listed, meaning there's less competition from other buyers. Finding these opportunities requires a proactive approach, including networking, direct mail campaigns, and attending auctions and property expos.

Networking and Direct Mail Campaigns:

1. Building a Network: Networking with other investors, real estate agents, and industry professionals can lead to off-market opportunities. Attend local property investment groups, seminars, and networking events to build relationships and learn about potential deals before they hit the market.
2. Direct Mail Campaigns: Sending direct mail to property owners in your target area can be an effective way to uncover off-market deals. This approach involves sending letters or postcards expressing your interest in purchasing their property. While response rates can vary, direct mail can reach motivated sellers who are considering selling but haven't yet listed their property.

Auctions and Property Expos:

1. Auctions: Auctions can be a great way to purchase properties below market value, especially if the seller is motivated to achieve a quick sale. Attend local auctions to get a feel for the process, observe bidding strategies, and potentially identify a bargain. It's important to have your finances in order and set a maximum bid to avoid overpaying in the heat of the moment.
2. Property Expos: Property expos bring together developers, agents, and service providers in one place, offering a wealth of information and potential leads on new developments and off-market opportunities. Attending these events allows you to meet industry professionals, gather market insights, and discover investment opportunities that may not be widely advertised.

Inspecting Properties

Once you've identified potential properties, conducting thorough inspections is essential to ensure you're making a sound investment. Property viewings allow you to assess the condition of the property, identify any issues, and evaluate its suitability based on your investment criteria.

How to Conduct Effective Property Viewings:

1. Preparation: Before the viewing, review the property's listing details, floor plans, and photos. Make a list of questions to ask the agent or seller and bring a checklist of key features you want to inspect. It's also helpful to research the surrounding area to understand its appeal and potential drawbacks.
2. First Impressions: During the viewing, take note of your first impressions of the property's exterior and interior. Pay attention to the overall condition, layout, and flow of the space. Consider whether the property meets your criteria and whether it would appeal to your target tenants or buyers.

What to Look for During Inspections:

1. Structural Issues: Inspect the property for any signs of structural damage, such as cracks in walls, uneven floors, or signs of water damage. Structural issues can be costly to repair and may impact the property's value and safety.
2. Neighbourhood and Surroundings: Evaluate the neighbourhood during your visit. Consider factors such as noise levels, the condition of neighbouring properties, and the overall vibe of the area. Assess whether the neighbourhood is aligned with your target market and investment goals.
3. Condition of Fixtures and Fittings: Check the condition of fixtures and fittings, including plumbing, electrical systems, windows, doors, and appliances. Look for any signs of wear and tear that may require immediate attention or future repairs.
4. Renovation Potential: If you're considering a fixer-upper, assess the property's potential for renovations or upgrades. Consider the scope of work required, the costs involved, and the potential return on investment.
5. Compliance and Regulations: Ensure the property complies with local building codes and regulations, particularly if you're planning renovations. Check for required permits and any restrictions that could impact your investment plans.

Evaluating Property Value

Evaluating property value is a crucial step in making informed investment decisions. Whether you're a first-time investor or expanding your portfolio, understanding how to assess a property's value can significantly impact your investment outcomes. This process involves conducting a Comparative Market Analysis (CMA), calculating potential returns, and identifying any red flags that could signal issues with the property's future value.

Comparative Market Analysis (CMA)

A Comparative Market Analysis (CMA) is a method used by real estate professionals to estimate a property's value by comparing it to similar properties that have recently sold in the same area. This approach helps you determine if a property is priced fairly and whether it aligns with your investment criteria.

How to Compare Similar Properties in the Area:

1. Identify Comparable Properties: The first step in a CMA is to find properties that are similar in size, condition, location, and features to the one you're evaluating. These are often referred to as "comps." Ideally, the comparable properties should have been sold within the last six months to ensure the most accurate reflection of current market conditions. Look for properties within the same neighbourhood or within a close radius, as location is a critical factor in property valuation.
2. Analyse Key Metrics: Once you've identified a set of comparable properties, analyse key metrics such as the price per square metre, sale price, and time on the market. This will give you a benchmark for what similar properties are selling for in the area. For example, if a comparable property sold for $500,000 and is 100 square metres, the price per square metre would be $5,000. Compare this to the property you're interested in to see if it's priced competitively.

3. Adjust for Differences: Adjustments may be necessary to account for differences between the comparable properties and the one you're evaluating. For instance, if a comparable property has an extra bathroom, a larger lot size, or recent renovations, you'll need to factor these into your analysis. Adjusting for these differences helps you arrive at a more accurate value estimate for the property in question.

Understanding the Role of Appraisals:

Appraisals play a critical role in property valuation, especially when it comes to securing financing. An appraisal is a professional assessment of a property's value, typically conducted by a licensed appraiser. Lenders often require an appraisal to ensure the property's value aligns with the loan amount.

1. How Appraisals Work: An appraiser will inspect the property, review comparable sales, and consider factors such as location, condition, and market trends. The appraiser will then provide a report detailing their estimate of the property's market value. This appraisal is crucial for lenders to ensure they are not over-lending on a property.
2. Importance for Investors: For investors, an appraisal provides an independent assessment of a property's value, helping to confirm whether you're getting a good deal. It also protects you from overpaying for a property that may not provide the expected returns.

Calculating Potential Returns

Understanding the potential returns on a property is essential for evaluating its investment value. This involves calculating both the rental yield and the capital growth potential.

Rental Yield Calculations:

1. Gross Rental Yield: Gross rental yield is a straightforward calculation that gives you an overview of the income potential of a property. It's calculated by dividing the annual rental income by the property's purchase price and then multiplying by 100 to get a percentage. For example, if a property is purchased for $500,000 and rents for $500 per week, the annual rental income is $26,000. The gross rental yield would be ($26,000 / $500,000) * 100 = 5.2%.
2. Net Rental Yield: Net rental yield provides a more accurate reflection of the property's profitability by accounting for expenses such as property management fees, maintenance, insurance, and taxes. To calculate the net rental yield, subtract these annual expenses from the rental income, divide the result by the purchase price, and multiply by 100. For instance, if the annual expenses total $5,000, the net rental yield would be (($26,000 - $5,000) / $500,000) * 100 = 4.2%.

Capital Growth Potential:

1. Historical Price Trends: To estimate the potential for capital growth, analyse historical price trends in the area. Look at how property values have changed over the past 5-10 years. Areas with consistent price growth are likely to continue appreciating, offering a good opportunity for capital gains.
2. Future Market Predictions: Consider future market predictions and developments in the area. Infrastructure projects, population growth, and economic factors can all contribute to capital

growth. For example, areas slated for new transport links or commercial developments often experience higher capital growth as demand for housing increases.

Identifying Red Flags

When evaluating a property's value, it's essential to identify any red flags that might indicate potential problems. These could affect not only the current value but also the property's ability to generate income and appreciate over time.

Signs of Overpriced Properties:

1. Long Time on Market: Properties that have been on the market for an extended period may be overpriced. If similar properties in the area are selling quickly but one particular property lingers, it could indicate that the asking price is too high relative to its value.
2. Unjustified Premiums: Be cautious of properties priced at a premium without a clear justification. Sellers might overprice a property due to emotional attachment or unrealistic expectations, which can lead to difficulty reselling or securing tenants at profitable rates.

Potential Issues That May Affect Future Value:

1. Structural Problems: Structural issues, such as foundation cracks, roof damage, or plumbing problems, can be costly to repair and may deter future buyers or tenants. Always conduct a thorough inspection and consider the cost of necessary repairs before proceeding with a purchase.
2. Neighbourhood Decline: The quality of the neighbourhood plays a significant role in property value. Watch for signs of decline, such as increasing crime rates, poor maintenance of public spaces, or a lack of investment in local infrastructure. These factors can negatively impact both rental income and capital growth.
3. Economic and Environmental Risks: Evaluate the broader economic conditions and environmental risks in the area. Properties in regions prone to natural disasters, such as floods or bushfires, may face higher insurance costs and potential devaluation. Similarly, areas dependent on a single industry for employment can suffer property value declines if that industry falters.

Making an Offer and Negotiating

Making an offer and negotiating effectively are critical stages in the property buying process. These steps determine whether you secure a property at a favourable price and under suitable terms. A well-structured offer, combined with strategic negotiation, can make the difference between a good deal and a great one. In this section, we'll explore the offer process, effective negotiation strategies, and the importance of due diligence.

Understanding the Offer Process

Before you can negotiate, you need to understand how to make a formal offer. The offer process can vary depending on the property, the market conditions, and the seller's preferences, but there are general steps and types of offers that apply in most situations.

How to Make a Formal Offer:

1. Research and Preparation: Before making an offer, ensure you have done thorough research on the property's market value, recent comparable sales, and any insights from your real estate agent. This information will help you determine a competitive yet reasonable offer price.
2. Writing the Offer: A formal offer is usually submitted in writing, often through a real estate agent. The offer should include the proposed purchase price, any conditions of the sale (such as finance approval or building inspections), the settlement period, and the deposit amount. In some cases, a buyer's letter to the seller, explaining why you're interested in the property, can add a personal touch and potentially sway the seller in your favour.
3. Submitting the Offer: Once the offer is written, it is submitted to the seller or their agent. The seller will then review the offer and decide whether to accept it, reject it, or make a counteroffer. It's important to be prepared for all three possibilities.

Types of Offers:

1. Unconditional Offer: An unconditional offer is a straightforward proposal to purchase the property without any conditions attached. This type of offer is often more attractive to sellers because it indicates that the buyer is committed to the purchase and is not relying on financing or other contingencies. However, it carries more risk for the buyer, as they are obligated to proceed with the purchase regardless of any issues that may arise later.
2. Subject to Finance: A "subject to finance" offer means the buyer's offer is contingent on securing a mortgage or loan. If the buyer cannot obtain financing, they have the option to withdraw the offer without penalty. This type of offer provides security for the buyer but may be less appealing to sellers, especially in competitive markets.
3. Subject to Building and Pest Inspection: This type of offer is conditional upon a satisfactory building and pest inspection. It protects the buyer by allowing them to back out of the deal if significant structural issues or pest infestations are discovered. While this is a common condition, it can also lead to further negotiations if problems are found during the inspection.
4. Subject to Sale: In some cases, a buyer may need to sell their current property before they can complete the purchase of a new one. A "subject to sale" offer includes this contingency. Sellers may view this as a less desirable offer because it introduces uncertainty into the transaction.

Negotiation Strategies

Negotiation is an art that requires a balance of assertiveness and flexibility. Knowing when to push for a better deal and when to compromise is key to successful property negotiations.

Tips for Negotiating a Better Price:

1. Start with a Reasonable Offer: While it might be tempting to start with a lowball offer, this strategy can backfire by offending the seller or causing them to take your offer less seriously. Instead, start with a fair and reasonable offer based on your research. This sets a constructive tone for negotiations.
2. Highlight Your Strengths as a Buyer: If you're in a strong financial position, such as being pre-approved for a mortgage or able to make a cash offer, make sure the seller knows this. Similarly, if you're flexible on the settlement date, this can be a strong negotiating tool, especially if the seller is keen to close quickly.

3. Use Market Conditions to Your Advantage: In a buyer's market, where there are more properties available than buyers, you have more negotiating power. Use this to your advantage by pointing out similar properties on the market or recent sales that support a lower offer.
4. Be Willing to Walk Away: One of the most powerful negotiation tools is the willingness to walk away if the deal doesn't meet your needs. This approach shows the seller that you're serious and won't overpay or accept unfavourable terms.

How to Handle Counteroffers and Bidding Wars:

1. Responding to Counteroffers: If the seller makes a counteroffer, take time to consider it carefully. Evaluate whether the new terms are acceptable or if there's room for further negotiation. Sometimes, a small concession on your part, such as a slight increase in the offer price or a shorter settlement period, can close the deal.
2. Navigating Bidding Wars: In a competitive market, you may find yourself in a bidding war with other potential buyers. Set a firm maximum limit on what you're willing to pay for the property, and stick to it. It's easy to get caught up in the emotion of a bidding war, but overpaying can jeopardise the financial viability of your investment.
3. Escalation Clauses: An escalation clause is a strategy used in competitive markets. It states that your offer will automatically increase by a certain amount if another higher offer is received, up to a specified maximum. This can help you stay competitive without overcommitting from the start.

Due Diligence

Even after making an offer and engaging in negotiations, your work isn't done. Due diligence is the process of thoroughly investigating the property and its surrounding circumstances before finalising the purchase. This step is critical to ensure that you're making a sound investment.

Conducting Further Inspections and Checks:

1. Building and Pest Inspections: A thorough building and pest inspection should be conducted to identify any potential issues with the property. Look out for structural problems, water damage, electrical issues, and signs of pest infestations. The results of these inspections may affect your decision to proceed or give you leverage to renegotiate the price.
2. Property Title and Zoning: Verify the property's title to ensure there are no encumbrances, such as unpaid taxes or legal disputes. Also, check the zoning laws in the area to ensure that the property's intended use is permitted. Zoning restrictions can impact future renovations, expansions, or property usage.
3. Environmental Checks: Depending on the location, environmental checks may be necessary to assess risks like flood zones, soil contamination, or proximity to hazardous materials. These factors can affect the property's value and your insurance costs.

Reviewing Contracts and Legal Considerations:

1. Legal Review of the Contract: Before signing any contract, it's essential to have it reviewed by a legal professional specialising in property transactions. They will ensure that the terms are fair and that there are no hidden clauses that could cause issues later.

2. **Cooling-Off Period:** In many regions, there is a mandatory cooling-off period after signing a contract, during which the buyer can withdraw from the sale without penalty. Understand the specifics of this period in your jurisdiction, as it provides an additional layer of protection if new information comes to light after signing.
3. **Final Walkthrough:** A final walkthrough of the property is often conducted just before settlement. This is your last chance to ensure the property's condition hasn't changed since your offer was accepted and that any agreed-upon repairs or inclusions are in place.

Closing the Deal

After weeks or even months of searching, evaluating, and negotiating, closing the deal is the final step in purchasing a property. This stage involves a series of legal and financial processes that officially transfer ownership of the property to you. While it may seem straightforward, there are several important steps to ensure that everything goes smoothly, from finalising the purchase to managing post-purchase responsibilities. Here, we'll guide you through the critical components of closing the deal, settling the property, and preparing for the next steps in your property investment journey.

Finalising the Purchase

Once your offer has been accepted and all negotiations are complete, the process of finalising the purchase begins. At this stage, you'll need to focus on legal and financial aspects to ensure that the transfer of ownership is legally binding and all conditions are met.

Understanding the Closing Process:

1. **Contract Review:** The first step in finalising the purchase is reviewing the contract of sale. This document outlines all the terms and conditions of the sale, including the agreed price, settlement date, and any special conditions. It's crucial that you, along with your solicitor or conveyancer, thoroughly review this contract to ensure that it reflects everything agreed upon during negotiations.
2. **Cooling-Off Period (if applicable):** In some regions, buyers are granted a cooling-off period, during which they can withdraw from the purchase without facing penalties. This period usually lasts for a few days, providing a final opportunity to back out if new concerns arise. Make sure you understand whether a cooling-off period applies in your situation and when it ends.
3. **Financing Finalisation:** By this point, you should have secured financing approval for the property. If your offer was conditional upon obtaining finance, now is the time to provide the lender with all necessary documentation to finalise the loan. Ensure that your mortgage or loan is fully approved before proceeding to the next steps.

Coordinating with Your Solicitor or Conveyancer:

Your solicitor or conveyancer plays a critical role in finalising the legal transfer of the property. They handle much of the behind-the-scenes work to ensure that the title of the property is clear, and the ownership transfer is completed smoothly.

1. **Title Search and Legal Checks:** One of the first tasks your solicitor will undertake is performing a title search. This ensures that the property title is free of any encumbrances,

such as unpaid debts or legal disputes. Any issues that arise during the title search must be resolved before settlement.
2. **Preparing Legal Documents:** Your solicitor or conveyancer will prepare and review all necessary legal documents for the transfer of ownership. These include the transfer of land documents, mortgage documents, and other essential paperwork required by local authorities.
3. **Coordinating with the Seller's Legal Team:** Your legal representative will coordinate with the seller's solicitor to finalise details such as the settlement date, payment arrangements, and any other conditions that need to be met before closing.

Settling the Property

Settlement is the point at which the legal ownership of the property is officially transferred from the seller to the buyer. It marks the culmination of the entire buying process, and it's essential to understand what happens during settlement to ensure everything is handled correctly.

Transfer of Ownership:

1. **The Settlement Meeting:** In many cases, a settlement meeting will take place where both parties' legal teams, the buyer, the seller, and the respective lenders finalise the transaction. This can happen in person or electronically, depending on the location and specific processes in place. During this meeting, the agreed purchase price is transferred from the buyer to the seller, and all legal documents are signed to complete the sale.
2. **Transfer of Title:** After the settlement meeting, your solicitor or conveyancer will lodge the transfer of title documents with the local land registry office. This ensures that the property title is updated to reflect you as the new owner. At this point, the property officially becomes yours.
3. **Handover of Keys:** Once the settlement is complete and the title is transferred, you will receive the keys to the property. This is an exciting moment, as it signifies that the purchase is finalised and you are now the legal owner of the property.

Final Payments and Adjustments:

1. **Final Payment:** Before the settlement date, you will need to make the final payment for the property. This includes the balance of the purchase price (after the deposit), any applicable taxes, and other closing costs such as legal fees and stamp duty. Your solicitor or conveyancer will ensure that all payments are processed correctly and that the funds are transferred to the seller.
2. **Adjustments for Rates and Utilities:** In addition to the final purchase price, there may be adjustments for council rates, utility bills, and other ongoing costs associated with the property. These costs are typically calculated based on the settlement date, and you may need to reimburse the seller for any prepaid expenses, or vice versa.

Post-Purchase Tasks

After closing the deal and settling the property, there are still a few important tasks to ensure that your property investment runs smoothly. Whether you plan to live in the property, rent it out, or renovate it, proper management and preparation are key to maximising your investment.

Preparing for Property Management:

1. **Choosing a Property Manager:** If you're planning to rent out the property, one of the first tasks is to hire a reputable property manager. A property manager will handle tasks such as tenant selection, rent collection, and property maintenance, making your role as a landlord easier. Look for a property manager with a solid track record in the area where your property is located.
2. **Setting Rental Rates:** Work with your property manager to set a competitive rental rate. This should be based on local market conditions, the condition of the property, and the demand for rental properties in the area. The goal is to find the right balance between maximising rental income and attracting quality tenants.

Planning Immediate Renovations or Repairs:

1. **Assessing the Property's Condition:** After taking possession of the property, conduct a thorough inspection to assess its current condition. Identify any immediate repairs or upgrades that may be necessary to either bring the property up to standard for rental or increase its value for resale.
2. **Budgeting for Renovations:** If renovations are required, create a detailed budget and timeline. Focus on improvements that will enhance the property's appeal and rental yield, such as kitchen and bathroom updates, fresh paint, or landscaping. Keep in mind that renovations can also increase the property's value, which can provide additional equity for future investments.
3. **Compliance and Safety Checks:** Ensure that the property meets all local building and safety codes. This includes checking smoke alarms, electrical systems, and plumbing. Making sure the property is compliant not only protects you legally but also helps attract quality tenants.

Reviewing Insurance Policies:

Once you've settled the property, it's important to review your insurance policies. This includes ensuring you have comprehensive property insurance that covers not only the building but also landlord-specific coverage if you're renting out the property. This can protect you against damage, loss of rental income, or disputes with tenants.

Case Studies and Examples

When it comes to property investment, real-life examples often provide invaluable insights that theory alone cannot offer. By studying the successes and challenges faced by first-time investors, you can gain a clearer understanding of what works and what doesn't. In this section, we'll explore a few case studies of successful first property purchases, key takeaways from those experiences, and common mistakes to avoid in your property investment journey.

Successful First Property Purchases

Case Study 1: John's Strategic First Investment in a Growth Area

John, a 28-year-old marketing professional from Melbourne, was eager to get started in property investment but found his local market overpriced. He did his homework and researched growth areas across Australia, eventually narrowing his focus on the outskirts of Brisbane, where properties were still affordable, and the market was showing strong growth indicators such as population increase and infrastructure development.

John's first purchase was a three-bedroom house in a suburb that was experiencing an influx of new residents due to its proximity to a new transport hub. He bought the property for $400,000, well within his budget. He worked with a local real estate agent to negotiate the price, bringing it down by $15,000 from the asking price.

Within two years, the property's value had appreciated by nearly 20%, and John had built enough equity to refinance and purchase his second property. Additionally, the rental income from the house was more than enough to cover his mortgage payments, making this a positively geared investment.

Key Takeaways from John's Experience:

1. Research Pays Off: John's success came from identifying a growth area with strong fundamentals, allowing him to purchase a property that appreciated quickly.
2. Negotiation Skills Matter: By negotiating the price, John was able to secure a better deal and enter the market with instant equity.
3. Long-Term Vision: John's focus on capital growth rather than just cash flow helped him build equity quickly, allowing him to grow his portfolio faster.

Case Study 2: Sarah's Fix-and-Flip Strategy for Instant Profit

Sarah, a 32-year-old teacher from Sydney, was interested in making quick profits rather than holding onto a property long-term. She identified a fixer-upper in a lower-demand area that had potential but needed cosmetic upgrades. The two-bedroom apartment was priced at $300,000, significantly lower than similar properties in the area due to its poor condition.

Sarah used her savings to renovate the kitchen and bathroom, spending around $30,000 on improvements. After just six months, she listed the property for sale and sold it for $380,000, making a net profit of $50,000 after expenses. She used the profit from the sale as a deposit for her next property, repeating the fix-and-flip strategy in a different neighbourhood.

Key Takeaways from Sarah's Experience:

1. Renovation Can Add Value: Sarah's ability to identify a property with potential and strategically renovate it for resale helped her make a significant profit in a short time.
2. Short-Term Strategies Can Work: The fix-and-flip strategy can yield quick returns if done correctly, but it requires a good understanding of renovation costs and the local market.
3. Budgeting for Renovations: Sarah's success hinged on staying within her renovation budget, which maximises her profit margins.

Common Mistakes to Avoid

While there are many success stories in property investment, first-time investors can also face challenges and make mistakes. Below are some common pitfalls and examples of how they can impact your investment, as well as strategies to avoid them.

Mistake 1: Overpaying for a Property

One of the most common mistakes is overpaying for a property due to a lack of market knowledge or emotional attachment. For example, Alex, a 30-year-old IT consultant, was eager to buy his first investment property and fell in love with a beachfront apartment. Without fully understanding the local market or comparing similar properties, he made an offer of $450,000, which was accepted. However, the apartment was later appraised at $420,000, meaning Alex had overpaid by $30,000.

This impacted his ability to build equity quickly, as the property's value stagnated over the next few years. To avoid this mistake, it's essential to conduct a comparative market analysis (CMA) and understand the true market value of the property before making an offer.

How to Avoid:

- Always conduct thorough market research and compare similar properties.
- Be cautious of emotional decisions; focus on the financials.
- Seek advice from professionals such as real estate agents or property valuers.

Mistake 2: Underestimating Maintenance and Renovation Costs

Another common pitfall is underestimating the costs of repairs or renovations. For instance, Michael, a 35-year-old accountant, purchased a 1960s home for what seemed like a bargain price. However, he quickly discovered that the property required major electrical rewiring and plumbing work, which cost him an unexpected $25,000. This significantly reduced his cash flow and delayed his ability to save for his next investment.

To avoid this, it's crucial to conduct thorough inspections and budget accurately for any renovations or repairs needed.

How to Avoid:

- Always conduct a professional inspection before purchasing.
- Budget for unexpected repairs, and ensure you have a financial buffer.
- Consider properties with only cosmetic upgrades if you're working on a limited budget.

Mistake 3: Ignoring Cash Flow for Capital Growth

Many first-time investors focus solely on capital growth and ignore cash flow, which can lead to financial strain. For example, Emma, a 29-year-old nurse, purchased a property in a high-growth area but didn't account for the fact that the rental income wouldn't cover her mortgage payments. As a result, she was out of pocket every month, and her personal finances became stretched.

While capital growth is important, ensuring that your property is cash flow positive or at least neutral is essential for maintaining a sustainable investment strategy.

How to Avoid:

- Conduct a cash flow analysis to ensure rental income covers expenses.
- Consider properties with strong rental yields as well as growth potential.

- Factor in all ongoing costs, such as property management fees, maintenance, and vacancy periods.

Chapter 3: Financing Your Investments

Introduction:

Introduction to Financing in Property Investment

When it comes to property investment, financing is the lifeblood of your strategy. While many aspiring investors believe that they need a large amount of upfront cash to get started, the truth is that smart financing allows you to leverage other people's money (OPM) and build wealth over time. In fact, financing is one of the most powerful tools at your disposal, enabling you to grow a property portfolio much faster than relying on your own savings alone.

Why Financing Matters: Leveraging Other People's Money (OPM)

One of the key principles in property investment is the ability to use other people's money—typically through bank loans or other financial products—to fund your property purchases. This concept is powerful because it allows you to control high-value assets without needing to pay the full amount upfront. By securing a mortgage, for example, you may only need to pay a fraction of the property's value as a deposit while borrowing the remainder.

Leveraging OPM enables you to:

- Accelerate Portfolio Growth: Instead of saving for years to buy a property outright, you can spread your funds across multiple properties by borrowing from lenders. This means you can control more assets and generate returns from a wider base of investments.
- Maximise Returns: The returns you generate from rental income or capital appreciation are based on the full value of the property, not just the portion you paid for. This means that the profits from your investment can significantly exceed the amount of your initial outlay, creating what's known as *gearing*—a powerful form of leveraging.
- Diversify Investments: By using financing, you can spread your risk across different properties and locations. For instance, instead of putting all your funds into one expensive property, you could finance multiple smaller, more affordable properties across various growth markets, diversifying your portfolio and minimising risk.

However, it's important to understand that financing is a tool that must be used wisely. Mismanaged debt can quickly lead to financial trouble, but with careful planning and proper risk management, leveraging OPM can propel you toward long-term financial success.

Common Myths About Property Investment Financing

One of the major barriers to entry for new investors is a set of common myths around financing property investments. These misconceptions often prevent people from even attempting to start their investment journey.

Myth 1: You Need a Large Amount of Cash to Get Started Many aspiring investors believe they need to save up for years or have a massive cash reserve to buy property. While a deposit is usually required, it doesn't have to be as large as most people think. Various loan options, including low-deposit loans or guarantor loans, allow investors to enter the market with as little as 5-10% of the property's value. Additionally, using equity from an existing property can serve as a deposit for a new purchase, minimising the need for upfront cash.

Myth 2: You Must Pay Off a Property Completely Before Buying Another. A common misconception is that you need to pay off your mortgage before buying another property. However, seasoned investors often *refinance* their existing properties to unlock equity, using that equity as a deposit for new investments. This allows you to scale your portfolio much faster than if you waited to pay off each property entirely.

Myth 3: Only High-Income Earners Can Secure Financing While income is an important factor in securing a loan, lenders consider a variety of factors when assessing borrowing capacity. A steady job, a good credit score, and solid financial management can go a long way in securing financing, even if your income isn't sky-high. Moreover, various loan products are tailored to different income levels, allowing a wide range of investors to enter the market.

Myth 4: All Debt Is Bad Many people associate debt with financial instability, but not all debt is created equal. *Good debt*—such as a mortgage for a cash-flow positive investment property—can generate income and increase your wealth over time. The key is managing the debt effectively and ensuring that the returns from your investment exceed the cost of borrowing.

By debunking these myths, potential investors can approach property investment with confidence, knowing that smart financing strategies can enable them to enter the market and grow their wealth.

The Role of Financial Literacy

To succeed in property investment, understanding the intricacies of financing is critical. Financial literacy—the ability to understand and make informed decisions about financial matters—plays a vital role in your success as an investor. This goes beyond basic budgeting; it includes understanding the terms and structures of loans, interest rates, and debt management.

Here are the key areas where financial literacy matters:

1. Understanding Loans: Not all loans are created equal. As a property investor, you'll need to be familiar with the different types of loans available, such as fixed-rate, variable-rate, interest-only, and principal-and-interest loans. Each loan type has its own advantages and disadvantages depending on your investment strategy. For instance, interest-only loans are often used by investors looking to maximise cash flow in the short term, while principal-and-interest loans help build equity over time. Understanding these differences will allow you to choose the best financing option for your needs.

2. Interest Rates and Their Impact: Interest rates directly affect the cost of borrowing. A small difference in interest rates can significantly impact the overall cost of your loan over time. Therefore, it's crucial to keep an eye on the market and understand how interest rate movements can affect your cash flow and long-term profitability. When interest rates are low, it might be a good time to lock in a fixed-rate loan, while variable rates can be more favourable during certain economic conditions.

3. Debt Management: One of the most critical aspects of financial literacy is learning how to manage debt effectively. As a property investor, you'll likely be carrying multiple loans at the same time. This requires careful planning to ensure that your debts are manageable and that your properties remain

cash-flow positive. Tools like offset accounts and debt recycling strategies can help reduce the interest you pay and improve your financial position.

4. Risk Mitigation: Understanding the risks associated with financing is just as important as understanding the potential rewards. Financial literacy equips you with the knowledge to assess risks, such as over-leveraging or changes in market conditions, and make informed decisions about when and how to take on debt. For example, borrowing too much without accounting for potential interest rate rises could lead to cash flow issues. By staying informed, you can create a buffer that protects your investment even in challenging times.

Understanding Different Loan Types

One of the most critical aspects of property investment is choosing the right type of loan. The loan you select will impact your cash flow, the cost of your investment, and your long-term wealth-building strategy. Understanding the differences between various loan types and how each one works can empower you to make informed decisions that align with your investment goals.

Fixed vs. Variable Rate Loans

When choosing a loan, one of the first decisions you'll face is whether to opt for a fixed-rate loan or a variable-rate loan. Each has its advantages and disadvantages, depending on market conditions and your investment strategy.

Fixed-Rate Loans

A fixed-rate loan locks in the interest rate for a set period, usually between one and five years. During this time, your repayments remain the same, regardless of changes in the broader market.

Pros of Fixed-Rate Loans:

- Predictability: The most significant benefit of a fixed-rate loan is the predictability it offers. Your repayment amount will remain the same for the fixed term, which makes it easier to budget and plan your finances.
- Protection from Interest Rate Rises: If interest rates rise during the fixed period, your repayments will stay the same, shielding you from increasing borrowing costs.

Cons of Fixed-Rate Loans:

- Less Flexibility: Fixed-rate loans often come with restrictions on additional repayments and may charge penalties for early repayments or refinancing.
- No Benefit from Rate Cuts: If interest rates fall, you won't benefit from lower repayments, as you're locked into your fixed rate.

Fixed-rate loans are ideal for investors who want stability and predictability in their repayments. However, they may not be suitable if you're looking for flexibility to make extra payments or capitalise on falling interest rates.

Variable-Rate Loans

Variable-rate loans have an interest rate that can change in response to fluctuations in the broader market. Your repayments will go up or down depending on whether interest rates rise or fall.

Pros of Variable-Rate Loans:

- Flexibility: Variable-rate loans often offer more flexibility, such as the ability to make extra repayments, redraw funds, or refinance without penalty.
- Benefit from Rate Cuts: If interest rates fall, your repayments will decrease, improving your cash flow.

Cons of Variable-Rate Loans:

- Uncertainty: The biggest downside to variable-rate loans is that your repayments can increase if interest rates rise, potentially putting a strain on your finances.

Variable-rate loans are a good option for investors who value flexibility and are comfortable with some level of risk. However, they require careful financial planning to account for the possibility of rising interest rates.

Which Is Better for Property Investors?

The decision between fixed and variable loans often depends on your risk tolerance and investment strategy. If you prefer stability and certainty in your repayments, a fixed-rate loan may be the better choice. On the other hand, if you're looking for flexibility and are comfortable with some market risk, a variable-rate loan can offer significant advantages, especially in a falling interest rate environment. Some investors choose to split their loan, fixing a portion while leaving the rest variable, which allows them to enjoy both predictability and flexibility.

Interest-Only Loans

An interest-only loan is a loan where you only pay the interest on the loan for a set period, usually between one and five years. After the interest-only period ends, the loan typically reverts to a standard principal and interest loan, where you begin paying off both the interest and the principal.

How Interest-Only Periods Can Improve Cash Flow: Interest-only loans are popular among property investors because they significantly reduce the monthly repayment amount during the interest-only period. This improves cash flow, as you're not paying down the principal. Instead, you can use the extra cash flow for other investments, property renovations, or to build a financial buffer.

Pros of Interest-Only Loans:

- Maximised Cash Flow: Lower repayments mean more cash in your pocket, which can be reinvested or used to cover other costs.
- Tax Benefits: For investors in many countries, the interest payments on investment properties are tax-deductible, which makes interest-only loans an attractive option.

Cons of Interest-Only Loans:

- No Equity Growth: During the interest-only period, you're not reducing the loan principal, which means you're not building equity through loan repayments.
- Higher Payments Later: Once the interest-only period ends, your repayments will increase significantly as you begin paying off both the principal and the interest.

Interest-only loans are ideal for investors looking to maximise cash flow in the short term, especially if they plan to sell the property before the loan switches to principal and interest repayments. However, they do come with higher long-term risks if property values don't appreciate as expected or if you don't have a strategy for managing higher future repayments.

Principal and Interest Loans

With a principal and interest loan, you pay off both the interest and a portion of the principal each month. This gradually reduces the amount you owe and helps you build equity in the property over time.

Balancing Loan Repayments with Equity Growth: Principal and interest loans are a more traditional type of loan, and they ensure that your loan balance decreases over time. This builds your equity in the property and reduces the overall amount of interest you'll pay over the life of the loan.

Pros of Principal and Interest Loans:

- Equity Growth: By paying off both the interest and principal, you gradually own more of the property, which can be leveraged for future investments.
- Lower Total Interest: Since you're reducing the loan balance over time, you'll pay less interest overall compared to an interest-only loan.

Cons of Principal and Interest Loans:

- Higher Monthly Repayments: The repayments on a principal and interest loan are higher than those of an interest-only loan, which can strain cash flow, especially in the early stages of your investment.

Principal and interest loans are better suited for investors who prioritise building equity in their property and who have a long-term investment horizon. This type of loan provides stability and reduces the risk of being caught with a large principal balance at the end of the loan term.

Line of Credit

A line of credit is a flexible loan option that allows you to borrow up to a certain limit, using the equity in your property as collateral. Unlike a traditional loan, where you receive a lump sum and make regular repayments, a line of credit gives you access to funds that you can draw from as needed.

How Investors Can Use a Line of Credit for Multiple Properties: Lines of credit are especially useful for property investors who want to finance multiple deals or cover renovation costs. You only pay interest on the amount you've drawn from the line of credit, which means you have more flexibility to manage your finances.

Pros of a Line of Credit:

- Flexibility: You can draw funds as needed, making it an excellent option for investors who may need to access capital for renovations or to cover other investment expenses.
- Interest Only on Withdrawn Amounts: You only pay interest on the funds you've used, which can help reduce interest costs compared to a traditional loan.

Cons of a Line of Credit:

- Temptation to Overspend: The easy access to funds can lead to overspending if not managed carefully, which could increase your debt load.
- Higher Interest Rates: Lines of credit often come with slightly higher interest rates compared to traditional mortgages.

A line of credit is a powerful tool for seasoned investors who need financial flexibility. However, it's essential to use this loan type responsibly, as the convenience of easy access to funds can lead to increased debt if not managed carefully.

Offset Accounts and Redraw Facilities

Offset accounts and redraw facilities are features that can be attached to a mortgage, helping you reduce interest payments and offering more financial flexibility.

Offset Accounts

An offset account is a transaction account linked to your home loan. The balance in the offset account is deducted from the loan balance when interest is calculated. For example, if you have a $300,000 loan and $50,000 in your offset account, you'll only pay interest on $250,000.

Pros of Offset Accounts:

- Reduced Interest: The more money you keep in your offset account, the less interest you pay on your mortgage.
- Flexibility: You can still access the funds in your offset account for other purposes, such as renovations or emergencies.

Redraw Facilities

A redraw facility allows you to make extra repayments on your loan and then withdraw those funds if needed. This is a good option for investors who want to reduce their interest but still retain access to their funds.

Pros of Redraw Facilities:

- Interest Savings: By making extra repayments, you reduce the loan balance and the amount of interest you pay.
- Access to Funds: You can withdraw the extra repayments if needed, offering flexibility.

Cons:

- Limited Access: Some redraw facilities may have fees or limits on how often you can access your funds.

Offset accounts and redraw facilities are valuable tools for reducing interest and improving financial flexibility. Both options allow you to make the most of your mortgage, minimising costs and maximising your control over your investment strategy.

Assessing Your Borrowing Capacity

Before diving into property investment, one of the most crucial steps is understanding your borrowing capacity. Your ability to secure financing for a property is determined by several factors, and knowing these can help you set realistic expectations and make informed decisions. Understanding borrowing capacity not only ensures that you don't over-leverage yourself but also puts you in a stronger position when negotiating with sellers and lenders. In this section, we'll explore the key factors lenders consider, how to understand your debt-to-income ratio, the importance of pre-approval, and strategies to maximise your borrowing power.

Key Factors Lenders Consider

Lenders assess multiple aspects of your financial situation before approving a loan. These factors help them determine how much risk they are taking by lending to you, and they will affect the amount they are willing to offer.

1. Income

Your income is one of the most significant factors in determining your borrowing capacity. Lenders look at your total income, including salary, bonuses, rental income, and any other regular earnings. The higher your income, the more likely you'll be able to afford larger loan repayments, which increases your borrowing capacity.

- Salary: Lenders prefer borrowers with stable, full-time employment. If you're self-employed, they may ask for additional documentation, such as tax returns, to verify your income.
- Additional Income: Rental income from other properties, investment dividends, or government benefits can also be factored into your borrowing capacity, depending on the lender's criteria.

2. Expenses

Lenders will review your regular expenses, including rent or mortgage repayments (if applicable), utility bills, insurance premiums, groceries, and other living costs. They want to ensure you have enough disposable income after these expenses to comfortably afford loan repayments.

- Living Expenses: Lenders typically use standard benchmarks to estimate your living costs. However, if your expenses are significantly higher than the average, this may reduce your borrowing capacity.
- Children and Dependents: Having children or dependents increases your expenses, which can lower your borrowing capacity as it affects your disposable income.

3. Existing Debt

Any existing debts, such as credit card balances, car loans, or personal loans, will reduce the amount you can borrow. Lenders calculate your debt-to-income ratio to assess how much of your income is already committed to debt repayments.

- Credit Cards: Even if you pay off your credit card balance every month, lenders will often consider the card's credit limit when assessing your borrowing capacity. For example, if you have a $10,000 credit limit, lenders assume you could potentially rack up $10,000 in debt, which impacts your borrowing power.
- Personal Loans and Car Loans: Ongoing repayments for personal or car loans reduce your disposable income, limiting the amount of additional debt you can take on.

4. Credit Score

Your credit score is a key indicator of your creditworthiness. Lenders use your credit score to assess how reliably you've managed debt in the past. A high credit score demonstrates financial responsibility and increases your chances of securing a loan with favourable terms.

- Good Credit History: If you've consistently paid off your debts on time, this will reflect positively in your credit score, increasing your borrowing capacity.
- Bad Credit History: Missed payments, defaults, or having too many credit applications can damage your credit score, making it harder to secure a loan or limiting the amount lenders are willing to offer.

5. Loan-to-Value Ratio (LVR)

The Loan-to-Value Ratio (LVR) is the percentage of the property's value that you're borrowing. Lenders generally prefer an LVR of 80% or less, meaning you provide a 20% deposit, although some may offer loans with a higher LVR if you have mortgage insurance.

- Lower LVR: A lower LVR means you're borrowing less compared to the value of the property, which makes you less risky to lenders. It can also help you avoid paying Lenders Mortgage Insurance (LMI).
- Higher LVR: While higher LVRs can make it easier to enter the market with a smaller deposit, they come with higher risks and may increase your borrowing costs, including mandatory LMI.

Debt-to-Income Ratio (DTI)

One of the most important metrics lenders use to assess your borrowing capacity is the debt-to-income (DTI) ratio. The DTI ratio compares your total monthly debt payments to your gross monthly income.

It gives lenders a clear picture of how much of your income is already committed to repaying debt and how much capacity you have to take on new loans.

Calculating Debt-to-Income Ratio

To calculate your DTI ratio, divide your total monthly debt payments (including mortgage payments, car loans, personal loans, and minimum credit card payments) by your gross monthly income. Multiply the result by 100 to get the percentage.

For example:

- Monthly debt payments: $2,000
- Gross monthly income: $7,000

DTI ratio = ($2,000 / $7,000) * 100 = 28.6%

What Is a Good DTI Ratio?

Lenders typically prefer a DTI ratio of below 36%. If your DTI is too high, it indicates that too much of your income is going toward existing debt, which makes you a higher-risk borrower. Some lenders may still approve loans with higher DTIs, but it could limit how much they're willing to lend and result in higher interest rates.

Pre-Approval Process

Obtaining pre-approval from a lender is an essential step in the property investment process. Pre-approval gives you a clear idea of how much a lender is willing to loan you, helping you set a budget for your property search. It also shows sellers and agents that you are a serious buyer with financing ready to go, which can give you an advantage in negotiations.

Why Pre-Approval Is Important

1. Sets Your Budget: Pre-approval provides a clear estimate of how much you can borrow, which allows you to focus on properties within your price range. This saves time and prevents the disappointment of finding out later that you can't afford the property you've chosen.
2. Boosts Your Credibility: Sellers and agents are more likely to take your offer seriously if you have pre-approval. It shows that you've already been vetted by a lender and have the financial backing to proceed with the purchase.
3. Speeds Up the Buying Process: Having pre-approval in place speeds up the loan approval process once you find a property, allowing you to act quickly and confidently.

How to Get Pre-Approval

To get pre-approval, you'll need to provide the lender with documentation, including:

- Proof of income (e.g., payslips, tax returns)
- Details of your assets and liabilities (e.g., savings, other properties, debts)
- Identification documents (e.g., passport, driver's licence)

The lender will assess your financial situation and give you a pre-approval letter that outlines how much they're willing to lend, usually valid for 3-6 months.

Maximising Your Borrowing Power

There are several strategies you can use to maximise your borrowing power and improve your chances of securing a larger loan at favourable terms.

1. Reduce Personal Debt

The less personal debt you have, the more borrowing capacity you'll have for property investments. Pay down credit card balances, personal loans, or car loans to improve your DTI ratio and free up more of your income for mortgage repayments.

2. Improve Your Credit Score

Boosting your credit score can significantly enhance your borrowing power. Simple strategies like paying bills on time, reducing your credit card limits, and avoiding multiple credit applications can help improve your score. A higher credit score can lead to better loan terms and increase the amount you can borrow.

3. Increase Your Income

If possible, increasing your income through additional work, a raise, or leveraging rental income from existing properties can boost your borrowing capacity. Lenders will take into account any regular, stable income streams when assessing how much you can borrow.

4. Save for a Larger Deposit

Saving for a larger deposit reduces your LVR and makes you less risky to lenders. A lower LVR can increase your borrowing capacity and may also help you avoid paying LMI, saving you thousands of dollars.

5. Choose the Right Loan Type

Selecting the right loan type can also maximise your borrowing power. For example, interest-only loans may reduce your monthly repayments in the short term, allowing you to qualify for a larger loan.

Structuring Your Loans for Property Investment

When investing in property, how you structure your loans can significantly impact your financial flexibility, risk management, and ability to grow your portfolio. Loan structuring involves choosing the right combination of loan products, terms, and arrangements to meet your financial goals. In this section, we'll explore different loan structuring options, including the risks and rewards of cross-collateralization, the benefits of separating each property's financing, how split loans can provide a balance of risk and reward, and the importance of keeping personal and investment loans separate.

Cross-Collateralization: Risks and Rewards

Cross-collateralization is a loan structuring strategy where multiple properties are used as security for one or more loans. Essentially, you're securing multiple properties under a single loan agreement, which can help investors with limited equity unlock more funds for new purchases. While this approach can provide certain benefits, it also comes with notable risks.

The Rewards

- **Maximising Borrowing Capacity**: By using the equity in multiple properties as collateral, you may be able to borrow more money than if you had used just one property as security. This can help you expand your portfolio more quickly, as the lender views the combined assets as lower risk.
- **Simplified Loan Management**: With one loan secured against multiple properties, you have fewer loan accounts to manage, which can simplify your financial tracking and reduce administrative work.
- **Access to Additional Equity**: Cross-collateralization can unlock more equity from your existing properties, allowing you to use that equity to finance the purchase of new properties.

The Risks

- **Reduced Flexibility**: One of the biggest downsides of cross-collateralization is that it limits your flexibility. If you want to sell one property, the lender may require you to either pay down part of the loan or offer additional security before they agree to release the property from the loan.
- **Increased Risk**: If one property in your portfolio declines in value, it could affect the entire loan, putting all your properties at risk. This structure can create a domino effect, where the negative performance of one property impacts the security of others.
- **Complicated Refinancing**: Cross-collateralized loans can make it more difficult to refinance individual properties, as all assets are tied into one loan agreement. This limits your ability to access better interest rates or switch lenders without reconfiguring the entire loan structure.

Portfolio Loan Structures: Separating Each Property's Financing

An alternative to cross-collateralization is structuring your loans so that each property has its own individual loan. This is known as a **portfolio loan structure**, where each investment is financed separately, providing more flexibility and control over your portfolio.

The Benefits

- **Greater Flexibility**: By keeping each property's financing separate, you have more flexibility to sell, refinance, or make changes to individual loans without affecting the rest of your portfolio. For example, if you want to sell one property, you can do so without needing approval from the lender for other properties in your portfolio.
- **Reduced Risk**: With separate loans, the performance of one property doesn't impact the others. If one property decreases in value, it won't put your entire portfolio at risk. This structure allows you to better manage the risk associated with each investment.

- **Easier Refinancing**: Separate loans make it easier to refinance individual properties to take advantage of better interest rates or loan terms. You can strategically refinance properties with more equity while keeping higher-interest loans in place for others.

Considerations

- **More Loan Accounts**: One downside of this approach is that you'll have more loan accounts to manage, which can increase administrative complexity. However, this added complexity is often outweighed by the increased flexibility and control over your portfolio.

Split Loans: Combining Fixed and Variable Interest Rates

Split loans offer a way to combine the stability of fixed interest rates with the flexibility of variable rates. With a split loan, a portion of your loan is set at a fixed interest rate, while the remainder is set at a variable rate. This structure allows you to balance the benefits and risks of both types of loans.

The Benefits

- **Interest Rate Stability**: The fixed-rate portion of the loan provides you with certainty about your repayments. You'll know exactly what your payments will be for that part of the loan, which helps with budgeting and cash flow management, especially during periods of economic uncertainty or rising interest rates.
- **Potential for Savings**: The variable-rate portion of the loan gives you the opportunity to benefit from any decreases in interest rates. If rates fall, your repayments on the variable part of the loan will decrease, allowing you to save money.
- **Flexibility**: Variable-rate loans typically offer more flexibility than fixed-rate loans, allowing you to make additional repayments without penalty. By keeping a portion of your loan at a variable rate, you maintain the ability to pay down your debt faster if you have surplus cash flow.

The Risks

- **Rising Interest Rates**: While the variable-rate portion of the loan offers potential savings if rates fall, there's also a risk that rates could rise, increasing your repayments. It's important to assess whether you can afford higher repayments if rates increase.
- **Limited Repayment Flexibility on Fixed Rates**: Fixed-rate loans often come with restrictions on how much extra you can repay during the fixed term. If you want to make significant additional repayments, you may be penalised on the fixed-rate portion.

When to Consider Split Loans

Split loans are often a good option for investors who want to balance the certainty of fixed rates with the flexibility of variable rates. This structure is particularly useful if you're concerned about potential interest rate rises but also want the option to pay down your loan more quickly if rates remain stable or decrease.

Personal vs. Investment Loans: Keeping Finances Separate

When structuring your loans, it's essential to keep your **personal loans** and **investment loans** separate. Mixing personal and investment finances can lead to tax complications and make it harder to track the performance of your property portfolio.

Why Separating Loans Matters

- **Tax Deductibility**: Interest on loans for investment properties is generally tax-deductible, while interest on personal loans (e.g., for your home or car) is not. If you mix personal and investment loans, it can become difficult to determine which portion of the interest is deductible, leading to potential issues with the tax office.
- **Clear Financial Tracking**: Keeping your personal and investment loans separate allows you to more easily track the financial performance of your properties. You'll have a clearer picture of how much your investments are costing you and what returns they are generating.
- **Improved Financial Planning**: Separate loans enable better financial planning. You can focus on paying down non-deductible debt (such as your home loan) first, while using interest-only or lower-interest loans for investment properties to maximise your cash flow.

How to Separate Personal and Investment Loans

- **Dedicated Accounts**: Use separate bank accounts for personal and investment finances. This makes it easier to track expenses and ensures that you're keeping your finances distinct.
- **Seek Professional Advice**: Work with an accountant or financial advisor who specialises in property investment to ensure your loan structures are tax-efficient and compliant with relevant regulations.

Creative Financing Strategies for Property Investors

In the world of property investment, financing is key to scaling your portfolio and maximising returns. While traditional bank loans are the most common financing option, savvy investors often employ creative strategies to acquire more properties, manage cash flow, and reduce risk. This section explores five creative financing strategies: using equity from below-market-value (BMV) properties, forming joint ventures, utilising vendor financing, employing rent-to-own strategies, and seeking alternative funding from private lenders and hard money loans.

Using Equity to Buy More Properties

One of the most powerful ways to grow your property portfolio is by leveraging the **equity** in your existing investments to finance additional purchases. Equity refers to the difference between a property's current market value and the outstanding loan balance. By using equity from BMV properties, investors can unlock the potential to fund further acquisitions without needing to save large amounts of cash for deposits.

How to Leverage Equity

Once you've accumulated sufficient equity in a property, you can approach your lender to **refinance** the loan. This involves reassessing the property's current value, allowing you to borrow against the increased equity. For example, if a BMV property has appreciated in value or you've made improvements that increase its market price, the equity grows accordingly. You can then use this additional borrowing power as a deposit for your next property.

The Benefits

- **No Need for Extra Savings**: Instead of waiting to save up for another deposit, you can use your existing assets to fast-track your next investment.
- **Exponential Portfolio Growth**: Leveraging equity allows you to acquire more properties faster, accelerating your wealth-building potential.
- **Tax Efficiency**: In many cases, the interest paid on the additional borrowing for investment purposes is tax-deductible, improving your cash flow position.

Example: An investor purchases a BMV property for $300,000 with a loan of $250,000. After renovations, the property's value increases to $400,000. With $150,000 in equity, they refinance the property and borrow an additional $100,000 to use as a deposit for a second property.

Joint Ventures: Partnering with Other Investors

Joint ventures (JVs) offer a way for investors to pool resources, share risks, and split profits on property deals. This strategy is particularly useful for those who may not have sufficient funds or experience to go it alone but still want to reap the benefits of property investment. In a joint venture, two or more investors come together to purchase and manage a property, with each partner contributing capital, expertise, or both.

How Joint Ventures Work

In a typical JV, each party agrees on the terms of the partnership, including their respective roles, financial contributions, and how profits or losses will be shared. These terms are often formalised through a legal agreement. One partner might provide the majority of the capital, while the other handles the day-to-day management of the investment.

The Benefits

- **Shared Costs and Risks**: By partnering with another investor, you can split the financial burden, making it easier to afford more significant investments.
- **Access to Expertise**: If you're new to property investment, partnering with an experienced investor can provide valuable mentorship and knowledge.
- **Increased Buying Power**: A JV allows you to pool funds, enabling you to purchase larger or more profitable properties that would be out of reach on your own.

Example: A first-time investor with $50,000 teams up with a seasoned investor who contributes $100,000. Together, they purchase a $400,000 investment property, splitting profits and responsibilities according to their initial agreement.

Vendor Financing: Seller-Financed Deals for Flexibility

Vendor financing, also known as **seller financing**, is a creative financing method where the property's seller acts as the lender, allowing the buyer to pay for the property over time rather than securing a traditional mortgage. This strategy is beneficial when the buyer has difficulty qualifying for a loan or when both parties seek more flexible terms than those offered by a bank.

How Vendor Financing Works

In a vendor-financed deal, the seller and buyer agree on a purchase price and payment terms. The buyer makes regular payments directly to the seller, often with an agreed interest rate. This arrangement can be structured as a lease-purchase agreement or a contract for deed, where the seller retains the property title until the buyer pays the agreed amount in full.

The Benefits

- **Flexible Payment Terms**: Seller financing offers more flexibility in terms of interest rates, down payments, and repayment schedules.
- **No Need for Traditional Loans**: Buyers who don't qualify for traditional financing can still acquire property through this method.
- **Faster Transactions**: Without waiting for bank approvals and mortgage processing, vendor-financed deals can close more quickly.

Example: A buyer with poor credit is unable to secure a bank loan for a $250,000 property. The seller agrees to finance the purchase, requiring a $25,000 down payment and monthly payments of $1,500 over 10 years, with an interest rate of 6%.

Rent-to-Own Strategies: Flexibility for Buyers and Investors

Rent-to-own, or **lease option**, is a financing strategy that allows tenants to rent a property with the option to buy it later. This option is attractive to buyers who may not have sufficient funds for a down payment or who need time to improve their credit score. Investors use rent-to-own as a way to generate rental income while securing a potential future sale at a pre-agreed price.

How Rent-to-Own Works

In a rent-to-own arrangement, the tenant pays rent as usual, with a portion of the rent often credited toward the purchase price. At the end of the lease period, the tenant has the option to buy the property at the agreed-upon price. If the tenant decides not to purchase the property, the investor keeps the rent paid during the lease term, including any option fees.

The Benefits

- **Secure a Future Sale**: Investors benefit from having a tenant who is committed to potentially purchasing the property, reducing the likelihood of vacancy.
- **Rental Income with Potential for Capital Gain**: Rent-to-own agreements typically involve a higher rent than standard leases, generating additional income while giving the tenant time to qualify for a mortgage.
- **Flexibility for Buyers**: Rent-to-own agreements provide buyers with the opportunity to lock in a purchase price while they build up a deposit or improve their financial situation.

Example: An investor rents out a $300,000 property for $1,800 per month, with $300 credited toward the purchase price. After three years, the tenant has the option to buy the property at the pre-agreed price of $320,000.

Private Lenders and Hard Money Loans: Alternative Funding Options

For investors who don't meet the strict lending criteria of traditional banks, **private lenders** and **hard money loans** offer alternative sources of financing. Private lenders are individuals or organisations that provide loans, often with less stringent requirements but at higher interest rates. Hard money loans, on the other hand, are short-term loans typically used for property flips or renovations.

Private Lenders

Private lenders are often more flexible than banks and may consider factors beyond credit scores and income levels when approving a loan. However, they usually charge higher interest rates to offset the increased risk. These loans are particularly useful for investors with bad credit or those looking for fast financing.

Hard Money Loans

Hard money loans are typically used by investors who need to finance a property quickly, such as in the case of a flip. These loans are based on the value of the property rather than the borrower's creditworthiness. Hard money lenders charge higher interest rates and offer shorter repayment terms, often between six months and three years.

The Benefits

- **Faster Approvals**: Private lenders and hard money loans often have quicker approval times than traditional loans, allowing investors to act fast on opportunities.
- **Flexible Terms**: These loans can be tailored to fit specific investment strategies, whether it's a short-term fix-and-flip or a long-term buy-and-hold.
- **Access to Capital**: Investors who don't qualify for bank loans due to credit issues or lack of documentation can still access funds.

Example: An investor plans to flip a distressed property purchased at auction. They secure a $200,000 hard money loan with a 12-month term and an interest rate of 10%. After six months of renovations, they sell the property for $300,000, repaying the loan and pocketing the profit.

Understanding Interest Rates and Loan Repayments

When it comes to financing property investments, understanding how interest rates and loan repayments work is crucial. Interest rates directly affect your monthly payments, long-term financial commitment, and overall profitability. This section will cover the different types of interest rates, their impact on your investment cash flow, loan amortisation schedules, and key factors to consider when comparing loans.

How Interest Rates Work

Interest rates are essentially the cost of borrowing money from a lender. In property investment, the interest you pay on your mortgage plays a significant role in determining your cash flow and long-term profitability. The two primary types of interest rates are **fixed** and **variable**, and many investors also choose a **split-rate** mortgage, combining the benefits of both.

Fixed-Rate Mortgages

A **fixed-rate mortgage** locks in the interest rate for a set period, typically ranging from 1 to 5 years. During this period, your loan repayments remain consistent, providing stability and predictability, regardless of any changes in the broader economic environment.

Advantages:

- **Stability**: Fixed repayments make it easier to budget, especially for new investors.
- **Protection from Rate Increases**: You won't be affected by rising interest rates during the fixed period.

Disadvantages:

- **Lack of Flexibility**: If interest rates fall, you won't benefit from lower repayments.
- **Higher Break Costs**: If you wish to refinance or pay off the loan early, you may face high fees for breaking the fixed contract.

Variable-Rate Mortgages

A **variable-rate mortgage** means your interest rate fluctuates with the market. When the central bank adjusts interest rates, lenders typically follow suit, raising or lowering the rates on your loan.

Advantages:

- **Flexibility**: Variable-rate loans often come with more flexible features like redraw facilities and offset accounts.
- **Lower Rates in Favourable Markets**: If interest rates drop, your repayments will decrease, improving your cash flow.

Disadvantages:

- **Unpredictability**: Changes in interest rates can make budgeting more difficult, especially if rates rise.
- **Exposure to Rising Rates**: If rates increase, your repayments can rise significantly, affecting your profitability.

Split-Rate Mortgages

A **split-rate mortgage** combines both fixed and variable rates. This allows you to lock in a portion of your loan at a fixed rate, while the rest is subject to market fluctuations. Investors often choose split-rate loans to balance stability with the potential benefits of variable rates.

Advantages:

- **Best of Both Worlds**: You can hedge against rising interest rates while still benefiting from any rate decreases.
- **Budgeting Flexibility**: Part of your repayments remains consistent, making it easier to plan.

Disadvantages:

- **Complexity**: Managing two types of interest rates and repayments can be more complicated.
- **Potential for Fees**: Depending on the lender, split loans may come with additional costs.

The Impact of Interest Rates on Cash Flow

Interest rates play a pivotal role in determining your monthly loan repayments, which directly impacts your cash flow. For property investors, maintaining a positive cash flow is essential for covering expenses like maintenance, insurance, and property management fees.

Rising Interest Rates

When interest rates rise, your mortgage repayments increase. This can significantly reduce your cash flow, making it harder to cover your ongoing costs. In extreme cases, rising rates can lead to negative cash flow, where your property is no longer profitable month to month.

Example:

- A $400,000 loan at a 3% interest rate requires monthly repayments of approximately $1,700. If rates rise to 4.5%, those repayments increase to about $2,025—an extra $325 per month.

Falling Interest Rates

Conversely, falling interest rates lower your monthly repayments, improving your cash flow and profitability. Lower repayments mean you can more easily service your loan and potentially invest in additional properties.

Example:

- On the same $400,000 loan, a drop from 3% to 2% reduces monthly repayments to approximately $1,480, freeing up an additional $220 per month for reinvestment or savings.

Loan Amortisation and Repayment Schedules

Loan amortisation refers to the process of paying off a loan over time, with each payment covering both the interest and a portion of the principal (the original loan amount). The repayment schedule shows how much of each payment goes toward the principal and how much goes toward interest.

Amortisation Over Time

At the beginning of a loan term, a significant portion of your repayments goes toward interest, with only a small amount reducing the principal. Over time, as the loan balance decreases, more of your repayments go toward paying down the principal, which reduces the overall interest you pay.

Example:

- On a 30-year loan, in the first few years, around 70-80% of each repayment may go toward interest. By the end of the term, nearly the entire repayment will go toward reducing the principal.

The Cost of Long-Term Interest

Although monthly repayments may be manageable, the total interest cost over the life of the loan can be substantial. The longer the loan term, the more interest you'll pay in the long run. For this reason, some investors choose to make extra payments when possible, which reduces the principal faster and lowers total interest costs.

Example:

- On a $400,000 loan at 3% interest over 30 years, you'll pay around $207,000 in interest. Reducing the loan term to 20 years would lower the interest paid to approximately $134,000.

Comparing Loans: What to Look For

When selecting a loan, it's essential to compare more than just interest rates. Additional factors like fees, repayment flexibility, and loan features can significantly impact your overall financial position.

Fees and Charges

Many loans come with a range of fees, including application fees, ongoing maintenance fees, and exit fees. Some lenders may also charge fees for features like redraw facilities or offset accounts. It's essential to factor these into your calculations when comparing loans.

Key Fees to Watch:

- **Application Fees**: One-time fee for setting up the loan.
- **Ongoing Fees**: Monthly or annual charges for maintaining the loan.
- **Early Exit Fees**: Fees for paying off the loan early or refinancing.

Repayment Flexibility

Some loans offer more flexibility than others in terms of repayment options. Features like **redraw facilities** and **offset accounts** can help reduce your overall interest costs or provide access to funds in case of emergency.

Redraw Facility:

This feature allows you to make extra repayments on your loan and then redraw those funds if needed. This can be useful for building up an emergency fund while still reducing your interest costs.

Offset Account:

An offset account is a transaction account linked to your mortgage. The balance in this account is deducted from your loan balance when calculating interest, reducing the amount of interest you pay over time.

Fixed vs. Variable vs. Split Options

When comparing loans, consider whether a fixed, variable, or split-rate option best suits your investment strategy. Each type of loan has advantages and disadvantages depending on market conditions and your cash flow requirements.

Loan Features and Conditions

Finally, review the specific conditions attached to each loan. Some loans may have restrictions on extra repayments, while others offer repayment holidays or flexible payment schedules. It's essential to match the loan's features to your personal financial situation and investment goals.

The Role of Deposit and Loan-to-Value Ratio

In property investment, understanding the relationship between your deposit and the loan-to-value ratio (LVR) is essential. These factors influence not only how much you can borrow but also the terms of your loan, including interest rates and repayment schedules. In this section, we will explore what LVR is, how it's calculated, the impact of deposit size on loan terms, and how equity can be used as a deposit for future property purchases.

What is LVR?

The **loan-to-value ratio (LVR)** is a metric used by lenders to assess the risk involved in lending money for property purchases. It is calculated as the percentage of the property's value that is being financed through a loan. The remainder of the property's value must be covered by your deposit.

The formula for LVR is:

LVR is calculated by dividing your loan amount by the value of the property, then multiplying by 100. For example, if you took out a $500,000 loan for a house worth $600,000, then your LVR would be $500,000 divided by $600,000 which is 83%.

Lenders use the LVR to assess how much risk they are taking on by offering the loan. A higher LVR means more risk for the lender, as the borrower is contributing a smaller deposit.

Why LVR Matters in Property Investment

LVR plays a significant role in property investment for both the lender and the borrower. For lenders, it helps them determine how much of the property's purchase price they are willing to finance and at what terms. For investors, understanding LVR is crucial because it affects not only your borrowing capacity but also your ability to manage risk and maximise returns.

Typical LVR Thresholds

Most lenders have set thresholds for LVR, which influence the loan terms offered. A **standard LVR** for property investment is around 80%, meaning the borrower is expected to contribute a 20% deposit. However, there are low-deposit loans available that allow for higher LVRs, up to 95%, with some additional conditions.

Impact of LVR on Loan Terms

LVR directly affects the terms of your loan, including interest rates, borrowing capacity, and potential fees. The size of your deposit is closely tied to your LVR, and larger deposits generally result in more favourable loan terms.

How Deposit Size Impacts Interest Rates

One of the most significant impacts of LVR is on **interest rates**. A lower LVR (meaning a larger deposit) typically results in lower interest rates. This is because the lender perceives the loan as less risky when the borrower contributes more equity. Lower interest rates mean lower monthly repayments and less overall interest paid over the life of the loan.

Borrowing Capacity and LVR

LVR also affects your **borrowing capacity**. A lower LVR allows you to borrow more, while a higher LVR limits the amount you can borrow. This is because lenders are more cautious about lending large amounts to borrowers with smaller deposits, as they have less of a financial stake in the property.

For example, with a 20% deposit (80% LVR), you can typically borrow more than if you only have a 5% deposit (95% LVR). In addition, lower LVRs open up access to more favourable loan products, which can further enhance your borrowing power.

Lender's Mortgage Insurance (LMI)

If your LVR exceeds 80%, many lenders will require you to pay **Lender's Mortgage Insurance (LMI)**. LMI is an insurance policy that protects the lender if you default on your loan. While LMI does not protect you, the borrower, it is a cost that must be factored into the overall expense of purchasing a property with a smaller deposit.

LMI can add several thousand dollars to the cost of the loan, depending on the size of the loan and the LVR. While it's possible to capitalise LMI into the loan, meaning it's added to the total loan amount and paid off over time, this will increase your monthly repayments and the total interest paid.

Low-Deposit Loans: Pros and Cons

For many first-time investors, saving up a 20% deposit can be challenging. Low-deposit loans, which allow for higher LVRs (up to 95%), can be an attractive option. However, they come with both benefits and drawbacks.

Pros of Low-Deposit Loans

- **Entering the Market Sooner**: A smaller deposit means you can purchase a property sooner, allowing you to take advantage of market growth and start building your portfolio.
- **Leverage**: A low deposit increases the amount of leverage you have, meaning you control a large asset with a smaller financial outlay.
- **Capital Growth**: If property prices rise, you can benefit from capital growth without having tied up a large portion of your funds in the deposit.

Cons of Low-Deposit Loans

- **Higher Interest Rates**: As mentioned earlier, high-LVR loans come with higher interest rates, increasing your monthly repayments and total loan costs.
- **Lender's Mortgage Insurance (LMI)**: As discussed, high-LVR loans often require LMI, adding to the overall cost of the loan.
- **Increased Risk**: With less equity in the property, you are more exposed to market fluctuations. A downturn in property values could result in negative equity, where your loan amount exceeds the property's value.

For investors considering a low-deposit loan, it's essential to weigh these pros and cons and evaluate whether entering the market early justifies the additional costs and risks.

Using Equity as a Deposit

One of the most powerful tools for property investors is the ability to use **equity** from an existing property as a deposit for purchasing a new property. This strategy allows you to grow your portfolio without needing to save for a deposit each time you want to buy.

What is Equity?

Equity is the difference between the value of a property and the outstanding balance of the loan secured against it. For example, if your property is valued at $500,000 and you have $300,000 remaining on your mortgage, you have $200,000 in equity.

Leveraging Equity for New Investments

Many lenders allow investors to use the equity in one property as a deposit for another. This is done by refinancing the original loan and borrowing against the equity you've built up.

Example:

Let's say you purchased a property worth $400,000, and its value has increased to $500,000. You have an outstanding mortgage of $300,000, giving you $200,000 in equity. If you refinance the property at

80% LVR, you can borrow up to $400,000 (80% of $500,000). Since you already owe $300,000, this allows you to access $100,000 in equity to use as a deposit for your next property.

Benefits of Using Equity as a Deposit

- **No Need for Cash Savings**: Instead of saving for a deposit, you can use your equity to fund new purchases, allowing you to scale your portfolio faster.
- **Increased Borrowing Power**: Equity provides a source of funds for deposits, meaning you can take on larger or more properties than if you were relying solely on cash savings.
- **Tax Efficiency**: In some cases, interest on the equity used to purchase investment properties may be tax-deductible, enhancing the financial benefits of this strategy.

Risks of Using Equity

While leveraging equity can be a powerful tool, it comes with risks:

- **Increased Debt**: Using equity means taking on more debt, which can increase your financial exposure, especially in a market downturn.
- **Negative Equity**: If property values fall, you could end up owing more than the property is worth, making it difficult to refinance or sell without a loss.

Navigating the Mortgage Application Process

Applying for a mortgage is a crucial step in financing your property investment, and understanding the application process can help you secure favourable terms and avoid common pitfalls. This section will guide you through what lenders look for, the steps involved in the application process, common mistakes to avoid, and how to handle rejection.

What Lenders Look For

When you apply for a mortgage, lenders assess several key factors to determine your suitability for a loan. They are looking to ensure that you can afford the loan and that you pose a manageable risk. Here's what they typically focus on:

Income Verification

Lenders need to verify your income to ensure that you can make your mortgage repayments. This usually involves providing recent payslips, tax returns, and possibly bank statements. For self-employed individuals, lenders may require additional documentation, such as business financial statements and tax returns for the past two to three years.

Tax Returns

Tax returns provide a comprehensive view of your income and financial stability. Lenders use them to verify your income, assess your financial history, and gauge your ability to repay the loan. Ensure your tax returns are up-to-date and accurately reflect your financial situation.

Personal Financial Details

Lenders will also review your personal financial details, including:

- **Assets and Liabilities**: A summary of what you own (e.g., savings, investments, properties) and what you owe (e.g., existing loans, credit card debt).
- **Credit Score**: Your credit score is a crucial factor that reflects your creditworthiness and financial behaviour. A higher score improves your chances of approval and may qualify you for better interest rates.
- **Employment History**: Lenders prefer stable employment. They'll look at your job history to ensure you have a consistent income stream.

Steps in the Application Process

Navigating the mortgage application process involves several key steps, each critical to securing a loan. Here's a breakdown of what to expect:

1. Pre-Approval

Before you start house hunting, getting pre-approved for a mortgage is essential. This involves providing basic financial information to a lender, who will then assess your borrowing capacity and offer a pre-approval amount. Pre-approval helps you understand your budget and demonstrates to sellers that you are a serious buyer.

2. Gathering Documents

Once you decide to proceed with a mortgage application, you'll need to gather and submit various documents, including:

- Proof of income (payslips, tax returns)
- Bank statements
- Identification (passport, driver's licence)
- Details of existing debts and assets
- Property information (if you have already selected one)

3. Application Submission

Submit your completed application along with the required documents. Your lender will review the information and may request additional documentation or clarification.

4. Assessment and Approval

The lender assesses your application, including your credit history, financial stability, and the property value. They will also conduct a property valuation to ensure it meets their lending criteria. If everything is satisfactory, they will issue a formal loan approval.

5. Loan Offer and Acceptance

Once approved, you'll receive a loan offer outlining the terms and conditions. Review the offer carefully, considering interest rates, fees, and repayment terms. If you accept the offer, you will need to sign the loan agreement.

6. Settlement

After accepting the loan offer, the settlement process involves transferring ownership of the property and finalising the mortgage. You'll need to coordinate with your solicitor or conveyancer to ensure all legal requirements are met, and final payments are made.

Common Mistakes to Avoid

Avoiding common mistakes in the mortgage application process can prevent delays and improve your chances of approval. Here are some pitfalls to watch out for:

1. Incomplete or Incorrect Documentation

Submitting incomplete or incorrect documentation can delay your application or result in a denial. Ensure all documents are accurate, up-to-date, and complete.

2. Failing to Check Your Credit Report

Before applying, check your credit report for any errors or discrepancies. Address any issues and improve your credit score if necessary. A poor credit score can negatively impact your application.

3. Overextending Your Budget

Applying for a loan that stretches your budget too thin can lead to financial strain. Ensure that the loan amount is manageable and that you can comfortably afford the repayments, including any potential changes in interest rates.

4. Making Large Purchases

Avoid making large purchases or taking on new debts before or during the mortgage application process. Significant changes in your financial situation can impact your loan approval.

5. Not Comparing Loan Options

Don't settle for the first loan offer you receive. Compare different lenders and loan products to find the best terms and rates for your situation.

Dealing with Rejection

If your loan application is rejected, it's important to understand why and how to address the issues. Here's what you can do:

1. Understand the Reason

Ask the lender for feedback on why your application was rejected. Common reasons include a low credit score, insufficient income, or high debt levels.

2. Address the Issues

Once you understand the reasons for rejection, take steps to address the issues. Improve your credit score, reduce existing debts, or save for a larger deposit.

3. Seek Professional Advice

Consider consulting a mortgage broker or financial advisor for personalised advice on improving your application and exploring alternative financing options.

4. Reapply When Ready

After addressing the issues, you can reapply for a mortgage. Ensure that your financial situation has improved and that you have a strong application before reapplying.

Refinancing Your Property Investments

Refinancing is a strategic financial move that can significantly impact your property investment journey. It involves revising the terms of your existing mortgage to better suit your current needs and financial situation. This section delves into what refinancing is, its benefits, when it might not be the best option, and provides a real-life case study to illustrate its potential advantages.

What is Refinancing?

Refinancing involves replacing your existing mortgage with a new loan, often from a different lender, but it can also be with your current lender. The primary goal is to alter the terms of the mortgage to better align with your financial objectives.

When and Why You Should Consider Refinancing:

1. **Interest Rates Have Dropped:** If market interest rates have fallen since you took out your original loan, refinancing can allow you to secure a lower rate, reducing your monthly payments and overall interest expense.
2. **Improved Credit Score:** A better credit score since your initial loan approval might qualify you for more favourable terms, including lower interest rates.
3. **Increased Property Value:** If your property's value has increased, you might be able to refinance to access some of that increased equity for other investments or to reduce your loan-to-value ratio (LVR).
4. **Change in Financial Goals:** If your financial goals have shifted, such as moving from a fixed-rate to a variable-rate loan to take advantage of lower rates, refinancing can help align your mortgage with your current strategy.
5. **Consolidating Debt:** Refinancing can also be used to consolidate high-interest debts into your mortgage, potentially lowering your overall interest payments.

Benefits of Refinancing

Refinancing can offer several significant benefits, depending on your financial situation and goals:

1. **Accessing Lower Interest Rates:**
   - **Cost Savings:** Lower interest rates reduce your monthly mortgage payments and the total amount of interest paid over the life of the loan. For instance, if you refinance a $400,000 mortgage from a 5% to a 3% interest rate, you could save thousands in interest over the term of the loan.
   - **Increased Cash Flow:** Lower payments free up cash that can be redirected towards other investments or personal expenses.
2. **Pulling Out Equity:**
   - **Home Equity Loans:** If your property's value has increased, refinancing allows you to pull out equity (a cash-out refinance). This cash can be used for further property purchases, renovations, or other investments.
   - **Portfolio Expansion:** Accessing equity to reinvest in additional properties can accelerate your investment growth. For example, using equity from one property to fund a deposit on a new investment can leverage your portfolio.
3. **Improving Cash Flow:**
   - **Interest-Only Options:** Refinancing to an interest-only loan period can temporarily improve cash flow, though it's important to plan for the transition to principal repayments.
   - **Extended Loan Terms:** Extending the term of your loan can reduce monthly payments, improving your cash flow, though it might increase the total interest paid.

When Not to Refinance

While refinancing can be advantageous, it's not always the best option. Understanding when to avoid refinancing is crucial:

1. **High Costs and Fees:**
   - **Application Fees:** Refinancing involves application and processing fees, which can offset the savings from a lower interest rate. Ensure the long-term benefits outweigh these initial costs.
   - **Break Costs:** If you're breaking a fixed-rate loan, you may incur break costs, which can be substantial.
2. **Short-Term Savings vs. Long-Term Costs:**
   - **Extended Loan Term:** Extending the term of your loan might reduce monthly payments but can increase the total amount of interest paid over the life of the loan. Evaluate whether the short-term benefits justify the long-term costs.
3. **Prepayment Penalties:**
   - **Penalties:** Some mortgages come with prepayment penalties, which can make refinancing less attractive if these penalties are significant.
4. **Poor Credit Score:**
   - **Unfavourable Terms:** If your credit score has declined, you might not qualify for better terms. In such cases, refinancing could result in higher rates or less favourable conditions.

Refinancing Case Study

Scenario: Sarah, an experienced property investor, purchased a two-bedroom apartment for $300,000 five years ago. At the time, she secured a 5% fixed-rate mortgage. The property's value has since increased to $450,000, and current market interest rates have dropped to 3%.

Refinancing Decision:

- **Current Loan:** $250,000 remaining on the original loan.
- **New Loan:** Refinance to a new mortgage at 3% interest rate for the remaining term.

Steps Taken:

1. **Appraisal and Equity Calculation:** Sarah had her property appraised and confirmed its current value at $450,000. With $250,000 remaining on her loan, she had $200,000 in equity.
2. **New Loan Terms:** She refinanced to a new 3% interest rate loan, reducing her monthly payments and saving on interest. She also opted for a cash-out refinance to access $50,000 of her equity for further investments.

Outcomes:

- **Interest Savings:** Sarah's monthly payments decreased from $1,600 to $1,200, saving $400 per month. Over the remaining term, this equated to thousands in interest savings.
- **Equity Utilisation:** The $50,000 cash-out allowed Sarah to purchase a new property, further expanding her investment portfolio and accelerating her wealth growth.

Lessons Learned:

- **Evaluate Costs vs. Benefits:** Sarah's decision to refinance was driven by the significant savings on interest and the opportunity to leverage her equity for new investments.
- **Market Conditions:** Timing her refinance when interest rates dropped and her property value increased allowed her to maximise benefits.

Managing Debt in Property Investment

Managing debt is a crucial aspect of property investment. When approached strategically, debt can be an empowering tool to grow your portfolio and generate wealth. However, mismanagement of debt can lead to financial strain and missed opportunities. This section will explore the difference between good and bad debt, strategies for reducing debt, and how to maintain healthy debt ratios while expanding your investment portfolio.

Good Debt vs. Bad Debt

Understanding the distinction between good and bad debt is fundamental to property investment success. The right kind of debt can help you build wealth, while the wrong kind can become a financial burden.

Good Debt:

- **Definition:** Good debt refers to borrowing that is used to acquire assets that appreciate in value or generate income. In the context of property investment, this typically includes mortgages on properties that produce rental income and increase in value over time.
- **Wealth Creation:** Property investment debt is often considered good debt because it allows investors to leverage other people's money (OPM) to purchase assets they may not be able to afford outright. The rental income can cover loan repayments, and over time, capital appreciation builds equity.
- **Tax Benefits:** In many countries, interest on loans for investment properties is tax-deductible, further enhancing the financial benefits of carrying property investment debt.

Bad Debt:

- **Definition:** Bad debt refers to borrowing that is used to purchase items that depreciate in value or do not generate income. Examples include credit card debt, personal loans for consumer goods, or car loans.
- **Financial Strain:** Bad debt is often high-interest and does not offer a return on investment. It can erode your financial stability, making it harder to service good debt like property loans.

For property investors, the goal is to accumulate good debt—debt that is productive, manageable, and contributes to wealth creation.

Strategies for Reducing Debt

While good debt can be advantageous, it is important to manage and reduce it where possible. There are several strategies that investors can use to keep their debt levels manageable and improve their financial position.

1. **Paying Down Principal:**
    - **Accelerated Repayments:** Making extra payments towards the principal of your loan can significantly reduce the total interest paid over the life of the loan. Even small, additional payments each month can shorten the loan term and save thousands in interest.
    - **Lump-Sum Payments:** If you come into extra money, such as a bonus or an inheritance, consider using it to make a lump-sum payment towards your mortgage. This can lower the outstanding balance and reduce your ongoing monthly payments.
2. **Refinancing:**
    - **Lowering Interest Rates:** As mentioned earlier, refinancing can help you secure a lower interest rate, which reduces your monthly payments and the total amount of interest paid over time. This is especially useful if market interest rates have fallen or your credit score has improved since you initially took out the loan.
    - **Shortening the Loan Term:** If your financial situation has improved, consider refinancing to a loan with a shorter term. While this will increase monthly payments, it can save you a substantial amount in interest and help you pay off the loan faster.
3. **Consolidating Loans:**
    - **Simplifying Debt Management:** If you have multiple loans, consolidating them into a single loan can simplify repayments and potentially lower your overall interest rate.

This strategy works particularly well if your debts include high-interest personal loans or credit card debt.
- **Reduced Interest Payments:** By consolidating higher-interest debts into your mortgage or a lower-interest loan, you can reduce the total amount of interest you pay and free up cash flow for other investments.

Maintaining Healthy Debt Ratios

As you grow your property portfolio, it is crucial to maintain healthy debt ratios to ensure that your investments remain manageable and financially sustainable.

1. **Debt-to-Income Ratio (DTI):**
   - **Definition:** Your debt-to-income ratio is a measure of your total monthly debt payments compared to your gross monthly income. Lenders often use this ratio to assess your ability to take on additional debt.
   - **Maintaining a Healthy DTI:** Ideally, your DTI should remain below 36%, although some lenders may allow higher ratios for property investors. Keeping your DTI within this range ensures that your debt is manageable and reduces the risk of financial strain.
   - **Improving DTI:** To lower your DTI, focus on reducing bad debt and increasing your income, either through salary growth or additional rental properties.

2. **Loan-to-Value Ratio (LVR):**
   - **Definition:** The loan-to-value ratio is the percentage of the property's value that is financed through a loan. For example, if you have a $400,000 loan on a $500,000 property, your LVR is 80%.
   - **Target LVR:** A lower LVR is generally better, as it indicates that you have more equity in the property. Lenders typically prefer an LVR of 80% or lower for investment properties. Keeping your LVR below this threshold can help you secure better loan terms and avoid paying for lender's mortgage insurance (LMI).
   - **Managing LVR:** To reduce your LVR, consider using excess rental income or additional savings to pay down the mortgage, or refinance if your property's value has increased.

3. **Cash Flow Management:**
   - **Positive vs. Negative Gearing:** Positive gearing occurs when your rental income exceeds your mortgage and other property-related expenses, while negative gearing means you are making a loss. While negative gearing can provide tax benefits, positive gearing ensures that your investment generates a profit and contributes to your financial stability.
   - **Cash Buffer:** Maintaining a cash buffer or emergency fund is essential for managing unforeseen expenses, such as property repairs or periods of vacancy. This buffer protects your investments and ensures you can continue servicing your debt even in challenging times.

Tax Considerations in Property Financing

Understanding the tax implications of property investment is essential for maximising your returns and ensuring compliance with tax laws. Proper tax planning can significantly enhance your overall profitability, and failing to take full advantage of tax-saving opportunities can result in missed benefits. In this section, we'll explore key tax considerations for property financing, including tax-deductible interest, depreciation benefits, negative gearing, and capital gains tax (CGT).

Tax-Deductible Interest

One of the primary benefits of property investment is the ability to claim tax deductions on interest paid for investment loans. By understanding how to leverage tax-deductible interest, you can significantly reduce your taxable income and improve cash flow.

What is Tax-Deductible Interest?

- **Investment Loans:** The interest paid on loans used to finance investment properties is typically tax-deductible. This applies to loans for purchasing the property, as well as loans taken out for property-related expenses, such as repairs, renovations, and maintenance.
- **Personal Loans:** It's important to note that interest on personal loans (such as a mortgage on your primary residence) is not tax-deductible. This is why it's crucial to separate personal and investment loans to avoid any confusion when filing taxes.

How It Works:

- **Claiming Deductions:** Each year, you can deduct the interest portion of your investment loan repayments from your taxable income. This effectively lowers your tax liability and allows you to retain more of your rental income. For example, if you paid $10,000 in interest on an investment loan, that $10,000 is deducted from your income, reducing the amount of tax you owe.
- **Interest-Only Loans:** Some investors choose interest-only loans because they provide higher tax deductions in the short term, as the entire repayment is considered interest. This strategy can improve cash flow while maximising the immediate tax benefits.

Strategies to Maximise Deductions:

- **Interest Prepayment:** In some cases, prepaying the interest on your investment loan for the upcoming financial year can allow you to claim a larger deduction in the current year. This strategy can be especially useful if you expect your income to increase in the future, moving you into a higher tax bracket.
- **Loan Structuring:** It's important to keep investment loans separate from personal loans, as mixing the two can complicate your tax situation and make it difficult to claim the full deductions you're entitled to.

Depreciation Benefits

Depreciation is another powerful tool for reducing your tax liability as a property investor. By claiming depreciation on your property, you can deduct the decreasing value of the building and its assets over time.

What is Depreciation?

- **Building Depreciation:** Buildings naturally wear out over time, and the tax code allows property investors to claim deductions for this "wear and tear." This applies primarily to the structure of the building, as well as any permanent fixtures.
- **Asset Depreciation:** In addition to the building itself, you can also depreciate certain assets within the property, such as appliances, carpeting, and light fixtures. These are referred to as "plant and equipment" assets.

How Depreciation Works:

- **Capital Works Deduction (Division 43):** The capital works deduction allows investors to claim a portion of the construction costs of the building each year. Residential properties built after 1985 typically qualify for this deduction, which is spread out over 40 years.
- **Depreciating Assets (Division 40):** For items like appliances, investors can claim a deduction for the depreciation of these assets based on their expected lifespan. A tax depreciation schedule, prepared by a qualified quantity surveyor, outlines these deductions and helps ensure you're claiming all eligible depreciation.

Benefits of Depreciation:

- **Non-Cash Deduction:** Depreciation is a non-cash deduction, meaning you don't have to spend any money to claim it. It simply recognizes the decreasing value of your property and assets over time, which can reduce your taxable income and improve your cash flow.
- **Tax-Deferred Income:** By claiming depreciation, you effectively defer paying taxes on a portion of your rental income, allowing you to keep more of your money working for you.

Negative Gearing

Negative gearing is a popular strategy among property investors, especially in markets where rental yields are lower than mortgage repayments. Understanding how negative gearing works can help you optimise your tax position and improve your overall investment returns.

What is Negative Gearing?

- **Definition:** Negative gearing occurs when the cost of owning an investment property (including mortgage interest, property management fees, and maintenance expenses) exceeds the rental income generated by the property. This creates a taxable loss, which can be offset against other income, such as salary or wages.
- **Benefit:** The primary benefit of negative gearing is that it reduces your taxable income, which can lower your overall tax liability. The strategy is particularly useful for high-income earners looking to minimise their tax bill.

How Negative Gearing Works:

- **Offsetting Income:** If your property generates a $20,000 annual rental income but your expenses (including loan interest and maintenance) total $25,000, you have a $5,000 loss. This loss can be used to reduce your taxable income, effectively lowering your tax bill.

- **Long-Term Strategy:** While negative gearing results in a short-term loss, investors typically rely on long-term capital gains to offset these losses. The idea is that, over time, the property will appreciate in value, and the tax benefits of negative gearing will help improve cash flow until the property becomes positively geared.

Risks of Negative Gearing:

- **Market Fluctuations:** Negative gearing assumes that property prices will rise over the long term, which isn't always guaranteed. Market downturns can result in lower capital gains, making it harder to offset the losses from negative gearing.
- **Cash Flow Management:** Negative gearing can strain your cash flow, especially if you're relying on personal income to cover property losses. It's important to have a solid financial plan in place to ensure you can sustain the strategy over the long term.

Capital Gains Tax (CGT)

Capital gains tax (CGT) is a tax on the profit made from the sale of an investment property. Understanding how CGT works is crucial for planning your exit strategy and ensuring you don't get caught off-guard by a large tax bill when you sell a property.

What is Capital Gains Tax?

- **Definition:** CGT is the tax levied on the profit (or capital gain) made from selling an investment property. The gain is calculated as the difference between the sale price and the property's original purchase price, plus any costs associated with buying and selling the property.
- **Exemptions:** The sale of your primary residence is typically exempt from CGT, but investment properties are subject to this tax.

How CGT Works:

- **Calculating Capital Gains:** To calculate your capital gain, subtract the property's purchase price (plus any costs, such as stamp duty and legal fees) from the sale price. If you've held the property for more than 12 months, you may be eligible for a CGT discount.
- **50% CGT Discount:** In many countries, including Australia, investors who hold a property for more than one year are eligible for a 50% CGT discount. This means you only pay tax on half of the capital gain, which can significantly reduce your tax liability.

Impact of Refinancing:

- **Equity Release:** Refinancing a property to pull out equity does not trigger CGT because the property isn't being sold. However, if you eventually sell the property, the capital gain will be calculated based on the original purchase price, not the refinanced amount.
- **Selling After Refinancing:** If you sell a property after refinancing, any capital gain will be subject to CGT. It's important to plan for this eventual tax liability when using equity from a property to finance other investments.

Reducing Your CGT Liability:

- **Hold for Longer Than 12 Months:** The most common way to reduce CGT is to hold the property for at least 12 months, which qualifies you for the 50% discount.
- **Offsetting Gains with Losses:** If you have other investments that have incurred a capital loss, you can use these losses to offset your capital gains, further reducing your CGT liability.

Case Studies: Financing Strategies That Worked

The world of property investment can be complex, especially when it comes to financing strategies. Successful investors often rely on innovative financing techniques to maximise returns and expand their portfolios. In this section, we'll explore three real-world case studies that highlight how different financing approaches can lead to property investment success.

Case Study 1: Leveraging Equity for Rapid Portfolio Growth

The Investor's Strategy: In this case, a first-time property investor named Sarah managed to grow her portfolio quickly by leveraging the equity in her properties. After purchasing her first below-market-value (BMV) property, Sarah utilised the concept of instant equity to finance additional acquisitions.

How It Worked:

1. **Initial Purchase:** Sarah purchased her first property, a BMV deal, in a high-growth area for $300,000, with an 80% loan-to-value ratio (LVR). The market value of the property was assessed at $350,000, giving her $50,000 in instant equity.
2. **Refinancing:** After holding the property for just 12 months, Sarah saw a further rise in the property's market value due to strong capital growth in the area. The property was now worth $400,000. Sarah approached her lender to refinance the property and accessed 80% of the new value, releasing $80,000 in equity.
3. **Using Equity for a Second Property:** With $80,000 in equity, Sarah used this as a deposit to purchase a second property. She again targeted a BMV property, purchasing it for $250,000 while its market value was estimated at $280,000. By repeating the strategy, Sarah was able to secure multiple properties in a short period.

Key Takeaways:

- **Equity Recycling:** Sarah's use of instant equity allowed her to avoid saving for deposits each time and rapidly scale her portfolio.
- **High-Growth Areas:** Investing in high-growth locations enabled her to maximise capital appreciation and unlock more equity through refinancing.

Case Study 2: Creative Financing with Joint Ventures

The Investor's Strategy: Two investors, Jack and Emily, wanted to enter the property market but lacked sufficient individual funds to purchase a higher-yield property. Instead of going it alone, they formed a joint venture (JV) partnership, pooling their financial resources to acquire a larger, higher-yield investment.

How It Worked:

1. **Pooling Resources:** Jack and Emily each contributed $50,000, giving them a combined deposit of $100,000. With a total budget of $500,000, they were able to secure an 80% LVR loan, using their combined capital as the deposit.
2. **Acquiring a Multi-Family Unit:** Rather than purchasing single-family homes, they opted for a multi-family unit with five apartments. This property offered a strong rental yield and long-term potential for capital growth.
3. **Joint Ownership Agreement:** To protect both parties' interests, they set up a joint venture agreement. This legal document outlined the roles and responsibilities of each partner, including how profits would be shared and how the property would be managed. They also clarified exit strategies, detailing what would happen if either party wished to sell their share of the property.
4. **High Rental Income:** The multi-family unit provided a higher rental income than they could have achieved individually. The rental income covered the mortgage, maintenance, and other costs, while still generating a healthy cash flow for both Jack and Emily.

Key Takeaways:

- **Joint Ventures:** Pooling resources allowed Jack and Emily to access larger, higher-yield properties that would have been unattainable individually.
- **Risk Sharing:** A well-structured joint venture agreement ensured both investors had clear expectations and legal protection, minimising potential conflicts.

Case Study 3: Overcoming Loan Rejection

The Investor's Strategy: In this case, Mark, a self-employed investor, faced rejection from a major bank when applying for a mortgage. However, instead of giving up on his property investment goals, he explored alternative lending options and successfully secured financing through a different lender.

How It Worked:

1. **Loan Rejection:** Mark, who ran his own small business, applied for a mortgage from a well-known bank to purchase an investment property. However, due to his irregular income and less-than-ideal credit score, the bank rejected his application. The bank was concerned about his ability to make consistent repayments based on his self-employment status.
2. **Assessing Financial Position:** Following the rejection, Mark took steps to improve his financial situation. He worked with his accountant to ensure his tax returns were up-to-date and reflected his true earnings. He also reviewed his personal expenses to demonstrate stronger financial management.
3. **Alternative Lenders:** Mark approached a mortgage broker who specialised in securing loans for self-employed individuals. The broker connected Mark with a second-tier lender that had more flexible lending criteria. Although the lender charged a slightly higher interest rate, they were willing to offer him a loan based on his adjusted income figures and the potential rental income from the investment property.
4. **Success Through Persistence:** Despite the initial rejection, Mark was able to secure a mortgage for the investment property with the second lender. The property's strong rental yield helped offset the higher interest rates, allowing Mark to continue building his portfolio.

Chapter 4: My Journey: From 1st to 3rd Property

Introduction:

Entering the world of property investment was a pivotal moment in my life. At the time, I didn't fully comprehend the significance of the decision I was making, but I knew it had the potential to transform my financial future. My first property investment was much more than just buying real estate; it was a turning point that redefined my approach to wealth-building, risk management, and financial independence.

I remember the overwhelming sense of excitement, mixed with a degree of uncertainty, as I stood at the crossroads of my investment journey. Buying my first property wasn't just a financial decision, it was the beginning of a long-term commitment to a path that would shape my future. It required research, planning, and a deep dive into an industry I was only beginning to understand. The leap from being an observer to becoming an active participant in the property market was an exhilarating and, at times, intimidating experience. Still, it was also an essential step in building a successful portfolio that I would later expand on in ways I hadn't initially imagined.

Reflecting on My First Investment

The decision to invest in my first property didn't happen overnight. I was intrigued by real estate from a young age, but when I finally made the move, it was driven by a clear understanding of the importance of long-term financial planning. I knew that owning property was one of the most reliable ways to build wealth, and I was ready to take the plunge. My first property wasn't a grand purchase; it was modest in size, a one-bedroom unit in a market that showed promise. But more importantly, it was within my means and allowed me to make the transition from dreaming about property investment to actually owning a piece of real estate.

I knew the significance of starting with something manageable, focusing on a property that had the potential for growth but wouldn't overstretch my finances. While the size of the property might not have been impressive to others, it was monumental to me. This initial purchase set the foundation for everything that followed. The feeling of owning an asset that could potentially increase in value over time was empowering, and it fueled my desire to continue learning and growing as an investor.

From the outset, I treated this first investment as a stepping stone rather than a final destination. I viewed it as an opportunity to gain hands-on experience in the property market. The lessons I learned from this first purchase would be instrumental in shaping my approach to future investments. I quickly realised that the property market was not a static landscape but a dynamic, ever-evolving one. Understanding market trends, buyer behaviour, and financial strategies were essential components of becoming a successful investor.

Lessons Learned from Taking the Leap

Diving into the property market for the first time taught me numerous valuable lessons, not just about property investment but about discipline, strategy, and perseverance. One of the most important takeaways was the significance of research. Before buying the property, I spent countless hours analysing market trends, property prices, and the area's growth potential. I learned that, in real estate, the location is critical, but timing is just as important. Identifying a market that was on the brink of growth was one of the smartest moves I made with this first purchase.

I also quickly learned the importance of financing strategies. Understanding loan structures, interest rates, and the role of leveraging were critical factors in ensuring I could afford not just the first property but the next ones. My first property wasn't just a purchase; it was the start of a financial strategy that involved carefully managing debt while maximising my investment returns.

Another significant lesson was learning to manage risk. No investment is without its challenges, and there were times when the uncertainties of the property market made me question my decisions. But every setback or moment of doubt became an opportunity to adapt, learn, and refine my strategies. For example, while my first property was a relatively smooth process, I encountered unexpected renovation costs and property management challenges that I hadn't fully anticipated. These hurdles were a reminder that flexibility and preparedness are vital in the property world. Adapting to changes and being ready for the unexpected are just as important as careful planning.

Perhaps the most crucial lesson was the importance of patience. In property investment, success doesn't come overnight. I realised that building a successful portfolio takes time, but with the right strategy and mindset, the rewards can be significant. Watching the value of my first property gradually increase over time reinforced the idea that property investment is a long game. It requires a mix of strategy, timing, and a willingness to wait for returns. This patience, combined with the knowledge I gained, laid the groundwork for expanding my portfolio.

Setting the Stage for Rapid Growth

My first property investment wasn't just a singular achievement; it was the catalyst that propelled me forward. After gaining a foothold in the property market, I realised that the strategies and lessons I'd learned could be applied to future purchases. The idea of rapidly growing my portfolio seemed achievable, but it required a disciplined approach and a clear understanding of how to leverage the equity from my first property.

The most exciting part of this journey was the realisation that each new property purchase could be easier and more financially rewarding than the last. By carefully managing my first investment, I was able to generate equity that allowed me to fund future deals. This concept of leveraging equity became a cornerstone of my strategy, enabling me to expand my portfolio without needing massive cash reserves for each new purchase.

With my first property, I gained the confidence to make bolder moves. I began to understand how to identify opportunities, negotiate better deals, and structure loans to maximise cash flow. Each success built on the last, and I found myself becoming more comfortable navigating the complexities of the property market.

The Excitement of Future Investments

Looking back, my first property investment was not just a financial decision; it was the beginning of a journey that would shape my future in ways I hadn't anticipated. It taught me that property investment is not just about acquiring assets but about developing a mindset of continuous learning and growth. Each property added to my portfolio represented a new chapter, filled with its own challenges, risks, and rewards.

What excites me the most is the prospect of future investments. The knowledge and experience I've gained from my first property have given me the confidence to pursue more significant opportunities and set higher goals. I'm no longer just an investor; I'm a strategist, continually refining my approach to property investment.

In many ways, my first property was the foundation upon which I've built a career in property investment. It was the catalyst for change, the spark that ignited a passion for real estate that continues to drive me today. And while that first purchase will always hold a special place in my journey, it's just the beginning of what I hope will be a long and rewarding path in property investment.

The First Property: One-Bedroom Unit

The decision to invest in my first property was a pivotal moment in my journey as a property investor. As a first-time buyer, I knew I had to make the right choice from the outset, particularly when it came to location, market conditions, and ensuring the property would offer a strong return on investment. Through research, strategic planning, and a willingness to take calculated risks, I was able to secure a one-bedroom unit that set the stage for my future success.

Choosing the Right Location

The first significant step in my property investment journey was selecting the right location for my first purchase. One of the most critical factors in real estate is the old adage: "location, location, location." I was aware that choosing a property in the right area could either make or break my investment, especially since I was just starting out.

Instead of looking at more expensive markets in major cities, where property prices were prohibitively high, I decided to focus on a market that was more affordable but still had growth potential. After carefully analysing several markets, I settled on a suburban area that offered the perfect balance between affordability and opportunity for capital growth.

While major cities were tempting due to their high demand, I realised that the higher entry costs and slower growth rates would limit my ability to scale my portfolio quickly. By choosing this particular area, I was able to capitalise on an emerging market that was still affordable, with property prices showing a steady upward trend. I specifically sought a neighbourhood with a mix of established infrastructure, schools, transport links, and planned developments, all of which indicated future growth potential.

Market Analysis and Growth Potential

Before committing to the purchase, I conducted extensive market analysis. This involved looking at historical property price trends, local employment rates, and population growth in the area. I learned that a key indicator of a healthy property market is steady demand, driven by factors like job opportunities, a growing population, and infrastructure development. The area I chose had all these factors, with property prices increasing modestly year on year.

I researched local government plans, such as infrastructure projects and amenities that would likely boost the area's appeal to tenants and homebuyers. By analysing these factors, I was able to forecast potential appreciation in property values and rental demand, ensuring that the investment was positioned for long-term growth.

Research Process: Assessing Market Trends

To ensure that I wasn't making decisions based on gut feeling alone, I delved deeply into the data. I used online property portals to track sale prices and trends over the previous five to ten years, consulted with local real estate agents to get their expert opinions, and reviewed market reports. One of the most important aspects of my research was comparing the area's property prices to other similar regions. I wanted to ensure that I was entering a market that was undervalued but had growth potential, rather than overpaying for a property in an already inflated market.

I paid particular attention to population growth projections, which are a key indicator of future housing demand. If more people were moving into the area, that meant increased demand for rental properties, which would ensure strong occupancy rates and potential rental increases over time. The data suggested that the area was transitioning from being overlooked by investors to becoming an attractive option for first-time buyers and renters.

The Purchase Process: Securing an Off-Market Deal

Once I had identified the right area, I focused on finding the right property. Rather than browsing listings available to the general public, I looked for off-market opportunities. Off-market deals are properties that are for sale but not widely advertised, giving buyers a chance to negotiate better terms without the competition of an open market.

To find such opportunities, I networked with local real estate agents, letting them know I was a serious buyer interested in below-market-value properties. By building relationships with agents, I positioned myself as someone they could trust to close a deal quickly, which led to one agent presenting me with a one-bedroom unit that had not yet been listed publicly.

Negotiating a Below-Market-Value (BMV) Property

The property was in need of some cosmetic repairs, which worked in my favour. Sellers often price properties lower when they require work, and in this case, the owner was looking for a quick sale, making it a prime candidate for negotiation. I knew from my research that the property was undervalued, but I still needed to secure it at the lowest possible price to create instant equity and reduce my overall financial risk.

During the negotiation process, I leveraged the property's condition to argue for a reduced price, highlighting the costs I would need to incur for renovations. After several rounds of negotiation, I managed to purchase the property for a price well below its market value, which instantly increased my equity position from the moment I closed the deal. This was a crucial factor in allowing me to later leverage the property's equity for future investments.

Key Challenges in Securing Financing as a First-Time Buyer

As a first-time buyer, securing financing wasn't without its challenges. Lenders tend to be more cautious with first-time investors, particularly if they have limited experience or savings. However, I was able to demonstrate financial discipline through a solid savings history and by showing the thorough market research I had conducted.

I approached multiple lenders to compare loan offers and chose one that offered the most favourable terms, including a competitive interest rate and the option for interest-only payments in the first few years. The interest-only loan allowed me to maximise my cash flow, which was essential as I worked to build a positive rental yield.

One of the challenges I faced was ensuring that my loan-to-value ratio (LVR) was within a range that made the bank comfortable lending to me. I had to make sure that my deposit and the property's valuation aligned with the bank's criteria, which took careful budgeting and financial planning.

Cosmetic Renovations: Enhancing the Property's Appeal

Once the purchase was completed, my next step was to enhance the property's value through cosmetic renovations. Given that the unit was structurally sound but outdated, I focused on upgrades that would improve its marketability to tenants without requiring significant financial outlay. The renovations included repainting the interior, updating the flooring, and modernising the kitchen and bathroom fixtures.

I budgeted approximately 5% of the property's purchase price for these renovations, which was a relatively modest investment that yielded significant results. These improvements not only increased the property's appeal to potential tenants but also allowed me to increase the rental asking price, improving my overall yield.

Rental Yield Improvement Post-Renovation

The renovations had an immediate impact on the property's rental yield. Before the upgrades, the expected rental income was modest, reflecting the unit's outdated condition. However, once the improvements were completed, I was able to raise the rent by nearly 20%, significantly increasing my cash flow.

The property, which was initially expected to deliver a modest rental yield, was now delivering returns that exceeded my expectations. The increase in rent also attracted more stable, long-term tenants, reducing vacancy periods and ensuring consistent income.

Current Performance: Market Value and Rental Returns Today

Today, the property has continued to appreciate in value, with its current market value significantly higher than the original purchase price. The increase in equity has not only boosted my net worth but has also provided the financial leverage needed to secure additional properties. The rental returns have remained strong, providing consistent cash flow and serving as a foundation for my property portfolio.

In hindsight, the decision to invest in this one-bedroom unit was one of the best choices I made. It provided a low-risk entry point into the property market while delivering solid financial returns. By selecting the right location, negotiating a BMV deal, and enhancing the property's appeal through renovations, I was able to create a highly profitable investment that continues to contribute to my overall portfolio growth.

The Second Property: Another Unit in a Growing Suburb

After successfully acquiring my first property, the journey toward building a property portfolio had truly begun. The lessons learned from my first investment laid the foundation for my next steps, including a clearer understanding of what to look for in future investments. The next challenge was to identify another affordable growth market, secure a second below-market-value (BMV) property, and leverage the equity from my first property to finance this new purchase.

Why I Chose This Suburb: Identifying Another Affordable Growth Market

When it came time to acquire my second property, I knew that I needed to apply the same principles that had worked for my first investment. I was looking for an area that was still undervalued, with strong potential for future growth, but without the high entry costs of major city markets. However, I also wanted to diversify slightly by focusing on a different region from my first property. The goal was to spread my investments geographically, which would help mitigate risks while maximising growth potential.

The suburb I eventually selected was a growing residential area located on the outskirts of a major city, known for its recent surge in population and development projects. I identified it as a potential hotspot based on a variety of factors, including local government plans for infrastructure improvements, a steady rise in population, and increasing demand for rental properties. It was also still affordable, which meant I could enter the market without overstretching my budget.

Analysing the Area's Potential and Comparing it with Other Suburbs

To ensure I was making an informed decision, I conducted a comparative analysis of several neighbouring suburbs, looking at their property prices, historical growth rates, and local amenities. The area I selected showed signs of being in the early stages of a growth cycle, with relatively low property prices but clear upward momentum. This was reflected in a modest but steady increase in property values over the past five years, alongside announcements of new infrastructure projects such as transportation links and commercial developments.

One of the key indicators that reinforced my decision was the demographic shift in the area. As younger families and professionals began to move away from the inner city in search of affordable housing, this suburb had become a desirable location for those looking for more space and better value for money. Additionally, the rental market in the area was thriving, with low vacancy rates and strong rental demand, making it an attractive option for property investors like myself.

By comparing the area with other potential suburbs, I was able to identify that it had a unique combination of affordability and growth potential, without the competition and inflated prices found in more established suburbs.

The Strategy Behind Acquiring a Second BMV Property

Once I had decided on the suburb, the next step was to find a property that met my investment criteria—namely, a below-market-value property that could deliver both capital growth and rental yield. As with my first investment, I looked for off-market opportunities where I could negotiate directly with the seller. I was again able to leverage relationships I had built with real estate agents to gain access to listings that had not yet hit the open market.

The property I eventually purchased was a two-bedroom unit that needed some cosmetic upgrades but was otherwise in solid structural condition. The owner was motivated to sell quickly due to financial pressures, which gave me an advantage in negotiating a lower price. The strategy was the same as my first property: buy below market value, make minor renovations, and rent the property out to generate consistent cash flow while waiting for capital appreciation.

By staying disciplined and not overpaying, I was able to purchase the unit for significantly less than its true market value. This immediately increased my equity position and reduced the risks associated with the investment.

Financing the Purchase: Using Equity from the First Property

A key advantage I had when purchasing the second property was the equity I had built up in my first property. The increase in the first property's market value, combined with the renovations I had made, meant that I had gained significant equity, which I could use as leverage for my next purchase.

I approached the same lender I had used for my first property and applied for a line of credit, secured against the equity in my first property. By refinancing the original loan, I was able to pull out enough equity to cover the deposit and associated costs for the second property, without having to dip into my personal savings.

This strategy of using equity to finance new investments is a powerful tool for property investors, as it allows you to grow your portfolio without needing to save large amounts of cash for each subsequent purchase. The key to making this work is ensuring that the first property continues to perform well, both in terms of rental income and capital appreciation, to support the additional debt taken on for the new purchase.

Navigating the Financing Process for Property Number Two

While leveraging the equity from my first property made the financing process easier, there were still some challenges to navigate. For instance, lenders are typically more cautious with second properties, especially if the investor has only recently acquired their first. To mitigate this, I had to present a strong financial case, demonstrating that I had a stable rental income from my first property and that the second property had strong cash flow potential.

I worked closely with my mortgage broker to ensure that I was securing the best possible loan terms for the second property. We discussed various loan structures, including the option of an interest-only period to improve cash flow during the first few years. In the end, I opted for a principal-and-interest loan, as it offered lower interest rates and allowed me to gradually pay down the mortgage while benefiting from capital growth.

The Importance of Due Diligence: Researching the Property Thoroughly

One of the most important lessons I learned from my first property was the need for thorough due diligence. Before committing to the purchase, I conducted a comprehensive inspection of the property, checking for any potential structural issues or hidden costs that might affect its long-term performance.

I hired a professional building inspector to assess the property, which gave me peace of mind that there were no major repairs needed. I also researched the local rental market, ensuring that there was sufficient demand for a two-bedroom unit in the area. This involved checking comparable rental listings, speaking with local real estate agents, and reviewing historical vacancy rates.

By doing this due diligence, I was able to avoid common pitfalls, such as purchasing a property with significant maintenance issues or in an area with low rental demand. While the process was time-consuming, it ultimately saved me from potential financial headaches down the road.

Avoiding Pitfalls and Learning from Minor Mistakes

Even with all the preparation and research, no property purchase is without its challenges. One minor mistake I made during the purchase of the second property was underestimating the costs of certain cosmetic renovations. While I had budgeted for painting and new flooring, I hadn't accounted for some unexpected costs, such as plumbing repairs and additional electrical work. These costs ate into my initial renovation budget, but fortunately, they didn't derail the overall profitability of the investment.

This experience taught me to always have a contingency fund for unexpected expenses, particularly when purchasing older properties that may have hidden maintenance issues.

Growth and Return: How the Second Property's Value Increased

The second property proved to be a successful investment. After completing the necessary cosmetic upgrades, I was able to secure a tenant within a week of listing the property for rent. The improvements not only enhanced the property's appeal but also allowed me to charge a higher rent than initially expected.

Over time, the property's value has appreciated significantly, thanks to the area's ongoing growth and development. The combination of strong rental income and capital growth has made the second property a key contributor to my portfolio's overall performance.

Current Market Value and Rental Income

Today, the second property continues to perform well. Its current market value has increased by more than 60% since I purchased it, thanks to both the initial BMV deal and the growth of the suburb. The rental income has remained stable, providing consistent cash flow and helping to offset the mortgage repayments.

By leveraging the equity from my first property, conducting thorough due diligence, and focusing on long-term growth markets, I was able to make the second property a profitable investment. This success further reinforced my confidence in the power of property investing and set the stage for my next acquisition.

The Third Property: One-Bedroom Villa

By the time I was ready to acquire my third property, my strategy had matured. The success of my first two investments had given me both the confidence and the financial leverage needed to expand my portfolio further. With a solid understanding of how to identify below-market-value (BMV) properties and a clear focus on cash flow and long-term growth, I set my sights on my next investment: a one-bedroom villa.

Using Equity to Finance the Purchase: The Power of Leveraging Property

One of the most powerful aspects of property investment is the ability to use existing assets to finance new purchases. Leveraging the equity from one property to buy another is a common strategy that allows investors to grow their portfolios without requiring large cash savings for each subsequent purchase. By the time I started looking for my third property, my second unit had appreciated in value, giving me enough equity to leverage for the next deal.

How I Used Equity from the Second Property to Buy the Third

After purchasing my second property and seeing its market value rise, I recognized that the equity I had accumulated could be put to work. I refinanced the second property to access a line of credit that would serve as the deposit for my third property. This strategy enabled me to continue expanding my portfolio without having to save for another deposit from my personal finances.

Refinancing allowed me to maintain liquidity while keeping my investment momentum going. The process involved reassessing the market value of the second property and securing a new loan based on its increased equity. By doing this, I was able to pull out a portion of the equity without selling the property, using it as leverage to finance my next purchase.

Refinancing: The Steps and Processes Involved

Refinancing to extract equity is a multi-step process, but one that can unlock significant opportunities for portfolio growth. The first step was obtaining an updated valuation of my second property. As it had increased in value since I purchased it, the valuation confirmed that I had enough equity to access a line of credit without negatively impacting my loan-to-value ratio (LVR).

I worked with my mortgage broker to explore my refinancing options, ensuring I secured a favourable interest rate and terms that aligned with my long-term investment goals. Refinancing typically comes with associated costs, such as loan application fees and valuation charges, but I factored these into my overall budget to ensure they didn't impact my cash flow too heavily.

Once the refinancing process was complete, I had access to enough equity to cover the deposit and related costs for my third property, allowing me to continue building my portfolio without depleting my savings.

Expanding the Portfolio with Confidence: Aiming for Sustainable Growth

With the third property, I aimed to expand my portfolio sustainably. Having learned valuable lessons from my previous two purchases, I was focused on finding a property that would offer strong rental returns while continuing to appreciate in value. This time, I shifted my focus slightly and sought out a property with higher cash flow potential.

By this stage, I understood that balancing capital growth with positive cash flow was essential for long-term success. While my first two properties had strong capital growth potential, I wanted the third property to contribute more to my monthly cash flow, which would help ensure the portfolio remained financially stable even during market fluctuations.

Shifting Focus to Properties with Rental Potential for Cash Flow

For my third property, I chose a one-bedroom villa in a suburb with strong rental demand and relatively low competition. Villas typically appeal to tenants looking for a balance between apartment living and the benefits of a standalone house, making them a popular choice for singles or couples. I saw this as an opportunity to diversify my portfolio with a property type that would offer consistent rental income.

The suburb I selected was experiencing a rise in rental demand due to its proximity to public transport, shopping centres, and local employment hubs. While it wasn't as trendy as other areas, the rental yields were higher, and the vacancy rates were low—exactly what I was looking for to enhance the cash flow from my portfolio.

How I Balanced Risk and Reward by Diversifying My Portfolio

One of the key strategies I employed with this third purchase was diversification. By adding a different type of property—a villa—into my portfolio, I spread my risk across multiple asset types. This diversification helped balance potential market fluctuations. For instance, while apartment prices in certain areas might stagnate, the villa market could remain buoyant due to different buyer and tenant demographics.

Additionally, I was conscious of maintaining a balanced mix of properties that offered both capital growth potential and strong rental returns. While my first two properties were primarily growth-focused, the villa was more of a cash flow-focused investment, providing immediate returns through rental income while still having the potential for long-term appreciation.

Overcoming Hurdles: Challenges During the Purchase and Renovation Process

Despite my experience with two prior properties, the purchase and renovation process for the villa wasn't without its challenges. One of the key hurdles I encountered was an unexpected delay in the settlement process. This was due to complications with the vendor's legal paperwork, which extended the timeline and caused some stress. However, I was prepared for such potential delays by keeping communication open with my solicitor and the vendor, which ultimately led to a successful settlement.

Renovation challenges also arose, as the villa required some upgrades to improve its rental appeal. While the initial inspection didn't reveal any major structural issues, there were some unexpected costs, such as plumbing and electrical repairs, which added to the renovation budget. These unforeseen expenses reinforced the importance of always budgeting for contingencies in property investments.

Despite these challenges, the renovations were completed within a reasonable timeframe, and I was able to enhance the villa's appeal significantly with a fresh coat of paint, modern fixtures, and updated flooring. The improvements not only increased the villa's rental value but also its market value, contributing to the overall success of the investment.

Lessons Learned from Unexpected Costs and Delays

The purchase of the third property taught me several valuable lessons. First, I learned the importance of patience and preparation when dealing with unexpected delays in the purchasing process. Having a clear communication strategy and working with experienced professionals—such as solicitors and property managers—can make all the difference when navigating unforeseen challenges.

Second, the renovation process reinforced the need to budget for unexpected expenses. No matter how thorough your due diligence is, there are always potential surprises during a renovation. Setting aside a contingency fund ensured that these surprises didn't derail my investment plans.

Finally, I learned that managing multiple properties required careful attention to cash flow and overall financial management. With three properties in my portfolio, I had to ensure that each was performing well in terms of rental income and capital growth, while also balancing mortgage repayments and other expenses.

Managing Multiple Properties and Ensuring Each Remained Positively Geared

Managing three properties presented a new level of complexity. I had to ensure that each property remained positively geared, meaning that the rental income exceeded the mortgage repayments and expenses. Positive gearing allowed me to cover my costs and even generate surplus income, which I reinvested into maintaining the properties and planning for future investments.

I also relied heavily on my property management team to handle tenant relations, maintenance requests, and rent collection. Delegating these tasks allowed me to focus on the broader strategy of growing and managing my portfolio while ensuring that the day-to-day operations of the properties were running smoothly.

Results and Returns: How the One-Bedroom Villa Performed in Terms of Value and Yield

The one-bedroom villa has proven to be a valuable addition to my portfolio. After completing the renovations and listing it for rent, I quickly secured a tenant, thanks to the villa's appeal and the strong rental demand in the area. The rental income exceeded my initial expectations, providing a healthy cash flow that contributed to the overall positive gearing of my portfolio.

In terms of capital growth, the villa has also appreciated in value, benefiting from the steady demand for properties in the suburb. While it hasn't experienced the same rapid growth as my first two properties, it has maintained a consistent upward trajectory, adding both value and stability to my portfolio.

The Property's Current Market Valuation and Rental Returns

Today, the villa continues to perform well both in terms of market value and rental returns. Its current market valuation has increased by around 27% since I purchased it, reflecting the ongoing growth in the suburb. The rental yield remains strong, providing consistent cash flow that supports the overall health of my portfolio.

By leveraging the equity from my second property, overcoming the challenges of the purchase and renovation process, and focusing on long-term sustainable growth, I was able to successfully add a third property to my portfolio. This investment marked another important milestone in my property journey, and it has positioned me well for future opportunities.

Key Strategies That Drove My Success

My property investment journey has been driven by a combination of strategic decisions, careful planning, and the ability to adapt and learn from each experience. While every investor's path is unique, there are certain key strategies that have been fundamental to my rapid portfolio growth. These strategies, from buying below market value (BMV) to leveraging equity, helped me scale my portfolio efficiently while managing risks. In this chapter, I'll break down the critical strategies that drove my success and explain how they can be applied by other investors.

Buying Below Market Value: Why BMV Deals Were Critical to My Rapid Portfolio Growth

One of the cornerstones of my property investment strategy has been consistently purchasing properties below their market value (BMV). BMV properties are those that are priced lower than their true market worth, often due to motivated sellers, distressed situations, or properties that need some cosmetic work to increase their appeal. Buying below market value was a critical factor in my ability to grow my portfolio rapidly because it allowed me to generate instant equity, which could then be leveraged for future investments.

How I Consistently Sourced and Secured BMV Properties

The key to consistently finding BMV deals was diligent market research and a readiness to act quickly when opportunities arose. I developed several methods for identifying BMV properties:

1. Building Relationships with Real Estate Agents: I worked to establish strong relationships with local real estate agents. Agents often have access to off-market properties or early listings, giving me the chance to secure deals before they reach the wider market. Networking with agents helped me stay informed about potential BMV opportunities.
2. Monitoring Property Portals: I used property portals to track listings closely and identify properties that had been on the market for extended periods. These properties were often priced lower or had motivated sellers looking to close quickly. I set up alerts for properties in my target areas to ensure I never missed an opportunity.
3. Direct Outreach and Networking: I also engaged in direct outreach, including letterbox drops in areas where I was actively searching. Reaching out to property owners directly helped me find motivated sellers who were looking for a quick sale, giving me the chance to negotiate favourable terms.

By consistently sourcing BMV properties, I was able to create immediate value in each purchase, ensuring that I was always ahead of the market curve. This strategy not only reduced my upfront costs but also enabled me to tap into equity that I could leverage for future acquisitions.

Renovating for Value: The Importance of Cosmetic Upgrades

Another essential component of my strategy was making cosmetic upgrades to enhance the value of each property. While structural renovations can be costly and time-consuming, cosmetic improvements are often quick, affordable, and can significantly boost both property value and rental appeal. Strategic renovations allowed me to increase rental income and, more importantly, improve the resale value of my properties.

How Strategic Renovations Boosted Both Property Value and Rental Income

For each property I purchased, I assessed the cosmetic changes that would have the most significant impact on its value. Common upgrades I focused on included:

- Painting and Flooring: A fresh coat of paint and new flooring can dramatically change the look and feel of a property, making it more appealing to both buyers and tenants. These are low-cost improvements that offer a high return on investment.
- Updating Kitchens and Bathrooms: Minor updates to kitchens and bathrooms, such as new countertops, fixtures, and cabinets, can elevate the perceived value of the entire property. I often targeted properties where these areas were outdated but structurally sound, allowing for cosmetic upgrades without major renovation costs.
- Improving Curb Appeal: First impressions are critical, and simple changes like landscaping, new doors, or modernising the facade of the property can make a significant difference. These enhancements also help attract quality tenants who are willing to pay higher rents for well-maintained properties.

By focusing on cosmetic upgrades that had the greatest visual and functional impact, I was able to boost rental yields and improve the resale value of my properties, further increasing the equity I could draw upon for future investments.

Leveraging Equity: Maximising the Power of Instant Equity for Financing Additional Purchases

One of the most powerful strategies I used to grow my portfolio was leveraging the equity I had built in each property. By purchasing BMV properties and enhancing their value through renovations, I was able to generate instant equity, which I could then use to finance additional purchases.

How I Structured My Loans to Unlock Equity and Finance Subsequent Properties

After purchasing each property and completing any necessary upgrades, I would work with my mortgage broker to refinance the property based on its new, higher value. This process involved reassessing the property's current market value and using the increased equity as collateral for a new loan or line of credit.

Key steps I followed in structuring my loans for future growth included:

1. Refinancing for Equity Access: Once the property had appreciated or after the renovation was complete, I would refinance to access the available equity. This allowed me to free up capital

that I could use as a deposit for my next investment, without having to save a large amount of cash.
2. Using Interest-Only Loans: For some properties, I opted for interest-only loans during the early years to maximise cash flow. This allowed me to minimise my monthly expenses while still benefiting from capital appreciation over time.
3. Portfolio Loan Structures: I was careful to structure each loan independently, ensuring that each property had its own financing. This provided flexibility and reduced the risk of cross-collateralization, where multiple properties are tied to the same loan.

By leveraging the equity in my existing properties, I was able to finance multiple purchases without needing large cash reserves for each one. This strategy helped me scale my portfolio more rapidly than would have been possible with traditional saving methods alone.

Focusing on High-Growth Areas: My Approach to Researching and Identifying Suburbs with Growth Potential

The final key strategy that drove my success was focusing on purchasing properties in high-growth areas. These areas were typically undergoing infrastructure development, experiencing population growth, or were up-and-coming suburbs with a rising demand for housing. By buying in the right locations, I was able to maximise both capital growth and rental yield.

The Indicators I Looked For That Led to the Choice of These Properties

When selecting investment locations, I looked for several key indicators that signalled future growth potential, including:

- Population Growth and Demographics: Areas with a growing population and a high demand for rental properties were always at the top of my list. I targeted suburbs with young professionals, students, or growing families, as these demographics often drive housing demand.
- Employment Opportunities: Proximity to employment hubs, business districts, or new infrastructure projects was another factor I considered. Areas with new job opportunities tend to attract a larger tenant pool and contribute to rising property prices.
- Infrastructure Development: I paid close attention to upcoming infrastructure developments, such as new transport links, schools, or shopping centres. These projects often signal future growth and can boost both property values and rental demand.
- Historical Trends and Future Predictions: I researched the historical price trends of each area and considered expert predictions for future growth. While past performance is not always indicative of future results, it provided a valuable reference point for selecting areas with strong potential.

By consistently targeting high-growth areas, I was able to secure properties that appreciated faster than average, further enhancing the value of my portfolio.

Challenges and Lessons Learned

As with any venture, my property investment journey hasn't been without its challenges. From navigating financing hurdles to managing multiple properties and balancing the risks inherent in property investment, I've learned many valuable lessons along the way. In this chapter, I'll reflect on some of the most significant challenges I faced and how I overcame them to continue growing my portfolio.

Financing Hurdles: Navigating Loan Approvals and Refinancing Challenges

One of the biggest challenges I encountered early on in my property investment journey was securing financing, especially as I began to scale my portfolio. While my initial purchase of a below-market-value (BMV) property gave me a strong start, acquiring subsequent properties required careful planning and a solid understanding of how the loan approval and refinancing processes work.

Understanding Lender Requirements and Maintaining Good Financial Health

When I first applied for a loan, I realised that lenders consider various factors when deciding whether to approve a mortgage, including credit scores, debt-to-income ratios, and the loan-to-value ratio (LVR). I quickly learned that maintaining a good credit score and reducing personal debt were essential for ensuring my borrowing capacity. Furthermore, having a pre-approval in place before making offers on properties gave me confidence in knowing how much I could borrow and speed up the purchasing process.

Navigating refinancing was another hurdle, especially when trying to leverage equity from one property to fund the next. Timing was crucial—I needed to ensure my properties had appreciated enough in value before approaching lenders for refinancing. Additionally, lenders often had strict criteria for refinancing, particularly when it came to investment properties. They scrutinised rental income, property performance, and my overall financial health before approving refinancing deals.

The Importance of Building Relationships with Lenders

Maintaining strong relationships with lenders and brokers was vital to overcoming financing challenges. Over time, I developed relationships with mortgage brokers who specialise in property investment. Their expertise and connections with multiple lenders allowed me to find the best loan products and navigate complex financial situations.

One of the key lessons I learned was the value of staying organised and having all financial documents readily available when applying for loans or refinancing. Lenders require extensive paperwork, including proof of income, tax returns, and detailed expense reports. Being proactive and organised in this regard helped streamline the loan approval process.

Property Management: Juggling the Responsibilities of Being a Landlord

Managing multiple properties meant taking on the responsibility of being a landlord, which brought its own set of challenges. From handling tenant relationships to staying on top of property maintenance, property management required significant time, effort, and organisational skills.

Tenant Management: Finding and Keeping Good Tenants

One of the biggest responsibilities of being a landlord is finding reliable tenants and maintaining good relationships with them. I learned that thorough tenant screening is critical to avoid problems down the road. Checking references, verifying employment, and ensuring tenants had a good rental history helped me avoid issues such as late payments or property damage.

Once I found reliable tenants, maintaining open communication and addressing their concerns promptly helped ensure long-term tenancy and minimal vacancy periods. Good tenants are often willing to stay for longer periods if they feel that their needs are being addressed, which reduces the risk of lost rental income due to vacancies.

Dealing with Maintenance and Unexpected Issues

Maintenance is an unavoidable part of property ownership. While I performed cosmetic upgrades to many of my properties to boost their value and rental appeal, ongoing maintenance and repairs were still necessary to keep the properties in good condition.

One lesson I quickly learned was the importance of setting aside a contingency fund for unexpected repairs. Even with newer properties, things can go wrong—whether it's a plumbing issue, electrical problem, or unexpected damage. Having a financial buffer to cover these costs ensured I could address issues quickly without disrupting my cash flow.

For larger or more time-consuming repairs, I also found it useful to build a network of trusted tradespeople who could handle various types of maintenance work. Having reliable contacts for plumbing, electrical, and general repairs saved me time and stress when issues arose.

Managing Risks: Mitigating Market Fluctuations and Property-Related Challenges

While property investment offers great potential for building wealth, it also comes with inherent risks. Market fluctuations, changes in interest rates, and unexpected property-related issues can all impact the performance of an investment. Understanding how to manage these risks was crucial to ensuring the long-term viability of my portfolio.

Navigating Market Fluctuations and Interest Rate Changes

Property markets can be unpredictable, and one of the biggest challenges I faced was navigating fluctuations in property values and rental demand. To mitigate these risks, I focused on buying properties in high-growth areas with strong underlying demand. This strategy helped insulate my portfolio from severe market downturns, as demand for housing in these areas remained relatively stable even during challenging economic times.

Interest rate changes were another risk I had to account for, especially since I had a mix of fixed and variable-rate loans. Rising interest rates can reduce cash flow and profitability, so I made sure to stress-test my portfolio by calculating how rising rates would impact my loan repayments. In some cases, I locked in fixed rates to provide stability during periods of uncertainty, while in other cases, I opted for variable rates to take advantage of lower interest costs in the short term.

Balancing Risk and Reward: Diversifying My Portfolio

Diversification played a key role in managing the risks associated with property investment. Rather than concentrating all my investments in one area or property type, I spread my investments across different suburbs and property types. This approach helped reduce my exposure to localised market downturns or property-specific risks. For example, if rental demand decreased in one area, I still had properties in other areas generating income.

I also diversified my portfolio in terms of rental yield and capital growth. Some properties were chosen for their strong rental returns, while others were selected for their long-term capital appreciation potential. This balance between cash flow and growth helped ensure my portfolio remained financially stable even when market conditions shifted.

Lessons Learned from Unexpected Property-Related Issues

Throughout my journey, I encountered several unexpected property-related issues, such as tenants vacating properties without notice or delays in renovation projects. Each challenge taught me the importance of being adaptable and having contingency plans in place. For example, I learned to budget for longer vacancy periods than initially expected and to thoroughly vet contractors before committing to renovation projects.

Another lesson I learned was the importance of staying informed about changes in property laws and regulations. Laws governing tenant rights, landlord responsibilities, and property taxes can change, and it's essential to stay up to date to avoid legal or financial complications.

Reflections on the Journey So Far

Reflecting on my property investment journey, it's clear that momentum has played a pivotal role in my growth from owning just one property to holding a portfolio of three within a relatively short span of time. What started as a cautious step into real estate turned into a rapid learning curve that not only built my confidence as an investor but also sharpened my strategies for success.

The Power of Momentum: From One to Three Properties

The transition from my first property purchase to acquiring the second and third properties was faster than I initially anticipated. When I bought my first one-bedroom unit, I knew that property investment could be a long-term wealth-building strategy, but I hadn't fully grasped the potential for rapid expansion. Once I saw the power of leveraging equity from my first property, I quickly realised how momentum could accelerate my portfolio growth.

Acquiring that first property was the most difficult step—getting familiar with the market, understanding financing options, and taking the plunge. However, once that hurdle was crossed, the rest came together much more smoothly. Using the instant equity I had built through buying below market value (BMV) and making strategic renovations, I was able to move on to my second purchase with greater ease and confidence. By the time I acquired my third property, I had refined my approach to financing and sourcing deals, making the process even more streamlined.

This momentum wasn't just financial but psychological as well. Each successful acquisition reinforced my confidence as an investor. I learned to trust my research, follow the data, and make decisions based on solid analysis rather than emotion. With each new property, I became more comfortable navigating the complexities of financing, property management, and the negotiation process.

Building Confidence as an Investor and Refining My Strategies

One of the key lessons I've learned along the way is that confidence comes from experience. Initially, I was cautious—spending a lot of time analysing every potential deal and worrying about whether I was making the right decisions. While that thoroughness was essential, I soon realised that action is just as important as analysis. No investment is completely risk-free, but by focusing on high-growth areas and buying BMV properties, I was able to mitigate many of the risks that initially concerned me.

As I moved from my first to my second and third properties, I refined my strategies based on what I had learned. For example, I became more adept at identifying BMV opportunities and was quicker to act on promising deals. I also learned the importance of leveraging equity to fund future purchases and how to maximise rental returns by making targeted, cost-effective renovations.

Additionally, I honed my skills in property management. Managing multiple properties comes with its own challenges, but I developed systems to stay on top of tenant relationships, property maintenance, and cash flow management. These skills are crucial for any investor looking to scale their portfolio.

Looking Ahead: Future Plans for Expanding the Portfolio

Looking ahead, my primary goal is to continue expanding my portfolio by applying the same principles that have worked for me so far. The first three properties have provided a solid foundation, not just in terms of equity and cash flow, but also in giving me the confidence and knowledge to tackle more complex deals.

My strategy going forward will be to maintain a balanced portfolio that includes both high-yield rental properties and properties with strong capital growth potential. I plan to continue focusing on BMV deals and properties in emerging suburbs with growth potential, while also diversifying into different property types. Additionally, as my portfolio grows, I'll be looking at opportunities to scale by leveraging more advanced financing strategies, such as using trusts and company structures for future purchases.

I'm also keen to explore the possibility of venturing into different property markets, both within my local area and potentially interstate. Diversifying into different markets will help spread risk and ensure my portfolio is more resilient to economic fluctuations.

Advice for New Investors: Key Takeaways

For anyone just starting out in property investment, the most important advice I can offer is to start with a clear strategy. Define your investment goals—whether it's cash flow, capital growth, or a combination of both—and ensure each property purchase aligns with those goals. Your strategy will evolve as you gain more experience, but having a plan will keep you focused and prevent you from making impulsive decisions.

Another critical takeaway is to educate yourself and stay informed. Property investment is a dynamic field, and markets can change quickly. By staying on top of property trends, economic indicators, and financing options, you'll be better equipped to make informed decisions and capitalise on opportunities as they arise.

Lessons from My Experience That New Investors Can Apply

1. **Start with BMV Properties:** Buying below market value sets you up for success by giving you instant equity. This equity can be leveraged for future investments, and it also provides a cushion in case market conditions change.
2. **Leverage Equity to Scale:** Once you have equity in your first property, use it to finance your next purchase. This is how you build momentum and grow your portfolio without needing large amounts of cash for each new investment.
3. **Focus on High-Growth Areas:** Do thorough research to find areas with strong growth potential. Look for indicators such as infrastructure development, population growth, and employment opportunities. Buying in these areas increases your chances of capital appreciation over time.
4. **Be Prepared for Challenges:** Property investment comes with challenges, whether it's financing hurdles or unexpected property repairs. Be prepared for these by having contingency plans and a financial buffer to handle the unexpected.
5. **Take Action:** While research and planning are essential, don't let analysis paralysis hold you back. The most important step in property investment is to take action—make that first purchase, learn from the experience, and use it as a stepping stone for future growth.

In conclusion, my journey from one to three properties has been an exciting and educational experience. By focusing on the right strategies, building momentum, and learning from challenges, I've been able to grow my portfolio and set the stage for continued success in the world of property investment. For new investors, the key is to start small, stay informed, and keep moving forward with confidence.

Chapter 5: Understanding the Market

Introduction:

In property investment, understanding the dynamics of the market is fundamental to making informed decisions that lead to long-term success. Market knowledge empowers investors to predict trends, mitigate risks, and capitalise on opportunities. A solid grasp of property market dynamics enables investors to align their strategies with prevailing conditions, ensuring they buy and sell at optimal times, maximise rental returns, and avoid costly mistakes.

The property market is complex and influenced by a variety of factors. These include economic conditions, supply and demand, interest rates, government policies, and global events. Recognizing how these forces interact is crucial for investors looking to build and maintain a profitable portfolio.

The Importance of Market Knowledge for Property Investors

For property investors, the ability to accurately assess market conditions is a key advantage. The property market does not operate in isolation; it is influenced by wider economic, social, and political factors. Investors who understand these variables are better positioned to time their purchases, maximise capital growth, and secure favourable rental yields.

One of the main benefits of market knowledge is the ability to identify opportunities in different market phases. Property markets are cyclical, typically moving through periods of growth, stagnation, decline, and recovery. Recognizing where the market is in its cycle allows investors to anticipate price trends. For example, purchasing during a slump, when prices are lower, can lead to significant capital appreciation when the market recovers. Similarly, selling during a boom maximises returns before prices plateau or decline.

Another aspect of market knowledge is understanding local conditions. While national trends provide a broad overview, real estate is fundamentally a local asset, and market dynamics can vary significantly between regions, cities, and even neighbourhoods. By researching local economic factors, such as employment growth, infrastructure developments, and population trends, investors can pinpoint high-growth areas with greater potential for appreciation.

In addition, market knowledge helps investors mitigate risks. Markets can be volatile, and sudden changes in interest rates, government policies, or global economic conditions can have a significant impact on property values and rental demand. Investors who are aware of these risks can take proactive steps to protect their investments, such as diversifying their portfolio or locking in favourable mortgage rates during periods of economic uncertainty.

How Market Conditions Affect Property Values, Rental Yields, and Investment Strategies

Market conditions play a crucial role in determining the value of property investments. When demand outpaces supply, property values tend to rise, creating opportunities for capital growth. Conversely, when supply exceeds demand, prices may stagnate or even decline. For investors, understanding the current supply-demand dynamic is vital for setting realistic expectations for both short-term and long-term returns.

In high-demand markets, property prices rise quickly, making it harder to find affordable deals. However, these markets often offer strong capital growth potential, which can compensate for higher entry prices. On the other hand, markets with less competition might provide opportunities to secure below-market-value (BMV) properties. While growth might be slower in these areas, the lower initial cost can lead to higher rental yields, especially if the property is located in an area with strong rental demand.

Rental yields, or the income generated by a rental property as a percentage of its value, are also heavily influenced by market conditions. In areas with high demand for rental properties, investors can command higher rents, which boosts yields. However, in regions with lower demand, investors may struggle to find tenants, resulting in vacancy periods and lower rental returns. Keeping a close eye on local market trends, such as employment rates and population growth, helps investors forecast rental demand and set competitive rental rates.

Market conditions also shape investment strategies. In a booming market, investors might focus on capital growth, aiming to buy properties that will appreciate significantly over time. In contrast, during periods of slower growth or downturns, investors might prioritise cash flow by focusing on properties with strong rental yields.

Another key consideration is financing. When interest rates are low, borrowing becomes cheaper, allowing investors to leverage their purchases more effectively. However, rising interest rates increase the cost of mortgages, which can erode profit margins. Investors need to adjust their strategies according to the prevailing interest rate environment, balancing the need for capital growth with the necessity of maintaining positive cash flow.

Key Factors That Drive Property Markets

Several key factors drive property markets, each influencing property values, rental yields, and investment opportunities:

1. **Economic Conditions**: The overall state of the economy has a significant impact on the property market. When the economy is strong, with low unemployment and rising wages, demand for housing increases, pushing property prices and rental rates higher. Conversely, economic downturns can lead to lower demand, falling property values, and rental vacancies.
2. **Interest Rates**: Interest rates are one of the most important factors for property investors. Lower interest rates reduce borrowing costs, making it easier for investors to finance property purchases. However, rising interest rates increase mortgage payments, potentially reducing an investor's cash flow. Monitoring central bank policies and predicting rate changes can help investors plan their financing strategies.
3. **Supply and Demand**: The balance between the supply of available properties and the demand for housing is a key determinant of property prices. Areas with limited housing supply and growing demand, such as major cities with strong job markets, typically experience higher property prices and rental yields.
4. **Government Policies**: Policies that impact property markets include zoning laws, taxation, and housing incentives. Government initiatives such as first-time buyer schemes, tax breaks for investors, or changes to stamp duty can either stimulate or dampen demand.

5. **Global Events**: Global economic trends, such as recessions or geopolitical events, can influence local property markets. For example, a global financial crisis might tighten lending criteria and reduce demand for property, while a sudden influx of foreign investors could drive up prices in certain markets.

The property market is cyclical, moving through distinct phases that can significantly impact property values, rental yields, and overall investment returns. Understanding these market cycles is crucial for property investors, as it allows them to time their purchases and sales more effectively and make informed decisions that maximise long-term profits. The four primary stages of a property market cycle are boom, slump, recovery, and stagnation. Each stage presents different opportunities and risks, making it essential for investors to recognize where the market is in its cycle and adjust their strategies accordingly.

Overview of Market Cycles: Boom, Slump, Recovery, and Stagnation

1. Boom

The boom phase is characterised by rapidly increasing property prices, high demand for real estate, and strong investor confidence. In this phase, buyers are eager to secure properties, often leading to bidding wars and properties selling above their asking price. Rental demand typically rises, pushing rents higher, and vacancy rates are low as more people compete for available housing. Investors are often drawn to the market during a boom, hoping to capitalise on price appreciation and rental income growth.

However, the boom phase also carries risks. Prices can become inflated, leading to concerns about a property "bubble," where values may exceed their sustainable level. Investors who buy at the peak of a boom may face difficulties if the market moves into a slump soon after, with prices correcting downward.

2. Slump

Following a boom, the market often enters a slump, where property prices stagnate or decline, and demand weakens. This phase is typically triggered by external factors such as economic downturns, rising interest rates, or government policy changes that reduce borrowing capacity or curb speculative buying. During a slump, investors may be reluctant to buy, and sellers may struggle to achieve their desired sale prices.

Rental demand can also soften, leading to higher vacancy rates and pressure on rental yields. In some cases, investors may experience negative cash flow if they are unable to secure tenants or if rents decline.

While the slump phase may seem challenging, it presents opportunities for investors who can identify underpriced properties or below-market-value (BMV) deals. Savvy investors often use this period to acquire properties at lower prices, anticipating that the market will eventually recover.

3. Recovery

The recovery phase is the period after a slump when the property market begins to stabilise and grow. Prices start to rise again, albeit at a more moderate pace compared to the boom phase. Investor confidence returns, and more buyers re-enter the market, leading to an uptick in property transactions. This phase is often accompanied by improvements in economic conditions, such as increased employment and wage growth, which contribute to greater demand for housing.

For investors, the recovery phase is an ideal time to buy, as properties are still relatively affordable compared to the peak prices seen during the boom. As demand increases and prices rise, investors who purchased during the slump or early recovery can benefit from capital appreciation and stronger rental yields.

4. Stagnation

The stagnation phase occurs when the market experiences little to no price growth, and demand for property levels off. This phase can last for several years, with minimal fluctuations in property values. Stagnation may follow a boom or recovery phase, especially if economic conditions are uncertain or if market fundamentals like supply and demand become imbalanced.

While the stagnation phase can be frustrating for investors seeking capital growth, it offers stability and predictability. Investors who focus on rental income may still find opportunities in this phase, as rents can remain steady even if property prices are flat. However, investors should be cautious about overextending themselves during stagnation, as prolonged periods of slow growth can erode returns if expenses such as maintenance and interest payments outpace rental income.

How to Identify Where the Market Is in the Cycle

Recognizing where the property market is in its cycle is a crucial skill for investors. While it is not always easy to pinpoint the exact phase, there are several indicators that can help investors assess the market's current condition.

1. **Price Trends**: One of the most obvious signs of a market cycle is the direction of property prices. Rapid price increases are indicative of a boom, while falling or stagnating prices suggest a slump or stagnation. In a recovery, prices typically begin to rise at a steady pace.
2. **Sales Volume**: During a boom, the number of property transactions tends to increase as buyers rush to secure properties. In contrast, sales volumes drop in a slump as demand weakens. A gradual increase in sales volume is often a sign of recovery.
3. **Rental Demand**: Strong rental demand and rising rents are often seen during a boom, while higher vacancy rates and falling rents are common in a slump. During recovery, rental demand usually stabilises and begins to improve.
4. **Interest Rates**: Changes in interest rates can signal shifts in the market cycle. Low interest rates typically fuel a boom by making borrowing more affordable, while rising rates can contribute to a slump by increasing the cost of mortgages.
5. **Economic Indicators**: Broader economic factors, such as employment rates, wage growth, and consumer confidence, can also provide clues about the property market cycle. A strong economy tends to support a boom or recovery, while economic uncertainty can lead to stagnation or a slump.

Case Studies of Past Property Market Cycles in Different Regions

Different regions experience property market cycles at different times, depending on local economic conditions, population growth, and housing supply. For example:

- **United States (2008 Financial Crisis)**: The U.S. housing market experienced a massive boom in the early 2000s, fueled by easy credit and speculative buying. When the bubble burst in 2008, the market entered a severe slump, with property prices plummeting by up to 50% in some areas. It took several years for the market to recover, and those who purchased during the downturn benefited significantly when prices began to rise again in the 2010s.
- **Australia (Early 2020s)**: After several years of strong price growth, driven by low interest rates and high demand, the Australian property market began to slow in 2022 as interest rates rose and inflation pressures mounted. While some regions experienced stagnation or price declines, others saw more modest growth, demonstrating the importance of understanding local market dynamics.

Importance of Timing Your Property Purchases in Line with Market Phases

Timing your property purchase to align with the market cycle is one of the most effective ways to maximise returns. Investors who buy during a slump or early recovery phase can benefit from capital growth as the market improves, while those who buy during a boom may face higher prices and increased competition.

However, timing the market perfectly is difficult, and even seasoned investors cannot always predict when a market will turn. Rather than attempting to "time" the market exactly, many investors adopt a long-term strategy, focusing on buying properties that offer solid fundamentals—such as good location, strong rental demand, and potential for capital growth—regardless of the current market phase. By holding onto properties through various phases of the cycle, investors can ride out short-term fluctuations and build wealth over time.

Supply and demand are the fundamental forces that drive property prices, rental yields, and market conditions in real estate. Understanding how these forces interact in a given market allows property investors to make more informed decisions about when and where to buy. By analysing both supply and demand, investors can gauge the potential for price appreciation and rental income growth, which are critical for long-term success in property investment.

How Supply and Demand Drive Property Prices

The balance between supply and demand in any property market determines price trends. When demand for properties exceeds supply, prices tend to rise, leading to a seller's market where buyers compete for a limited number of available properties. Conversely, when supply outpaces demand, prices typically fall, creating a buyer's market where properties may sit unsold for extended periods.

- **High Demand, Low Supply:** In markets with high demand and limited supply, property prices can escalate quickly. This is often seen in major cities, where population growth, job opportunities, and desirable amenities make certain areas highly attractive. As competition among buyers increases, property owners can raise their asking prices, and buyers are willing to pay a premium to secure a property.
- **High Supply, Low Demand:** When there is an oversupply of properties, especially in regions where demand is declining or stagnant, prices tend to drop. Developers may struggle to sell new units, and homeowners may have to lower their expectations to find buyers. In these markets, investors can often find properties at discounted prices, but they need to be cautious about the prospects for future demand and price recovery.

Factors Affecting Supply

Supply in the property market refers to the number of available properties for sale or rent. Several factors can impact supply, including government policies, new developments, and the availability of land for construction.

1. New Developments and Construction Activity

One of the most significant contributors to property supply is the level of new construction activity. In growing cities or suburbs, developers often respond to rising demand by building new housing projects. The number of new developments entering the market can lead to an increase in housing stock, which affects both prices and rental yields.

- **High Construction Activity:** When there is a surge in new housing developments, the supply of available properties increases, potentially driving down prices. This is especially common in areas where large-scale residential projects are being undertaken, such as urban renewal projects or the construction of high-rise apartment buildings.
- **Low Construction Activity:** In contrast, when construction slows down due to economic downturns, planning restrictions, or lack of available land, supply can become constrained. This often leads to upward pressure on prices, especially if demand remains strong.

2. Government Policies and Regulations

Government policies and regulations play a critical role in influencing the supply of properties. Zoning laws, building permits, and urban planning decisions can either stimulate or restrict new developments.

- **Relaxed Zoning and Planning Policies:** Governments that implement policies to encourage development, such as tax incentives for developers or streamlined approval processes, can increase the supply of properties. This can help balance markets experiencing housing shortages.
- **Restrictive Zoning Laws:** On the other hand, restrictive zoning laws or development controls can limit new housing projects, constraining supply and contributing to rising property prices. In cities with strict planning regulations, it can be difficult to add new housing stock, exacerbating housing shortages and driving up demand.

3. Existing Housing Stock and Turnover

The number of properties available for sale or rent at any given time depends on the existing housing stock and how frequently properties change hands. In some areas, homeowners may hold onto their properties for long periods, limiting the turnover of available homes. In contrast, areas with high mobility or significant investment activity may see more frequent property sales, increasing supply.

Factors Affecting Demand

Demand in the property market refers to the number of buyers or renters actively seeking properties. Several factors can influence demand, including population growth, employment trends, and economic conditions.

1. Population Growth

One of the most important drivers of property demand is population growth. As more people move into a city or region, the demand for housing increases, leading to higher property prices and rents. Areas with strong population growth, such as major metropolitan cities or regions experiencing inward migration, often see significant upward pressure on property demand.

- **Internal Migration:** People moving from rural areas to urban centres in search of job opportunities can fuel housing demand, particularly in cities with vibrant economies.
- **International Migration:** Immigration can also boost demand in key markets, especially in countries with favourable migration policies and strong employment prospects.

2. Employment Trends and Economic Conditions

Job availability and economic growth are directly linked to housing demand. Areas with strong job markets, low unemployment rates, and diverse industries tend to attract more people, driving up demand for both rental properties and homes for sale.

- **Job Growth and Property Demand:** Regions with expanding industries or large infrastructure projects tend to experience rising demand for housing as workers move to the area. This is particularly evident in areas with strong tech, finance, or manufacturing sectors.
- **Economic Downturns:** Conversely, economic downturns, layoffs, or industry closures can reduce housing demand, as fewer people are able to afford homeownership or rent at higher price points. In these situations, prices may stagnate or fall.

3. Interest Rates and Affordability

Interest rates have a significant impact on property demand by affecting mortgage affordability. When interest rates are low, borrowing becomes cheaper, making homeownership more accessible and increasing demand for properties. Low rates can also boost investor demand, as property investment becomes more affordable.

- **Low Interest Rates:** Lower interest rates encourage more people to take out mortgages, increasing demand for properties. This often leads to higher prices as more buyers enter the market.
- **High Interest Rates:** When interest rates rise, borrowing becomes more expensive, reducing affordability and cooling down property demand. In such environments, investors and homebuyers may delay purchases until rates stabilise.

How Investors Can Analyse Supply-Demand Dynamics

Understanding the balance between supply and demand in a specific market is critical for making smart investment decisions. To analyse supply-demand dynamics, investors can take the following steps:

1. Research Population Growth and Employment Trends

Before investing in a particular area, investors should research population growth projections and employment trends. Regions with strong population growth and low unemployment rates are likely to experience rising demand for housing, which can lead to price appreciation and higher rental yields.

2. Monitor Construction Activity

Investors should track the level of new construction activity in their target markets. High levels of construction may indicate an oversupply of properties, which could put downward pressure on prices and rents. On the other hand, limited new construction in a high-demand area could signal future price increases.

3. Evaluate Government Policies and Infrastructure Projects

Government initiatives, such as zoning changes or large infrastructure projects, can have a significant impact on both supply and demand. Investors should be aware of any major developments in their target markets, as these can affect long-term property values and rental demand.

4. Track Interest Rate Movements

Monitoring interest rates is essential for understanding shifts in demand. Investors should keep an eye on central bank policies and economic forecasts to anticipate changes in interest rates that may influence housing affordability and buyer sentiment.

Economic indicators are essential tools for property investors to gauge the health of the real estate market. Factors like interest rates, inflation, unemployment, and Gross Domestic Product (GDP) play a critical role in shaping property values, rental yields, and market trends. By understanding these key economic indicators, investors can better predict market shifts, make informed decisions, and mitigate risks during times of uncertainty.

Key Economic Indicators to Watch

1. Interest Rates

Interest rates are one of the most significant factors that affect property markets. They influence mortgage affordability, investor confidence, and overall demand for real estate. The interest rates set by central banks (such as the Federal Reserve in the U.S., the European Central Bank, or the Reserve Bank of Australia) affect the rates commercial lenders charge homebuyers and property investors.

- **Low Interest Rates:** When interest rates are low, borrowing becomes more affordable, leading to increased demand for property. Lower mortgage repayments make it easier for homebuyers and investors to enter the market, driving up property prices and stimulating real estate activity.
- **High Interest Rates:** When interest rates rise, borrowing becomes more expensive, reducing affordability and cooling down demand for property. Homebuyers are less likely to take on large loans, and investors may hesitate to expand their portfolios, leading to slower price growth or even price declines.

2. Inflation

Inflation refers to the rate at which the general level of prices for goods and services rises, eroding purchasing power. In the context of real estate, inflation can have both positive and negative effects on property values and rental income.

- **Rising Property Prices:** During periods of inflation, the cost of building materials and labour tends to increase, which raises the cost of new construction. This drives up property prices for both new and existing homes. For investors, inflation can lead to higher capital appreciation over time.
- **Impact on Rental Yields:** Inflation can also affect rental yields. As the cost of living increases, landlords may raise rents to cover rising expenses. However, if wages don't keep pace with inflation, tenants may struggle to afford higher rents, which can cap rental income growth.

3. Unemployment

Unemployment rates have a direct impact on housing demand and market sentiment. In a strong economy with low unemployment, people have stable incomes and are more confident in buying homes or renting properties. In contrast, during periods of high unemployment, property markets tend to slow down as fewer people can afford to purchase homes, and rental demand may weaken.

- **Low Unemployment:** In regions with strong job growth and low unemployment, there is often increased demand for housing, leading to rising property prices and higher rental yields. Investors target areas with robust job markets, as these areas tend to experience long-term growth in both property values and rental demand.
- **High Unemployment:** High unemployment can reduce demand for housing, leading to declining property prices and rental yields. Investors may face challenges in finding tenants, and vacancy rates may rise. In such conditions, property markets can stagnate, and investors need to carefully assess the risks of buying during economic downturns.

4. Gross Domestic Product (GDP)

GDP measures the overall economic output of a country and serves as a broad indicator of economic health. A growing GDP signals a strong economy, which often leads to higher demand for housing, while a shrinking GDP may indicate an economic downturn that can negatively impact property markets.

- **Economic Growth:** When GDP grows, wages tend to increase, consumer confidence rises, and people are more likely to invest in real estate. In strong economic periods, investors benefit from capital appreciation and rental income growth, as demand for housing increases.
- **Economic Contraction:** During periods of economic contraction or recession, GDP declines, and demand for housing can drop. Property prices may stagnate or fall, and rental yields may decrease due to weakened demand. Investors need to be cautious during these periods, as the risk of vacancies and falling property values increases.

How Changes in Interest Rates Affect Mortgage Affordability and Property Prices

Interest rates are perhaps the most direct economic indicator affecting the affordability of real estate. A change in interest rates can either stimulate or slow down the property market, depending on the direction of the rate movement.

1. Low Interest Rates: Boosting Affordability and Demand

When central banks lower interest rates, mortgage repayments become more affordable. This increase in affordability encourages more homebuyers and investors to enter the market, leading to increased competition for properties. As demand rises, so do property prices.

- **Increased Borrowing Power:** Lower interest rates mean that buyers can afford large mortgages, increasing their purchasing power. For example, a reduction in interest rates from 4% to 3% can significantly reduce monthly mortgage repayments, allowing buyers to stretch their budgets and bid more competitively on properties.
- **Higher Prices:** Increased demand due to lower borrowing costs often leads to price inflation. This creates a seller's market where properties are in high demand, pushing prices higher. Investors can benefit from capital gains during these periods, but they need to remain cautious about potential interest rate hikes in the future.

2. High Interest Rates: Reducing Affordability and Cooling the Market

When central banks raise interest rates to combat inflation or stabilise the economy, mortgage repayments become more expensive. This reduces affordability for homebuyers and can slow down demand in the property market.

- **Decreased Borrowing Power:** As interest rates rise, the cost of monthly mortgage repayments increases, reducing the amount buyers can afford to borrow. This leads to fewer buyers in the market, as homeownership becomes less affordable. Investors may also find it more difficult to finance new property purchases.
- **Cooling Property Prices:** As demand weakens, property prices tend to stabilise or even decrease. Investors who are over-leveraged may struggle to maintain positive cash flow, particularly if they have variable-rate mortgages that adjust upward with interest rate hikes.

Understanding the Impact of Inflation on Property Values and Rental Returns

Inflation plays a dual role in property investment, impacting both property values and rental returns. Investors need to understand how inflationary pressures affect their investments in the short and long term.

1. Inflation and Property Value Appreciation

Real estate is often viewed as a hedge against inflation because property values tend to rise over time as the cost of goods and services increases. Inflation drives up the cost of construction materials and labour, making new developments more expensive. As replacement costs rise, the value of existing properties tends to increase.

- **Positive for Long-Term Investors:** In inflationary periods, property investors benefit from capital appreciation. As property values rise, the investor's equity increases, and they can leverage this equity for future investments.
- **Negative for New Buyers:** For first-time homebuyers or investors, rising prices due to inflation can make it harder to enter the market, as affordability declines. High inflation can push prices to levels that outpace wage growth, creating barriers to entry.

2. Inflation and Rental Income Growth

In periods of inflation, landlords may raise rents to keep pace with the rising cost of living and property maintenance. However, rent increases are not always guaranteed, as rental income growth depends on tenant demand and their ability to pay.

- **Rising Rents:** Inflation often leads to higher rental income, as landlords adjust rents to cover increased expenses such as maintenance costs, insurance premiums, and property taxes. This can improve rental yields and overall returns for property investors.
- **Tenant Affordability:** If inflation outpaces wage growth, tenants may struggle to afford rent increases, limiting a landlord's ability to raise rents. This can cap rental income growth and increase the risk of vacancies.

Case Studies: How Economic Downturns or Booms Have Impacted Property Markets

1. The 2008 Global Financial Crisis (GFC)

The 2008 GFC is a prime example of how economic downturns can devastate property markets. In the lead-up to the crisis, low-interest rates and easy access to credit fueled a housing boom, particularly in the U.S. However, the collapse of the subprime mortgage market led to widespread foreclosures, plummeting property values, and a global economic recession.

- **Impact on Property Prices:** In the U.S., property prices dropped by more than 30% in some areas. Investors who had over-leveraged their properties faced financial ruin as property values fell below their mortgage balances.
- **Recovery:** Over the following decade, property markets gradually recovered, with prices reaching new highs in many regions. Investors who bought during the downturn were able to capitalise on significant price appreciation as markets rebounded.

2. The COVID-19 Pandemic

The COVID-19 pandemic caused a global economic shock in 2020, but its impact on property markets varied across regions. In some areas, government stimulus measures, low-interest rates, and a shift to remote work fueled demand for housing, particularly in suburban and regional markets.

- **Property Price Boom:** In countries like Australia and the U.S., low-interest rates and government incentives for homebuyers led to a property price boom during the pandemic. Despite economic uncertainty, property values surged as buyers sought more space and took advantage of cheap credit.

- **Rental Market Impact:** In some cities, rental demand declined as tenants moved to more affordable areas or left urban centres due to remote work. However, in other regions, demand for rental properties remained strong, leading to stable or rising rental yields.

Government policies play a crucial role in shaping property markets by influencing the supply and demand for housing, property prices, and investor behaviour. Policies related to zoning, property taxes, housing incentives, and tax regulations can either stimulate or slow down property market activity. As a property investor, understanding how these policies impact the market can help you make informed investment decisions and adapt your strategies to evolving regulations.

This section will explore how different government policies influence property markets, the impact of housing and tax policies on investors, and a case study illustrating how policy changes can lead to property market booms or busts.

Zoning Laws and Their Impact on Property Markets

Zoning laws regulate how land can be used in specific areas, whether for residential, commercial, or industrial purposes. These regulations are set by local governments and can significantly impact property values, development potential, and investment opportunities.

1. Residential Zoning: Limiting Housing Supply

In areas with strict residential zoning laws, the supply of new housing may be limited. For example, some cities restrict high-density developments, such as apartment complexes, to preserve the character of a neighbourhood. While this can protect existing property values, it also limits the availability of new housing, which can drive up property prices in high-demand areas.

- **Investment Impact:** For investors, restrictive zoning laws can create an opportunity for higher property appreciation in limited-supply areas. However, it can also limit the ability to develop or subdivide land, which may constrain growth potential for certain types of investments.

2. Mixed-Use Zoning: Encouraging Development and Growth

Mixed-use zoning, which allows for a combination of residential, commercial, and industrial development, encourages growth and increases the appeal of certain areas. By permitting a broader range of activities, mixed-use zoning can lead to the revitalization of neighbourhoods and boost demand for properties.

- **Investment Impact:** Investors in mixed-use zones often benefit from rising property values and rental demand as these areas attract more residents, businesses, and infrastructure. This type of zoning can create opportunities for higher rental yields and capital appreciation.

3. Greenfield and Brownfield Development

Government policies often encourage the development of underutilised land through greenfield (undeveloped land) and brownfield (previously developed land) projects. Incentives for developing these areas can stimulate housing supply, which in turn affects property prices.

- **Investment Impact:** Investors targeting these development zones may benefit from lower property acquisition costs and future price growth as infrastructure and amenities are developed in the area.

Property Taxes and Their Influence on Investment Decisions

Property taxes are a significant consideration for property investors, as they can affect cash flow, rental income, and the long-term profitability of an investment. Different regions have varying property tax structures, and changes in tax rates can influence property markets.

1. High Property Taxes: Reducing Investor Appeal

In areas with high property taxes, the costs of owning and maintaining a property can significantly reduce rental yields and overall returns. High property taxes can also deter buyers, especially first-time investors, as they increase the cost of homeownership.

- **Investment Impact:** Investors need to account for property tax rates when evaluating potential investments. In regions with high property taxes, it may be more difficult to generate positive cash flow, especially if rental income does not keep pace with rising tax expenses.

2. Tax Incentives and Deductions: Encouraging Investment

Many governments offer tax incentives to encourage investment in the property market. These incentives can include deductions for mortgage interest, depreciation of property, and other expenses related to property management. Tax breaks for first-home buyers or property investors can stimulate demand, driving up property prices and benefiting those who invest early.

- **Investment Impact:** Investors can use tax incentives to reduce their taxable income and improve cash flow. Deductions for interest expenses, depreciation, and maintenance costs can make property investment more financially viable, encouraging long-term investment in the housing market.

First-Home Buyer Schemes and Their Effect on Property Markets

Governments frequently introduce first-home buyer schemes to make homeownership more accessible to young or low-income buyers. These schemes may offer grants, stamp duty exemptions, or other financial assistance to help first-time buyers enter the property market.

1. Increased Demand for Entry-Level Properties

First-home buyer schemes typically increase demand for affordable properties, particularly in entry-level price ranges. This influx of demand can drive up prices for lower-cost homes, especially in popular first-home buyer markets.

- **Investment Impact:** For investors, first-home buyer schemes can create opportunities in the lower-end of the market, where demand is strong. However, increased competition from first-home buyers can make it more difficult to secure properties in this price range. Investors may need to act quickly or focus on other segments of the market to avoid bidding wars.

2. Long-Term Market Impact

While first-home buyer schemes can boost market activity in the short term, they may also create affordability issues if prices rise too quickly. As demand increases due to government incentives, property prices can surge, potentially pricing out future buyers and leading to a cooling of the market once the schemes end.

The Impact of Housing Policies on Investor Strategies

Governments often introduce housing policies aimed at increasing the supply of affordable housing, improving tenant protections, or stabilising property markets. These policies can have both positive and negative effects on property investors.

1. Rent Control and Tenant Protections

Some governments implement rent control policies to limit the amount landlords can charge for rent, aiming to protect tenants from excessive rent increases. While these policies benefit tenants, they can negatively affect property investors by capping rental income and limiting the potential for growth.

- **Investment Impact:** Rent control can reduce the profitability of rental properties, particularly in high-demand areas where investors might otherwise charge higher rents. Investors need to carefully consider local rental regulations when selecting properties to ensure they can generate sufficient cash flow.

2. Affordable Housing Initiatives

Governments may introduce policies to increase the supply of affordable housing, such as subsidies for developers or requirements for a certain percentage of new developments to be designated as affordable. These policies can help address housing shortages but may also impact property values in certain areas.

- **Investment Impact:** In areas where affordable housing initiatives are in place, property prices may grow more slowly, as the influx of affordable units can reduce demand for existing properties. However, investors who focus on affordable housing developments may benefit from government incentives and a stable rental market.

Tax Incentives and Their Effects on Property Investment

Tax incentives are powerful tools that governments use to encourage investment in the property market. These incentives can significantly impact an investor's cash flow, returns, and long-term financial success.

1. Negative Gearing

Negative gearing allows property investors to deduct the cost of owning an investment property (including mortgage interest and maintenance expenses) from their taxable income. This is particularly beneficial for investors who own properties that are temporarily cash-flow negative but have long-term capital growth potential.

- **Investment Impact:** Negative gearing encourages investors to hold onto properties even if they are not immediately profitable, knowing that tax deductions can offset losses. This strategy can lead to significant long-term capital appreciation.

2. Depreciation Deductions

Depreciation deductions allow investors to claim a portion of the property's value, as well as fixtures and fittings, as a tax deduction over time. This reduces taxable income and improves cash flow.

- **Investment Impact:** Depreciation can be a powerful tool for reducing tax liabilities, especially in new or recently renovated properties where depreciation rates are higher. Investors can use these deductions to offset rental income and reduce their tax burden.

Case Study: Policy Changes That Led to a Property Market Boom or Bust

1. Australia's First-Home Buyer Grant and Boom of the Early 2000s

In the early 2000s, the Australian government introduced a First-Home Buyer Grant to help young buyers enter the property market. This grant, combined with low-interest rates, led to a surge in demand for entry-level homes, particularly in major cities.

- **Impact on Property Prices:** The First-Home Buyer Grant contributed to a significant increase in property prices, particularly in lower-priced suburbs. As first-home buyers flooded the market, property prices rose rapidly, leading to concerns about affordability in subsequent years.
- **Boom and Bust Cycle:** While the grant initially boosted market activity, property prices eventually plateaued as demand slowed and affordability issues emerged. Investors who capitalised on the early stages of the boom benefited from significant capital appreciation, while those who entered the market later faced a cooling market and slower price growth.

In property investment, having in-depth knowledge of local markets is crucial for making informed decisions that can lead to higher returns. While national trends may provide a general overview, local property markets often behave differently due to various regional factors. Focusing on local markets allows investors to uncover hidden opportunities and gain a competitive edge.

In this section, we will explore why local market knowledge is essential, the tools and resources available for local market analysis, how to identify high-growth suburbs, and the influence of factors like infrastructure projects, gentrification, and urban development on property values.

The Importance of Local Market Knowledge vs. National Trends

While national property trends—such as overall house price growth, interest rate changes, or economic indicators—are important, they do not paint a full picture of individual markets. Different regions, cities, and suburbs can perform quite differently depending on a range of local factors. Understanding these nuances can help investors maximise their returns and mitigate risks.

1. National vs. Local Trends

National trends can be useful for understanding the broader economic context and the general direction of the property market, but they often overlook the unique drivers of specific localities. For example, a nationwide housing downturn may not affect areas undergoing rapid urbanisation or benefiting from major infrastructure projects.

- **Example:** While national house prices might be declining, a suburb near a new transport hub or undergoing significant gentrification could still experience price growth.

2. Finding Niche Opportunities

Focusing on local markets can reveal niche opportunities that are not reflected in national data. Investors who thoroughly understand local market dynamics can identify areas with growth potential before they become widely known, enabling them to enter markets at the right time.

- **Example:** An investor who monitors local job growth, population trends, and new developments may spot high-potential suburbs well before other investors, positioning themselves for higher returns as these areas appreciate.

Tools and Resources for Local Market Analysis

Effective research is key to uncovering the best property investment opportunities in local markets. Investors have access to a variety of tools and resources that provide valuable insights into local market conditions, trends, and potential growth areas. Below are some of the most important tools for conducting local market research.

1. Property Portals

Property portals such as Zillow, RealEstate.com, and Domain are invaluable for gathering local market data. These platforms provide information on property listings, recent sales, rental prices, and market trends. Investors can filter data by location to focus on specific suburbs or neighbourhoods, making it easier to compare prices and yields.

- **How to Use:** Use property portals to track the average property prices in an area, assess the time properties spend on the market, and evaluate rental demand. These platforms also offer historical data, helping investors understand long-term trends.

2. Real Estate Reports and Market Research

Many real estate agencies, such as CoreLogic, offer detailed reports on local market performance, including price movements, rental yields, and vacancy rates. These reports are an excellent resource for investors looking to make informed decisions based on hard data.

- **How to Use:** Download or purchase local market reports to analyse past and current property performance. Focus on areas with steady or increasing growth, as well as suburbs with strong rental demand and low vacancy rates.

3. Census Data

Census data provides crucial insights into the demographics of a suburb, including population growth, household composition, and income levels. This information helps investors identify areas with high demand for housing or neighbourhoods likely to grow as a result of demographic shifts.

- **How to Use:** Analyse census data to understand who lives in a particular area (e.g., young families, professionals, students) and determine what type of housing is in demand. Growing populations, rising incomes, or an influx of young professionals can signal future growth potential.

4. Local Real Estate Agents

Speaking to local real estate agents can provide a wealth of qualitative insights that are not captured in data reports. Agents often have intimate knowledge of a neighbourhood's trends, planned developments, and buyer or tenant preferences.

- **How to Use:** Engage with agents to gain insider information on the area, such as upcoming infrastructure projects, demand for specific property types, and common buyer profiles. This can provide valuable context for your investment decisions.

Identifying High-Growth Suburbs and Areas on the Rise

Investing in a high-growth suburb can significantly increase your chances of capital appreciation and rental yield growth. Identifying these areas requires a combination of data analysis, local knowledge, and an understanding of the key drivers that contribute to growth.

1. Population Growth

Population growth is one of the strongest indicators of a high-growth suburb. Suburbs that attract more residents typically experience greater demand for housing, which in turn drives up property prices and rental rates.

- **Example:** Look for suburbs where population growth is above the national average, as this often signals an increase in housing demand.

2. Employment Opportunities

Suburbs with growing employment opportunities are also likely to see property price increases. Areas close to business hubs, major employers, or industries experiencing expansion tend to attract workers who need housing nearby.

- **Example:** A suburb that is located near a new business park or industrial centre will likely experience increased demand for both rental and owned properties, making it a prime target for investment.

3. Infrastructure Development

New infrastructure projects such as roads, public transport, schools, and hospitals can significantly increase the desirability and accessibility of a suburb. Investors who buy in areas slated for infrastructure development often benefit from a boost in property values once these projects are completed.

- **Example:** A new train station or highway that connects a suburb to a city centre can reduce commute times and attract more residents, leading to rising property prices and higher rental demand.

4. Gentrification

Gentrification occurs when an older or run-down neighbourhood experiences redevelopment and an influx of wealthier residents. This process often leads to higher property values as demand for housing in the area grows. Investors who identify early signs of gentrification can purchase properties at lower prices and benefit from long-term capital growth.

- **Example:** Signs of gentrification include an increasing number of renovations, new restaurants or cafes opening, and rising rental rates. These are all indicators that an area is becoming more desirable.

How Infrastructure Projects, Gentrification, and Urban Development Influence Local Property Markets

Understanding the broader influences on local property markets, such as infrastructure projects, gentrification, and urban development, can help investors make strategic decisions. These factors have a direct impact on property values, rental demand, and the long-term growth prospects of an area.

1. Infrastructure Projects

Infrastructure projects are a key driver of property price growth. New roads, public transport, schools, hospitals, and recreational facilities all enhance the livability of a suburb and increase its appeal to potential buyers and renters.

- **Example:** When a new train line or highway is built, suburbs that were once considered too far from major employment centres suddenly become more accessible, leading to increased demand for housing. Investors who purchase properties in these areas before the infrastructure is completed often see significant capital appreciation.

2. Urban Development and Renewal

Urban development initiatives, such as the regeneration of old industrial areas or the construction of new housing estates, can create opportunities for property investors. These projects often involve the development of mixed-use neighbourhoods that combine residential, commercial, and recreational spaces, attracting new residents and businesses.

- **Example:** The redevelopment of a former industrial area into a modern residential and commercial hub can transform a previously undesirable location into a vibrant community, driving up property prices and rental demand.

3. Gentrification's Long-Term Impact

Gentrification can be a slow process, but it often leads to significant property price appreciation over time. Investors who buy in gentrifying neighbourhoods can benefit from rising rents and increasing demand as the area becomes more desirable. However, it's important to carefully assess whether gentrification will continue or if the area is reaching its peak.

- **Example:** Gentrifying suburbs often experience a wave of young professionals, artists, and small business owners moving into the area, which can lead to the revitalization of the local economy and a boost in property values. Investors who enter these markets early can achieve significant gains.

Identifying high-growth areas is one of the most important strategies for property investors seeking long-term capital gains and rental income. While property markets can be unpredictable, there are key indicators that signal future growth potential in specific neighbourhoods or suburbs. These indicators include population growth, employment rates, infrastructure development, and affordability. This section will explore these factors in detail, provide case studies of suburbs that experienced rapid growth, and offer insights into how investors can spot emerging neighbourhoods before they peak.

Key Indicators of Future Growth Areas

There are several key factors that help investors identify areas poised for growth. Recognizing these indicators allows you to enter a market before property prices and rents increase significantly, maximising your return on investment.

1. Population Growth

Population growth is one of the strongest indicators of a high-growth area. As more people move to a suburb, demand for housing increases, driving up property prices and rental demand. Population growth can be driven by factors such as:

- **Migration:** Areas that attract international or interstate migration often see a surge in housing demand.
- **Urbanisation:** As cities expand, the suburbs on the outskirts often experience an influx of new residents.
- **Baby Booms:** Some areas experience growth due to higher birth rates or the influx of young families.

Investors can track population growth using census data and government reports on projected population increases.

2. Employment Opportunities

High employment rates and the availability of well-paying jobs in an area can significantly boost demand for housing. Suburbs near employment hubs, business districts, or regions with expanding industries are likely to experience increased demand from workers seeking homes nearby. Key factors include:

- **Proximity to Major Employers:** Suburbs located near central business districts (CBDs), industrial parks, or large corporations tend to attract professionals who want to live closer to work.
- **Growing Industries:** Areas where industries such as technology, healthcare, or manufacturing are expanding may see increased demand for housing as workers move closer to job opportunities.

Tracking local employment data and studying industry trends can help investors pinpoint areas with job growth potential.

3. Infrastructure Development

Infrastructure projects, such as the construction of new transport links, roads, schools, and hospitals, have a significant impact on property prices. When new infrastructure is built, it improves the accessibility and desirability of an area, often leading to property value increases. Examples of key infrastructure developments include:

- **Public Transport:** New train lines, bus routes, or tram systems that improve commuting options often make previously inaccessible suburbs more attractive to buyers and renters.
- **Road Upgrades:** The construction of new highways or major road upgrades can reduce travel times and make an area more accessible to employment hubs.
- **Social Infrastructure:** New schools, hospitals, shopping centres, and recreational facilities can make a suburb more livable, increasing its appeal to families and young professionals.

Investors should pay attention to government announcements and local council plans for infrastructure development to identify areas likely to experience growth.

4. Affordability

Affordability plays a crucial role in determining whether an area has growth potential. As property prices rise in major cities and desirable suburbs, buyers and renters may seek more affordable options in outer suburbs or less popular neighbourhoods. This migration can drive up prices in areas that were previously considered less desirable. Key indicators of affordability include:

- **Price Comparisons:** Areas where property prices are significantly lower than nearby suburbs may attract buyers looking for better value.
- **Rental Yields:** High rental yields in an affordable area indicate strong rental demand, suggesting future capital growth potential.

Investors can use property portals and real estate reports to assess affordability metrics and compare different suburbs.

Case Studies of Suburbs that Experienced Rapid Growth

The following case studies illustrate how different factors—such as population growth, employment opportunities, and infrastructure development—can contribute to rapid property price growth in certain suburbs.

1. Case Study: Melbourne's Outer Suburbs

In the past decade, several outer suburbs of Melbourne, such as Tarneit and Werribee, experienced rapid growth due to significant infrastructure investments, population increases, and affordability. New train lines and freeway upgrades improved accessibility to Melbourne's CBD, while the areas remained relatively affordable compared to inner-city locations. As a result, these suburbs saw property prices rise significantly, with Werribee's median house price increasing by over 40% between 2015 and 2020.

2. Case Study: Sydney's Western Suburbs

Western Sydney suburbs such as Parramatta and Blacktown underwent substantial growth in recent years. Parramatta, in particular, benefited from being positioned as Sydney's "second CBD" with major infrastructure projects like the Parramatta Light Rail and WestConnex. The area attracted professionals working in the city and surrounding business districts, driving property prices up.

Blacktown, with its relatively affordable housing options and proximity to new transport links, also experienced an influx of new residents, leading to strong price growth.

How to Spot Emerging Neighbourhoods Before They Peak

Timing is critical when it comes to property investment. Identifying and purchasing in emerging neighbourhoods before they become fully developed allows investors to benefit from capital appreciation as the area grows in popularity. The following strategies can help investors spot emerging neighbourhoods before they peak:

1. Look for Early Signs of Gentrification

Gentrification often transforms underdeveloped or working-class neighbourhoods into desirable areas for young professionals, artists, and families. Early signs of gentrification include:

- **Increased Renovation Activity:** Older homes being renovated or redeveloped.
- **New Cafes and Restaurants:** The opening of trendy cafes, restaurants, and boutique shops indicates changing demographics.
- **Increased Public Investment:** Local governments investing in beautification projects or upgrading public spaces such as parks.

2. Monitor Infrastructure Announcements

As mentioned earlier, infrastructure projects have a significant impact on property values. Investors should monitor government announcements and local council plans for new transport links, roads, and social infrastructure. Areas slated for these improvements often experience price growth before the projects are even completed, as buyers anticipate future benefits.

3. Track Population and Employment Trends

Population and employment growth are critical indicators of an emerging neighbourhood. Areas experiencing a steady increase in new residents or job opportunities are likely to see increased demand for housing. Investors should track population statistics and employment data to identify these trends early.

4. Analyze Vacancy Rates and Rental Yields

Low vacancy rates and high rental yields indicate strong demand for rental properties, which often leads to future capital growth. Investors should track these metrics to identify areas where rental demand is outpacing supply, signalling potential for price appreciation.

5. Research Planned Developments

Beyond infrastructure projects, large-scale commercial or residential developments can signal future growth. These projects can bring new residents and businesses to an area, boosting demand for housing. Investors should research upcoming developments and consider how they will impact property values.

Balancing Growth Potential with Affordability

While high-growth areas offer the potential for significant capital gains, it is essential to balance this growth potential with affordability. Properties in rapidly growing areas can become expensive, which may reduce rental yields or make it difficult to generate positive cash flow. To achieve a balanced investment portfolio, consider the following factors:

- **Entry Price:** Look for suburbs where the entry price is still affordable compared to neighbouring areas with similar growth potential.
- **Rental Demand:** Ensure there is strong rental demand in the area to generate consistent cash flow while you wait for capital growth.
- **Affordability for Buyers and Renters:** Consider whether buyers and renters can afford to live in the area. Areas that become too expensive may see demand decline as buyers and renters seek more affordable options.

Understanding rental demand is crucial for property investors aiming to maximise returns on their investments. Rental demand directly influences rental yields, occupancy rates, and overall investment profitability. By analysing rental demand and identifying the demographics and trends driving it, investors can make informed decisions that enhance their property portfolio's performance. This section will delve into the factors influencing rental demand, explore key demographics, and provide case studies of areas with strong rental demand.

Analysing Rental Demand and Its Impact on Property Investment Returns

Rental demand is a key driver of investment returns, impacting both rental income and property values. High rental demand often translates to lower vacancy rates and higher rental yields, which can significantly improve an investment's cash flow and overall return on investment (ROI). Here's how rental demand affects property investment:

1. Rental Yields

Rental yield is the return on investment calculated as a percentage of the property's value. High rental demand can lead to increased rental rates, thus improving rental yields. Investors should focus on areas where rental yields are strong to ensure steady cash flow. Key metrics include:

- **Gross Rental Yield:** Calculated by dividing the annual rental income by the property's purchase price. High gross rental yields indicate strong rental demand and a good return on investment.
- **Net Rental Yield:** Accounts for expenses such as property management fees, maintenance, and insurance. A high net rental yield signifies that rental income covers expenses and provides a positive return.

2. Occupancy Rates

High rental demand typically results in lower vacancy rates, meaning properties are rented out more quickly and remain occupied for longer periods. Low vacancy rates reduce the risk of lost rental income and provide greater stability for investors. Investors should aim for properties in high-demand areas to ensure high occupancy rates and minimal downtime.

3. Property Value Appreciation

Areas with strong rental demand often experience property value appreciation due to increased investor interest and demand from potential buyers. As demand for rental properties rises, property prices may also increase, leading to potential capital gains for investors.

Understanding Demographics and Trends Driving Rental Demand

Rental demand is influenced by various demographic factors and trends. Understanding these influences helps investors identify the types of properties and locations that are likely to attract tenants.

1. Student Housing

In cities with large universities or colleges, there is often a consistent demand for rental properties from students. Key factors influencing student rental demand include:

- **Proximity to Educational Institutions:** Properties close to campuses or with easy access to public transport are highly sought after.
- **Affordability:** Student renters often look for affordable accommodation options with reasonable rent.
- **Amenities:** Features such as study spaces, high-speed internet, and communal areas can attract student tenants.

Investors can benefit from high rental yields and low vacancy rates by purchasing properties near educational institutions.

2. Urban Professionals

Cities with thriving job markets attract urban professionals who seek convenient, well-located rental properties. Key factors driving rental demand from professionals include:

- **Proximity to Work:** Properties near business districts or major employers are attractive to professionals seeking short commutes.
- **Lifestyle Amenities:** Modern apartments with amenities such as gyms, cafes, and restaurants appeal to this demographic.

- **Transport Links:** Good public transport and access to major road networks enhance the attractiveness of rental properties.

Investors should consider high-growth urban areas with strong employment opportunities when targeting properties for professionals.

3. Retirees

As the population ages, there is growing demand for rental properties catering to retirees. Factors influencing rental demand among retirees include:

- **Accessibility:** Properties with easy access to healthcare facilities, public transport, and amenities such as shopping centres are attractive to retirees.
- **Low Maintenance:** Single-story homes or apartments with low maintenance requirements appeal to retirees.
- **Community Features:** Retirement communities with social activities and support services are in demand.

Investors can target retirement communities or suburbs with amenities tailored to retirees to capture this growing market segment.

Case Studies of Areas with Strong Rental Demand

Examining real-life examples of areas with strong rental demand provides insights into how investors can capitalise on these trends. The following case studies highlight successful investments in high-demand rental markets.

1. Case Study: Inner-City Apartments

In Sydney, the inner-city suburb of Surry Hills has experienced high rental demand due to its proximity to the central business district (CBD), vibrant lifestyle amenities, and strong job market. Investors who purchased apartments in this area benefited from high rental yields and low vacancy rates. The suburb's appeal to urban professionals seeking convenient living arrangements and proximity to work contributed to strong investment returns.

2. Case Study: Student Housing in Melbourne

The suburb of Carlton in Melbourne, located near the University of Melbourne, has a high demand for student accommodation. Investors who acquired rental properties in Carlton have seen consistent occupancy rates and attractive rental yields. Proximity to the university, along with the availability of amenities and public transport, makes this area highly desirable for students.

3. Case Study: Retirement Community in Queensland

The coastal town of Noosa in Queensland has seen increasing demand for retirement properties due to its pleasant climate, access to healthcare facilities, and lifestyle amenities. Investors in Noosa who targeted properties suitable for retirees, such as single-story homes and retirement communities, have benefited from strong rental demand and appreciation in property values.

How Investors Can Capitalise on Rental Demand

To maximise returns from rental demand, investors should adopt the following strategies:

1. Market Research

Conduct thorough research to understand the rental demand trends in target markets. Analyse demographic data, rental yield reports, and vacancy rates to identify high-demand areas.

2. Property Type Selection

Choose property types that cater to the needs of specific tenant demographics. For example, invest in student accommodation near universities, modern apartments for urban professionals, or accessible homes for retirees.

3. Location Analysis

Focus on locations with strong rental demand due to factors such as proximity to employment hubs, educational institutions, and lifestyle amenities. Evaluate infrastructure developments and local market trends to ensure long-term rental demand.

4. Regular Monitoring

Continuously monitor rental market trends and adjust your investment strategy as needed. Stay informed about changes in demographic patterns, employment rates, and local infrastructure projects that may impact rental demand.

Global events can have profound effects on local property markets, influencing property values, investment strategies, and economic stability. Understanding these influences helps investors navigate uncertainties and make informed decisions. This section explores the impact of global economic events, currency fluctuations, and international investment trends on local property markets, supported by case studies of affected markets and adaptive strategies.

The Impact of Global Economic Events

1. Recessions

Global recessions can trigger significant shifts in local property markets. During economic downturns, reduced consumer spending and higher unemployment rates often lead to decreased property demand, falling property prices, and increased rental vacancies. Investors need to be aware of the following effects:

- **Property Prices:** Recessions generally lead to lower property prices as demand weakens. Sellers may be forced to lower prices to attract buyers, impacting investment returns.
- **Rental Yields:** Increased vacancies and reduced rental income can negatively affect rental yields. Tenants may seek more affordable housing options, reducing rental income for investors.
- **Financing Challenges:** Recessions can lead to tighter lending standards and higher interest rates, making it more challenging to secure financing for new property investments.

2. Pandemics

Pandemics, such as the COVID-19 pandemic, can disrupt local property markets by altering demand patterns and affecting economic stability. Key impacts include:

- **Shifts in Demand:** Pandemics can shift demand from urban to suburban or rural areas as people seek more space and remote work options. This can lead to increased demand for properties in previously less popular areas.
- **Property Utilisation:** Changes in work and lifestyle habits may affect property utilisation, with increased demand for home office spaces and outdoor areas.
- **Economic Uncertainty:** Economic uncertainty during pandemics can lead to reduced consumer confidence, impacting property sales and rental demand.

Currency Fluctuations and International Investment Trends

1. Currency Fluctuations

Currency fluctuations can impact property markets by influencing foreign investment and property prices. For example:

- **Foreign Investment:** A stronger local currency makes properties more expensive for foreign investors, potentially reducing foreign investment. Conversely, a weaker local currency can make properties more attractive to international buyers, driving up demand and prices.
- **International Buyers:** Changes in currency exchange rates can alter the purchasing power of international buyers, affecting their investment decisions and influencing local property markets.

2. International Investment Trends

Global investment trends, such as increased interest from international investors or shifts in investment priorities, can affect local property markets. For instance:

- **Increased Foreign Investment:** An influx of international investment can drive up property prices and competition in local markets. Investors need to be aware of potential price increases and adjust their strategies accordingly.
- **Shifts in Investment Preferences:** Changes in international investment preferences, such as a focus on residential versus commercial properties, can impact local property markets. Investors should monitor these trends to identify opportunities and risks.

Case Studies of Local Markets Affected by Global Events

1. Case Study: Sydney During the Global Financial Crisis (2008)

During the global financial crisis of 2008, Sydney's property market experienced a temporary downturn. The crisis led to reduced consumer confidence, lower property prices, and increased vacancy rates. Investors faced challenges in securing financing and managing rental income. However, Sydney's property market showed resilience and recovered over time, highlighting the importance of long-term investment strategies and market research.

Adaptation Strategy: Investors in Sydney who focused on long-term growth and diversified their portfolios were better positioned to weather the downturn. Some investors took advantage of lower property prices to acquire additional properties at discounted rates, benefiting from subsequent market recovery.

2. Case Study: Melbourne During the COVID-19 Pandemic (2020-2021)

The COVID-19 pandemic had a significant impact on Melbourne's property market, with changes in demand patterns and economic disruptions. Urban areas saw reduced demand as people sought more space in suburban and regional areas. Property prices in some urban areas declined, while suburban and regional markets experienced increased demand.

Adaptation Strategy: Investors in Melbourne who adapted to changing demand patterns by focusing on suburban and regional properties were able to capitalise on new opportunities. Investors who adjusted their portfolios and considered remote work trends found success in emerging markets with high demand.

3. Case Study: London and Brexit (2016-2020)

The uncertainty surrounding Brexit had a notable impact on London's property market. Currency fluctuations and economic uncertainty led to a temporary slowdown in property sales and a decline in property prices. Foreign investors faced challenges due to currency volatility, impacting their purchasing decisions.

Adaptation Strategy: Investors in London who remained informed about market trends and currency fluctuations were able to navigate the uncertainties effectively. Some investors used the opportunity to acquire properties at lower prices, anticipating future market stabilisation and potential appreciation.

In the realm of property investment, the expertise of real estate agents and market analysts is indispensable. Their insights and knowledge can significantly influence investment decisions and help investors navigate the complexities of the market. Here's how these professionals can enhance your property investment strategy and why it's crucial to work with them effectively.

How Real Estate Agents Provide Valuable Insights into Local Market Trends

Real estate agents are crucial in offering a comprehensive understanding of local property markets. Their role extends beyond merely listing properties; they offer valuable insights that can help investors make informed decisions.

1. **Local Market Knowledge**: Real estate agents have an in-depth understanding of the neighbourhoods they work in. They are familiar with local trends, such as which areas are experiencing growth, which neighbourhoods are in demand, and where there might be opportunities for investment. This local knowledge is vital for identifying properties with the potential for appreciation.
2. **Access to Off-Market Deals**: Agents often have access to properties that are not listed on major property portals. These off-market deals can provide unique opportunities to acquire properties before they are available to the general public, potentially giving you an edge in competitive markets.

3. **Market Comparisons**: Through Comparative Market Analysis (CMA), agents compare similar properties in the area to determine the fair market value of a property. This analysis helps investors understand whether a property is priced appropriately, and it aids in making competitive offers.
4. **Negotiation Skills**: Experienced agents are skilled negotiators. They can advocate on your behalf, negotiating price and terms with sellers to secure the best possible deal. Their expertise in negotiation can lead to significant savings and more favourable purchase terms.
5. **Understanding Market Dynamics**: Agents stay abreast of changes in market conditions, such as shifts in demand, new developments, and changes in local policies. Their ability to interpret these dynamics helps investors make strategic decisions based on current and anticipated market conditions.

The Importance of Working with Reputable Agents and Analysts

Selecting the right real estate agent or market analyst is crucial for successful property investment. Working with reputable professionals offers several advantages:

1. **Credibility and Experience**: Reputable agents and analysts have established track records of success and are known for their credibility. Their experience ensures that you receive accurate and reliable advice. They are well-versed in market trends, legal considerations, and the nuances of property investment.
2. **Up-to-Date Information**: The property market is dynamic, with frequent changes in regulations, interest rates, and market conditions. Reputable professionals stay current with these changes, providing you with the most up-to-date information and analysis, which is essential for making informed investment decisions.
3. **Ethical Standards**: Working with reputable agents ensures that you are dealing with professionals who adhere to high ethical standards. They are committed to acting in your best interests, providing honest advice, and avoiding conflicts of interest.
4. **Network and Resources**: Experienced agents and analysts have extensive networks within the real estate industry. This includes connections with mortgage brokers, property inspectors, and legal experts. Access to this network can streamline the investment process and provide additional resources for due diligence.

How to Leverage Market Reports and Expert Insights for Better Decision-Making

To maximise the value of working with real estate agents and market analysts, it's essential to effectively leverage their insights and resources. Here's how:

1. **Utilise Market Reports**: Regularly review market reports provided by your agent or analyst. These reports include data on market trends, property values, and economic indicators. Analysing these reports can help you understand current market conditions and identify potential investment opportunities.
2. **Ask for Detailed Analysis**: Request detailed analyses of specific neighbourhoods or properties you are interested in. This can include information on recent sales, price trends, and rental yields. A thorough analysis will help you make informed decisions and avoid overpaying for a property.

3. **Engage in Strategic Discussions**: Have regular discussions with your agent or analyst about your investment goals and strategies. Their insights can guide you in refining your investment approach, identifying emerging trends, and making strategic adjustments based on market conditions.
4. **Monitor Market Changes**: Keep track of any changes in the market or new developments that could impact your investment. Your agent or analyst should keep you informed about significant market shifts or opportunities that may affect your portfolio.
5. **Leverage Expert Recommendations**: Take advantage of recommendations from your agent or analyst regarding potential investments, neighbourhoods to watch, or upcoming market trends. Their expertise can guide you towards high-potential investments and help you avoid pitfalls.

By effectively collaborating with real estate agents and market analysts, and leveraging their expertise and resources, you can enhance your property investment strategy, make informed decisions, and achieve better investment outcomes.

In the ever-evolving world of property investment, staying informed about market trends and data is crucial for making strategic investment decisions. The property market is influenced by a variety of factors including economic conditions, demographic shifts, and local developments. Here's how to effectively track market trends and data to ensure you make well-informed investment decisions.

How to Stay Up to Date with Market Trends

1. **News Sources**:
    - **Real Estate News Websites**: Regularly visit real estate news websites such as Real Estate Weekly, Property Week, or industry-specific news outlets. These sources provide timely updates on market conditions, industry trends, and significant property transactions.
    - **Financial News Platforms**: Major financial news platforms like Bloomberg, Reuters, and CNBC offer insights into broader economic conditions that affect property markets, including interest rates, inflation, and employment data.
2. **Market Reports**:
    - **Quarterly and Annual Reports**: Many real estate agencies and market analysts publish quarterly or annual reports that provide in-depth analyses of property markets. These reports often include data on property prices, rental yields, and market trends.
    - **Local Market Reports**: Subscribe to reports specific to the regions or suburbs you are interested in. These reports offer detailed insights into local market conditions and emerging trends.
3. **Property Platforms**:
    - **Online Property Portals**: Platforms like Zillow, Domain, and Realestate.com.au provide real-time data on property listings, price trends, and market statistics. Use these platforms to monitor changes in property values and track new listings.
    - **Investment Analysis Tools**: Utilise tools and apps designed for property investors that aggregate data from various sources and provide analytical insights. Examples include PropTrack, CoreLogic, and REI.

Importance of Continuously Monitoring Economic Indicators and Property Prices

1. **Economic Indicators**:
   - **Interest Rates**: Fluctuations in interest rates can significantly impact mortgage affordability and property investment returns. Monitor central bank announcements and interest rate trends to gauge how they might affect your investments.
   - **Inflation**: High inflation can erode the purchasing power of money and affect property values and rental yields. Keeping track of inflation rates helps you understand potential changes in property prices and costs.
   - **Employment and GDP**: Economic indicators such as employment rates and Gross Domestic Product (GDP) growth influence property demand. A strong job market and economic growth generally boost demand for property, leading to higher prices and rental yields.
2. **Property Prices**:
   - **Price Trends**: Regularly review data on property price movements to identify trends in the market. This helps in understanding whether prices are rising, falling, or stabilising, which can influence your investment decisions.
   - **Comparative Analysis**: Compare current property prices with historical data to assess whether a market is overvalued or undervalued. This comparison can guide you in making strategic purchasing or selling decisions.

Tools and Resources for Ongoing Market Analysis

1. **Property Data Services**:
   - **CoreLogic**: Provides comprehensive data and analytics on property markets, including price trends, rental yields, and demographic information.
   - **PropTrack**: Offers detailed property market insights, including price forecasts, market activity, and property trends.
   - **Real Estate Investment Software**: Invest in software that helps track and analyse property data, such as PropertyValue or REI Master, to manage and assess your investment portfolio.
2. **Economic Forecasts**:
   - **Government Reports**: Review reports and forecasts from government agencies and economic research institutes. These often include predictions about economic growth, housing markets, and key economic indicators.
   - **Economic Research Firms**: Subscribe to research from firms that specialise in economic forecasting and market analysis. Their insights can provide valuable context for your property investment decisions.
3. **Investment Forums and Networking**:
   - **Online Forums**: Engage with property investment forums and communities to share insights, ask questions, and learn from other investors' experiences.
   - **Industry Events**: Attend property investment seminars, conferences, and networking events to stay updated on market trends and connect with industry experts.

Chapter 6: Making Smart Decisions

Introduction:

Making smart, well-informed decisions is fundamental to success in property investment. The real estate market is highly dynamic, influenced by a variety of economic, social, and political factors. It is vital for investors to understand these influences and make decisions that will maximise returns and minimise risks. From selecting the right property to choosing the best financing option, every decision in property investment carries consequences that can either propel an investor toward financial freedom or result in costly setbacks.

The Importance of Well-Informed Decisions in Property Investment

Property investment is not merely about buying real estate and waiting for its value to increase. Successful property investment requires a deep understanding of the market, careful analysis of trends, and a strategic approach to decision-making. Every step, from choosing the right location to securing favourable financing, involves a series of critical decisions that impact the long-term profitability of your investment.

Making uninformed or impulsive decisions can lead to unnecessary risks and financial strain. For instance, purchasing a property in a declining market without researching the area's economic indicators or overlooking hidden costs during renovations could result in unexpected losses. On the other hand, well-informed decisions, supported by thorough research and market analysis, can help investors identify high-growth areas, negotiate favourable deals, and effectively manage their investments for maximum profitability.

One of the key pillars of property investment success is knowledge. Investors must keep up with evolving market conditions, economic changes, and legislative shifts that could impact their investments. Staying informed helps property investors make decisions that are based on facts, rather than emotions or assumptions, allowing them to capitalise on opportunities while mitigating potential risks.

Maximising Returns and Minimising Risks Through Smart Decisions

One of the most significant advantages of making smart decisions in property investment is the ability to maximise returns while minimising risks. Property investment, like any form of investment, carries inherent risks—property values fluctuate, interest rates rise and fall, and unexpected expenses can occur. However, investors who make thoughtful, informed decisions can mitigate these risks while positioning themselves to benefit from the market's upside potential.

Maximising returns involves more than just choosing properties in high-demand areas. It also includes negotiating favourable purchase prices, effectively managing rental properties, and ensuring that each property's cash flow is positive. Investors can also enhance returns through strategies such as adding value via renovations or strategically refinancing properties to free up equity for further investment.

To minimise risks, investors should focus on conducting thorough due diligence before making any purchase. This means researching market conditions, performing comparative market analysis (CMA), and understanding key economic factors that influence property prices. Additionally, smart investors develop a risk management strategy that includes maintaining a diverse portfolio, ensuring they have a healthy cash flow to cover unexpected expenses, and using appropriate financing structures that do not over-leverage their position.

For example, investing in property located in a diversified economic area with strong employment opportunities and infrastructure development can significantly reduce risks. Similarly, setting a realistic budget that accounts for all costs—including repairs, legal fees, and ongoing maintenance—can help protect the investor from financial strain. Smart investors also build contingency plans, such as having emergency funds or insurance to cover unforeseen issues like vacancy periods or costly repairs.

The Mindset of a Successful Property Investor

Success in property investment requires more than just knowledge and strategy—it demands a particular mindset. Successful investors think long-term, focusing on building sustainable wealth rather than chasing short-term gains. They understand that property investment is a marathon, not a sprint, and that consistency, patience, and discipline are key to long-term success.

One of the essential qualities of a successful property investor is the ability to remain calm and rational, especially in the face of market fluctuations or unexpected challenges. Emotional decision-making can lead to overpaying for properties, selling at a loss during downturns, or making hasty investment choices. A successful investor approaches each decision with a clear mind, backed by data and analysis rather than fear or excitement.

Another key element of the investor mindset is the willingness to learn continuously. The property market evolves, and successful investors stay ahead by constantly educating themselves, seeking out advice from experts, and learning from their own experiences. They invest in their knowledge, understanding that this investment pays dividends in the form of better decision-making, fewer mistakes, and more profitable outcomes.

Successful investors also recognize the value of building a strong network of professionals. They work closely with experienced real estate agents, property managers, accountants, and mortgage brokers, leveraging their expertise to make informed decisions. Surrounding themselves with a reliable team helps them navigate complex market conditions and provides valuable insights that can influence key investment choices.

Additionally, successful investors embrace a proactive approach to problem-solving. They anticipate potential issues—such as tenant disputes, maintenance problems, or cash flow shortages—and put measures in place to address these challenges before they arise. Rather than reacting to problems as they occur, they develop contingency plans that allow them to continue growing their portfolios without disruption.

In summary, smart decision-making in property investment is about being well-informed, disciplined, and strategic. By focusing on thorough research, maintaining a long-term perspective, and continuously enhancing their knowledge and skills, investors can navigate the complexities of the property market with confidence. This approach helps them maximise their returns, reduce risk, and achieve long-term success in building their property portfolios. With the right mindset and decision-making strategies, property investors can turn challenges into opportunities and steadily grow their wealth through real estate investment.

Setting clear investment goals is one of the most crucial steps in building a successful property portfolio. Without defined goals, it's easy to lose direction, make impulsive decisions, or overlook opportunities that align with your financial objectives. Defining both short-term and long-term goals will provide clarity on your investment strategy, help you stay focused, and enable you to measure your progress over time.

In property investment, there are several potential outcomes you can aim for, including cash flow, capital growth, or portfolio diversification. Each requires a different approach, and understanding how to balance these goals is key to ensuring long-term success. By aligning your property investment decisions with your personal financial objectives, you can chart a strategic path to wealth creation that suits your risk tolerance, timeline, and resources.

Importance of Defining Short-Term and Long-Term Goals

At the start of your property investment journey, it's essential to distinguish between short-term and long-term goals. Having both in place allows you to balance immediate needs with future aspirations, helping you to make more strategic decisions.

Short-term goals typically focus on acquiring your first few properties, improving cash flow, or generating quick returns through value-add strategies like renovations or flipping. These goals are generally achieved within a few years and often involve lower-risk investments to build a strong foundation for future growth. Examples of short-term property investment goals include:

- Buying one property within the first 12 months.
- Securing a positive cash flow from rental income to cover mortgage repayments.
- Increasing the value of a property through renovations or development.

Long-term goals, on the other hand, are centred on building a sustainable portfolio that generates wealth over a period of decades. These goals could include amassing multiple properties, achieving financial independence through passive income, or reaching a net worth target by a specific date. Long-term goals often require a focus on capital growth and may involve taking calculated risks to achieve higher returns. Examples of long-term goals include:

- Owning 5-10 properties within the next 10-15 years.
- Generating enough passive income to replace your salary.
- Achieving a specific portfolio value for retirement or legacy building.

Without defined goals, investors may struggle to find consistency in their strategy, leading to fragmented decisions that don't necessarily move them closer to financial independence. Clearly outlining what you want to achieve helps you make smarter, more focused decisions, and provides a framework to track your progress.

Differentiating Between Cash Flow, Capital Growth, and Portfolio Diversification

Once you've defined your short-term and long-term goals, the next step is to determine what kind of investments will help you achieve them. In property investment, most strategies are based on three main objectives: cash flow, capital growth, and portfolio diversification. Understanding the differences between these strategies and how they relate to your goals is essential to developing a clear investment plan.

1. **Cash Flow** Cash flow refers to the income generated from rental properties after expenses such as mortgage payments, maintenance, and property management fees. Positive cash flow properties can provide a steady stream of income and help investors cover expenses while building equity over time. If your goal is to generate enough rental income to replace your salary, then prioritising cash flow is a suitable strategy. These properties tend to be found in areas with strong rental demand and relatively affordable property prices.
   Key considerations for cash flow investments:
   - Focus on rental demand: Target areas with high demand for rentals, such as urban centres or university towns.
   - Analyse rental yields: Ensure the rental income exceeds expenses, producing a surplus (positive cash flow).
   - Prioritise stability: Look for low-risk properties that will consistently generate income, even during economic downturns.
2. For example, if your short-term goal is to generate $1,000 per month in passive income, you might focus on acquiring high-yield rental properties in regional or suburban areas where property prices are lower but rental demand remains strong.
3. **Capital Growth** Capital growth refers to the increase in the value of your property over time. This strategy is typically more long-term, as the goal is to buy properties in high-growth areas and benefit from the appreciation of property values. Investors focusing on capital growth often invest in metropolitan areas, emerging suburbs, or regions undergoing significant development or infrastructure improvements.
   Key considerations for capital growth investments:
   - Focus on high-growth areas: Identify suburbs or cities where property prices are expected to rise due to economic growth, population increases, or gentrification.
   - Consider timing: Entering the market during the early stages of growth can maximise returns, but be prepared for market fluctuations.
   - Balance cash flow: Capital growth properties may have lower rental yields, so you need to ensure you can cover costs in the short term.
4. If your long-term goal is to achieve financial independence through property appreciation, focusing on high-growth areas is a key strategy. For instance, investing in properties located near new transport links or in neighbourhoods experiencing gentrification could yield substantial profits over a 10-20 year period.
5. **Portfolio Diversification** Portfolio diversification involves spreading your investments across different types of properties, locations, and strategies to mitigate risk. A diverse portfolio is less likely to be severely impacted by market fluctuations, as the performance of one property or area may offset the risks in another. Diversification can also mean having a mix of cash flow-positive properties and capital growth-focused investments.
   Key considerations for portfolio diversification:
   - Geographic diversification: Invest in properties across different cities or regions to reduce risk exposure to a single market.
   - Diversify by property type: Consider a mix of residential, commercial, and industrial properties to tap into different market dynamics.
   - Balance risk and reward: Spread investments across different risk profiles, such as a mix of lower-risk cash flow properties and higher-risk growth properties.

6. If your goal is to build a large, sustainable portfolio over time, diversification is crucial. For example, combining inner-city apartments for capital growth with regional homes for cash flow can provide stability while still allowing for long-term appreciation.

Aligning Investment Decisions with Your Personal Financial Objectives

After setting clear investment goals and identifying your priorities (cash flow, capital growth, or diversification), the next step is to align your investment decisions with your broader personal financial objectives. Every property you purchase should move you closer to achieving your financial goals, whether that's financial independence, retirement planning, or wealth-building.

Start by mapping out your overall financial picture—your current income, expenses, debts, and savings—and determine how property investment fits into this framework. Consider the following questions when aligning your property investments with your financial objectives:

- **What is your risk tolerance?** Investors with a higher risk tolerance may prioritise capital growth and be more willing to invest in emerging markets, while those with lower risk tolerance may focus on cash flow stability.
- **What is your investment timeline?** If you plan to retire in 10 years, you may want to focus on strategies that will generate significant capital growth or passive income within that time frame.
- **How much leverage are you comfortable with?** Using leverage (borrowed money) is common in property investment, but it's essential to understand your debt capacity and ensure you don't become over-leveraged.
- **What are your tax considerations?** Depending on your financial situation, you may want to focus on tax-deductible expenses, such as interest on investment loans, or take advantage of government incentives.

By aligning your investment decisions with your personal financial objectives, you can create a cohesive strategy that optimises your financial resources and maximises your returns. For instance, if your goal is to achieve financial independence through passive income, you may prioritise high-yield cash flow properties while still including some capital growth properties to ensure long-term wealth accumulation.

In property investment, success often hinges on the ability to assess, manage, and balance risk against potential rewards. Every investment decision comes with trade-offs, and understanding these is crucial for building a resilient, profitable portfolio. Whether you're investing in high-growth areas, stable markets, residential properties, or commercial ventures, each choice presents unique risks and rewards. Learning how to balance these factors allows investors to navigate market fluctuations and achieve long-term wealth accumulation.

This chapter will explore how to assess risk in different property markets and types, as well as strategies to balance risk and reward. By understanding your risk tolerance and aligning it with your investment goals, you can create a robust portfolio that weathers market downturns while maximising returns.

Assessing Risk in Different Property Investments

Property investment is inherently risky, as markets can be unpredictable, interest rates fluctuate, and local factors like infrastructure development or employment trends can significantly impact the value of properties. However, the level of risk varies widely between different types of property investments. A thorough understanding of these risks helps investors make informed decisions and choose properties that align with their financial objectives and risk tolerance.

1. High-Growth Areas vs. Stable Markets

One of the most important decisions property investors face is choosing between high-growth areas and more stable markets. Both present distinct risks and rewards:

- **High-Growth Areas**: These are typically emerging markets where property values are rising rapidly due to factors like urban renewal, infrastructure development, or an influx of residents. Investing in high-growth areas can result in significant capital appreciation in a relatively short time. However, these areas also tend to be more volatile, and property values can fluctuate dramatically based on economic conditions or market sentiment. The risk of overpaying for a property in a heated market is also higher, which could lead to losses if the market cools off.
  Reward: High potential for capital growth, ideal for long-term wealth creation.
  Risk: High volatility and potential for market downturns, leading to value depreciation.
- **Stable Markets**: These are areas with established infrastructure, low vacancy rates, and steady property values. Investing in stable markets tends to be less risky, as these areas have a history of stable growth and consistent demand. However, the downside is that property values in these areas may not experience significant spikes in value, limiting the potential for rapid capital appreciation.
  Reward: Lower risk of market volatility, stable rental income, and gradual capital growth.
  Risk: Lower potential for rapid capital appreciation, slower wealth accumulation.

Investors should weigh their risk tolerance when choosing between high-growth and stable markets. Those with a high tolerance for risk might prefer high-growth areas for their potential to generate substantial returns, while more risk-averse investors might prioritise stable markets for their reliability and security.

2. Regional vs. Metropolitan Markets

Another dimension of risk in property investment is whether to focus on regional or metropolitan markets.

- **Metropolitan Markets**: These are typically large, well-developed cities with diverse economies and strong population growth. Properties in metropolitan areas tend to have higher prices and lower rental yields but offer more security and long-term growth potential due to high demand for housing. The key risk in metropolitan markets is the likelihood of price corrections during economic downturns or oversupply situations. Additionally, high entry costs can limit the potential for strong rental returns in the short term.
  Reward: Long-term capital appreciation, high rental demand.
  Risk: High entry costs, price volatility, and lower initial rental yields.

- **Regional Markets**: Regional areas often offer lower property prices and higher rental yields, making them attractive to investors seeking positive cash flow. However, regional markets can be more volatile and dependent on specific industries (such as mining or tourism), meaning they may be more vulnerable to economic downturns or changes in local employment conditions. Investors must be aware of these factors when choosing regional markets to mitigate the risk of prolonged vacancies or stagnant property prices.
  Reward: Lower entry costs, higher rental yields.
  Risk: Greater market volatility, potential reliance on specific industries, and slower capital growth.

3. Established Properties vs. Off-the-Plan Investments

Investors must also consider the difference between established properties and off-the-plan investments.

- **Established Properties**: These properties have a known history, are already built, and may even have tenants in place, providing immediate rental income. Established properties offer more certainty in terms of market value and rental yield, reducing the risk associated with unknown factors. However, the potential for substantial capital growth might be lower than for off-the-plan properties in a booming market.
  Reward: Certainty regarding market value and rental income, fewer unknowns.
  Risk: Lower potential for rapid appreciation, higher purchase prices.
- **Off-the-Plan Properties**: Buying off-the-plan refers to purchasing a property before it is built, usually from a developer. The appeal of these properties lies in the potential for capital growth between the time of purchase and completion. Investors may also enjoy stamp duty savings and a lower initial purchase price. However, off-the-plan purchases carry significant risks, such as construction delays, quality issues, or a downturn in the market before the property is completed.
  Reward: Potential for capital growth, lower upfront costs, and tax incentives.
  Risk: Construction delays, market changes, quality issues, and potential overvaluation.

Understanding the Risk Profile of Different Property Types

Different property types, such as residential, commercial, and industrial properties, each come with their own risk profiles. Understanding these differences is crucial for building a well-diversified and resilient portfolio.

1. Residential Properties

Residential properties are often considered the safest form of property investment. They are in constant demand, as people always need housing, and they provide a stable rental income. However, the trade-off is that residential properties typically offer lower yields compared to commercial or industrial properties, and their value is more influenced by the broader economic cycle.

Reward: Steady demand and consistent rental income.

Risk: Lower yields, more dependent on the health of the general economy, and subject to market fluctuations.

2. Commercial Properties

Commercial properties, such as office buildings or retail spaces, can offer higher rental yields than residential properties and longer lease terms. However, they are typically more sensitive to economic conditions. During a recession, for example, businesses may downsize or close, leading to longer vacancy periods. Additionally, commercial properties tend to have higher upfront costs and are subject to more significant market fluctuations based on business cycles.

Reward: Higher yields and longer lease terms.

Risk: Longer vacancies during downturns, higher initial costs, and market dependency on business conditions.

3. Industrial Properties

Industrial properties, such as warehouses and factories, tend to offer even higher yields than commercial properties and are often subject to long-term leases with large businesses. However, they come with specific risks, including higher maintenance costs and a more limited pool of potential tenants. The demand for industrial properties is often tied to the economic performance of specific sectors like manufacturing or logistics.

Reward: High yields and long-term leases.

Risk: High maintenance costs and reliance on specific industries for demand.

Balancing Risk and Reward to Create a Resilient Portfolio

To build a resilient portfolio, investors must carefully balance risk and reward. The key is diversification—spreading investments across various types of properties, locations, and strategies. Diversifying reduces the impact of any single market downturn or unexpected event, protecting your overall portfolio.

Here are strategies to balance risk and reward:

1. Diversify Across Property Types

By investing in a mix of residential, commercial, and industrial properties, you can spread risk across different market segments. Residential properties provide stability, while commercial and industrial properties offer higher yields. This blend ensures that your portfolio generates consistent returns while capitalising on high-growth opportunities.

2. Geographic Diversification

Investing in multiple regions or cities can protect your portfolio from localised economic downturns. For example, if one area experiences a drop in property values due to industry-specific issues, properties in other regions may continue to perform well, balancing the portfolio's overall risk.

3. Mix of Cash Flow and Capital Growth Investments

Balancing properties that provide steady cash flow with those expected to experience capital growth is another way to manage risk. Cash flow properties can cover mortgage repayments and other expenses, while capital growth investments increase your overall wealth over time.

4. Ongoing Market Analysis

Constantly monitoring the market and staying informed about economic trends, local developments, and policy changes is essential for managing risk. Being proactive allows you to adjust your portfolio as needed, whether by selling underperforming properties, refinancing, or buying in emerging markets.

In property investment, the concept of "due diligence" refers to the rigorous research and analysis that investors must conduct before purchasing a property. This process is crucial for making informed decisions and avoiding costly mistakes. The right investment can generate substantial returns, but a poorly researched property could lead to financial losses. Therefore, conducting thorough due diligence is a fundamental step in any successful property investment strategy.

This chapter will delve into the importance of due diligence, key areas of research that investors should focus on, and how to gather and analyse data to make informed, strategic property investments.

The Importance of Conducting Thorough Due Diligence

Buying a property without comprehensive research is akin to gambling. Property investment is a significant financial commitment, and while the rewards can be high, the risks are equally considerable. Thorough due diligence allows investors to mitigate risks and make decisions based on facts rather than assumptions or emotional impulses.

1. Mitigating Risk

One of the primary purposes of due diligence is to reduce the risk associated with property purchases. By thoroughly understanding the local market, property conditions, legal constraints, and potential for growth, you can avoid overpaying or buying a property with hidden problems. Due diligence uncovers issues that may not be immediately apparent, such as structural defects, zoning restrictions, or undesirable neighbourhood trends.

2. Maximising Return on Investment (ROI)

Proper due diligence ensures that your property investments align with your financial goals. For example, if you're aiming for capital growth, researching local market trends will help you identify areas with strong potential for appreciation. On the other hand, if you're seeking rental income, due diligence can reveal areas with high tenant demand and solid rental yields. By understanding the market, you position yourself to maximise your ROI.

3. Avoiding Legal and Financial Pitfalls

Investing in property involves navigating complex legal and financial landscapes. Without due diligence, you risk encountering legal issues such as title disputes, zoning violations, or hidden debts attached to the property. Additionally, failure to properly assess a property's financial standing (e.g., outstanding liens or unanticipated renovation costs) can erode your profit margin and put your entire investment strategy in jeopardy.

Key Areas to Research

Effective due diligence covers a wide range of factors. Below are the key areas you should focus on to make well-informed property investment decisions.

1. Local Market Conditions

Understanding local market conditions is critical for identifying the potential for growth, rental demand, and long-term profitability. This research involves analysing broader economic indicators, housing trends, and market demand in the area where you're considering purchasing a property.

a. Market Trends

Before buying, analyse the property market's current cycle. Is it in a growth phase, or has it reached a plateau? Understanding where the local market sits in the property cycle (boom, slump, recovery, or stagnation) will help you determine whether it's a good time to buy. Research past property price trends, average time on the market for listings, and the general trajectory of property values in the area.

b. Supply and Demand

High demand and limited supply often lead to rising property values and rental yields. Look at the supply of housing in the area: Are there many new developments under construction? If so, this could lead to oversupply, which might drive prices down in the future. Conversely, an area with limited new supply and high demand from tenants or buyers is likely to see property values and rental returns increase over time.

c. Population Growth and Demographics

Population growth is a reliable indicator of rising demand for housing. Areas experiencing an influx of residents, whether due to job opportunities, lifestyle appeal, or infrastructure projects, tend to see property values appreciate. Research the local population trends, including who is moving to the area (e.g., families, young professionals, retirees), as this will inform your decision about what type of property to buy and how to cater to future tenants or buyers.

2. Property Condition and Potential

Before purchasing a property, you must assess its physical condition and potential for improvements. This involves inspections, analysing repair needs, and considering how renovations could increase the property's value or rental yield.

a. Building and Structural Integrity

A thorough property inspection is essential to uncover any issues with the building's structure, plumbing, electrical systems, or roofing. Major problems like foundation damage or faulty wiring can result in significant repair costs that eat into your profits. By hiring a professional building inspector, you can get a detailed report on the property's condition and decide whether the investment is worthwhile.

b. Renovation Potential

If the property requires cosmetic improvements or minor repairs, consider whether these renovations will increase the property's value or rental income. Analyse the costs of renovation against the potential uplift in market value. Sometimes, strategic renovations such as kitchen upgrades or modernising bathrooms can result in higher rental yields or a quicker resale at a higher price.

3. Financial Analysis

Understanding the financial implications of a property purchase is a key component of due diligence. This involves calculating potential returns, assessing costs, and reviewing financing options.

a. Rental Yields and Cash Flow

If you're purchasing the property as a rental investment, it's important to analyse the rental yield and expected cash flow. Rental yield is calculated as the annual rental income divided by the purchase price of the property, expressed as a percentage. A high rental yield suggests that the property is generating strong returns relative to its cost, but don't forget to factor in ongoing expenses such as property management fees, maintenance, insurance, and taxes.

b. Capital Growth Potential

Capital growth refers to the increase in the value of the property over time. To estimate capital growth potential, research historical price trends for similar properties in the area and consider factors like planned infrastructure projects or gentrification. It's also helpful to look at comparable sales in the neighbourhood to determine whether the property you're considering is priced competitively.

c. Financing Costs

Understand the full financial implications of your investment, including the interest rate on your loan, associated fees, and mortgage conditions. Calculate the total cost of borrowing and how it impacts your expected returns. Comparing loan products and selecting the most favourable financing option is a key part of the due diligence process.

4. Legal Considerations

Before purchasing a property, you must ensure that all legal aspects of the deal are in order. Failure to address legal concerns can lead to costly problems down the road.

a. Title and Ownership

One of the most important steps in due diligence is confirming that the seller has clear ownership of the property. Conduct a title search to ensure there are no encumbrances or claims on the property, such as outstanding mortgages, liens, or easements that could affect your use of the property.

b. Zoning and Planning Restrictions

Verify the property's zoning status to ensure it aligns with your intended use. For example, if you're purchasing a property to rent out as a short-term rental or planning to subdivide and develop the land, you'll need to confirm that local zoning laws permit these activities. Additionally, check for any upcoming changes to zoning regulations that could affect the property's value or your investment strategy.

c. Building Permits and Regulations

If you're planning to renovate or develop the property, check with the local authorities to confirm that the necessary building permits are in place. Failing to obtain the correct permits can result in hefty fines or even force you to undo the work.

How to Gather and Analyse the Right Data

Gathering accurate, up-to-date data is critical for effective due diligence. There are several sources of information available to investors, both free and paid, that can help you make informed decisions.

1. Property Portals and Real Estate Websites

Sites like Zillow, Realtor.com, and CoreLogic provide extensive data on property prices, recent sales, rental yields, and market trends. These platforms are valuable for researching individual properties and gaining a broader understanding of local market conditions.

2. Public Records and Government Data

Government websites often provide free access to public records, such as property tax assessments, zoning regulations, and census data. These records can help you assess the property's financial standing and compliance with local laws.

3. Real Estate Agents and Property Analysts

Experienced real estate agents can offer insights into local market trends, comparable sales, and buyer demand. Some agents also have access to proprietary data from property research firms that can provide more in-depth market analysis.

4. Professional Property Inspectors

Hiring a professional property inspector is a key part of due diligence. These experts provide detailed reports on the property's condition, which can help you avoid purchasing a property with hidden defects.

5. Legal and Financial Advisors

Consulting with property lawyers and financial advisors can ensure that you're not missing any legal or financial red flags. These professionals can help you navigate complex contracts, financing options, and tax implications.

Effective property investment relies heavily on analysing and understanding cash flow and returns. These metrics are crucial for assessing whether a property will be a profitable addition to your portfolio. By calculating rental yield, cash flow, and overall return on investment (ROI), investors can make informed decisions that align with their financial goals. This section will provide a comprehensive guide to these calculations, discuss strategies for optimising cash flow, and explore tools that can aid in evaluating investment performance.

Calculating Rental Yield, Cash Flow, and Overall Return on Investment

1. Rental Yield

Rental yield is a key metric that helps investors determine the potential income generated by a rental property relative to its value. It is expressed as a percentage and provides a snapshot of the property's earning potential.

a. Gross Rental Yield

Gross rental yield is calculated by dividing the annual rental income by the property's purchase price and then multiplying by 100 to get a percentage.

Formula:

Divide your annual rent by the value of the property. Multiply that figure by 100 to get the percentage of your gross rental yield.

George purchased an investment property for $600,000. He rents it out at $450 per week. The gross rental yield is the annual rental income ($450 x 52) = $23,400 / $600,000 x 100 = 3.9%

b. Net Rental Yield

Net rental yield provides a more accurate picture of profitability by accounting for property expenses, such as maintenance, property management fees, insurance, and taxes.

Formula:

Sum up the annual rent you will receive from the property. subtract the total expenses from the annual rent. Divide it by the value of the property. Multiply by 100. George's net rental yield is calculated by subtracting his property costs from his rental income. $23,400 ($450 x 52) - $4920 / $600,000 = 0.031 x 100 = 3.1%

2. Cash Flow

Cash flow represents the net amount of cash generated by the property after all expenses and loan repayments are deducted from the rental income. Positive cash flow means the property generates more income than expenses, while negative cash flow indicates a shortfall.

Formula:

Since the formula for calculating cash flow is rental income minus payments and expenses, your cash flow would be: $46,080 (gross rental income) minus $29,448 (mortgage, tax, insurance) minus $685 (repair and maintenance) is equal to $15,947 or $1,329 in positive cash flow for 12 months.

3. Overall Return on Investment (ROI)

ROI measures the profitability of an investment relative to its cost. It considers both rental income and capital gains.

Formula:

To calculate the property's ROI: Divide the annual return by your original out-of-pocket expenses (the downpayment of $20,000, closing costs of $2,500, and remodelling for $9,000) to determine ROI. ROI = $5,016.84 ÷ $31,500 = 0.159. Your ROI is 15.9%.

Evaluating Cash Flow Projections and Capital Growth Potential

1. Cash Flow Projections

Accurate cash flow projections are essential for understanding a property's financial viability over time. To evaluate cash flow projections:

a. Estimate Rental Income

Research comparable rental properties in the area to estimate potential rental income. Consider factors such as property size, location, and amenities to set a competitive rental price.

b. Calculate Operating Expenses

Include all ongoing expenses such as property management fees, maintenance, insurance, taxes, and utilities. It's essential to be thorough and realistic about these costs to avoid unexpected shortfalls.

c. Assess Mortgage Repayments

Use mortgage calculators to estimate monthly repayments based on the loan amount, interest rate, and term. Include principal and interest payments to get an accurate picture of your monthly obligations.

2. Capital Growth Potential

Capital growth refers to the increase in a property's value over time. To assess capital growth potential:

a. Analyze Historical Data

Review historical property value trends in the area. Look for patterns of consistent growth or volatility and assess whether the current market conditions favour appreciation.

b. Evaluate Economic and Infrastructure Developments

Research upcoming infrastructure projects, such as new transport links, commercial developments, or urban renewal initiatives. These factors can drive demand and contribute to property value increases.

c. Consider Market Indicators

Look at key market indicators, such as population growth, employment rates, and housing supply. Areas with strong economic fundamentals and high demand for housing are more likely to experience capital growth.

Tools and Strategies for Optimising Cash Flow While Maintaining Growth Prospects

1. Property Management Tools

Effective property management can enhance cash flow. Use property management software or services to handle tenant inquiries, maintenance requests, and rent collection efficiently. Tools like Rentec Direct or PropertyMe can streamline these tasks and ensure consistent cash flow.

2. Renovation and Value-Add Strategies

Strategic renovations can boost rental income and property value. Focus on high-impact, cost-effective upgrades such as modernising kitchens, bathrooms, or improving curb appeal. Evaluate the potential return on investment for each renovation project to ensure it aligns with your cash flow goals.

3. Tax Optimization

Optimise your tax position to improve cash flow. Claim allowable deductions, such as mortgage interest, depreciation, and property management fees. Consult with a tax advisor to ensure you're maximising tax benefits and reducing your taxable income.

4. Diversification

Diversifying your property portfolio can help balance risk and improve cash flow. Consider investing in different property types (e.g., residential, commercial) or locations with varying growth prospects. This strategy can mitigate risks associated with market fluctuations and provide more stable cash flow.

5. Review and Adjust Rental Pricing

Regularly review and adjust rental pricing based on market conditions and property performance. Periodically reassess the rental market to ensure your property is competitively priced and reflects any improvements or changes.

Investing in property is a significant financial commitment that can evoke strong emotions, from excitement about potential gains to anxiety about risks. However, allowing emotions to drive investment decisions can lead to costly mistakes. To achieve long-term success in property investment, it's crucial to approach decisions with objectivity and a clear focus on data. This section explores the dangers of emotional decision-making, strategies for maintaining an objective approach, and ways to distinguish personal preferences from investment priorities.

The Dangers of Letting Emotions Influence Property Investment Decisions

1. Overpaying for Property

Emotional attachment to a property can lead to overpaying. Investors may fall in love with a property's aesthetics or location, causing them to disregard their budget and investment criteria. This emotional bias can result in paying more than the market value, reducing potential returns and affecting overall profitability.

2. Ignoring Objective Data

When emotions take over, investors might ignore crucial data and analytical insights. For instance, an emotional desire for a specific area might overshadow negative indicators such as declining rental demand or increasing vacancy rates. This can lead to poor investment choices based on sentiment rather than solid evidence.

3. Making Hasty Decisions

Emotional decision-making often results in hasty choices driven by a fear of missing out (FOMO) or excitement about a perceived opportunity. Rushed decisions can lead to inadequate due diligence, overlooked risks, and suboptimal investment outcomes. Taking the time to analyse and evaluate all aspects of a property is essential for making informed decisions.

4. Difficulty Accepting Losses

Emotions can cloud judgement when dealing with underperforming investments. Investors who are emotionally attached to a property may delay selling or holding onto a losing asset longer than is financially prudent. This reluctance to cut losses can result in further financial damage and missed opportunities for better investments.

Strategies to Remain Objective and Data-Driven in Your Decision-Making Process

1. Establish Clear Investment Criteria

Before beginning your property search, define your investment criteria based on objective factors such as return on investment (ROI), cash flow, location, and property type. By setting these criteria in advance, you create a framework that helps you evaluate properties systematically and avoid letting personal emotions sway your judgement.

2. Conduct Comprehensive Research

Thorough research is essential for making data-driven decisions. Gather and analyse information from multiple sources, including market reports, property comparables, economic indicators, and expert opinions. Use this data to assess the viability of potential investments and make decisions based on evidence rather than emotion.

3. Use a Checklist for Evaluations

Develop a checklist to evaluate each property against your investment criteria. This checklist should include factors such as purchase price, potential rental income, property condition, and market trends. By consistently applying the checklist, you ensure that each property is assessed objectively and according to predetermined criteria.

4. Consult with Professionals

Engage with real estate agents, property managers, and financial advisors to gain expert insights. Professionals can provide an objective perspective and help you navigate complex decisions. Their expertise can counterbalance emotional biases and offer valuable guidance based on market knowledge and experience.

5. Avoid Relying Solely on Personal Preferences

Separate your personal preferences from investment decisions. While it's natural to have personal tastes or attachments, prioritise factors that align with your financial goals and investment strategy. Focus on the property's potential for income generation, value appreciation, and alignment with your overall investment plan rather than personal likes or dislikes.

6. Implement a Decision-Making Process

Develop and adhere to a structured decision-making process. This process should include steps for gathering information, evaluating options, and making final decisions based on objective analysis. Avoid making decisions impulsively and take time to review all aspects of the investment thoroughly.

7. Stay Grounded with Financial Metrics

Use financial metrics such as rental yield, cash flow, and return on investment to guide your decisions. These metrics provide a quantitative basis for evaluating the performance of a property and help you stay focused on financial objectives rather than emotional responses.

How to Separate Personal Preferences from Investment Priorities

1. Define Investment Goals

Clearly outline your investment goals and priorities before beginning your property search. Consider factors such as desired return on investment, risk tolerance, and cash flow needs. Align your property choices with these goals rather than letting personal preferences dictate your decisions.

2. Seek Objective Feedback

Discuss potential investments with trusted advisors or mentors who can provide objective feedback. Their external perspective can help you evaluate properties based on rational criteria rather than personal attachment or preferences.

3. Consider the Bigger Picture

Focus on the broader financial picture rather than individual property attributes. Assess how each property fits into your overall investment strategy and portfolio. Evaluate its potential to contribute to your long-term goals and financial success, rather than getting caught up in specific features or aesthetics.

4. Conduct a SWOT Analysis

Perform a SWOT analysis (Strengths, Weaknesses, Opportunities, Threats) for each property. This analytical tool helps identify the property's strengths and weaknesses from an investment perspective, along with opportunities and threats in the market. By evaluating properties through a SWOT analysis, you ensure that decisions are made based on objective factors rather than personal biases.

When navigating the property investment landscape, you will encounter various opportunities, each with its own set of advantages and challenges. Evaluating multiple investment options requires a structured approach to compare and contrast properties effectively. This process helps in identifying the most promising investments that align with your financial goals and personal strategy. In this section, we'll explore how to assess and compare different property investment opportunities, develop a framework for evaluating properties across various locations and types, and prioritise investments based on financial returns and strategic fit.

How to Assess and Compare Different Property Investment Opportunities

1. Define Evaluation Criteria

Before diving into the specifics of each property, establish clear evaluation criteria. These criteria should reflect your investment goals, risk tolerance, and financial objectives. Common criteria include:

- **Return on Investment (ROI):** The expected return relative to the investment amount.
- **Rental Yield:** The annual rental income as a percentage of the property's value.
- **Capital Growth Potential:** The likelihood of property value appreciation over time.
- **Cash Flow:** The difference between rental income and expenses.
- **Location:** Factors like proximity to amenities, infrastructure, and growth potential.

2. Conduct Comparative Analysis

Perform a comparative analysis to assess properties against each other based on your criteria. This involves:

- **Gathering Data:** Collect information on property prices, rental rates, and historical performance for each investment option.
- **Benchmarking:** Compare properties using standardised metrics such as ROI, rental yield, and cash flow.
- **Analysing Market Trends:** Examine local market conditions, economic indicators, and future growth prospects.

3. Evaluate Risk Factors

Assess the risk associated with each property. Key risk factors to consider include:

- **Market Volatility:** How susceptible is the local market to economic fluctuations?
- **Property Condition:** Are there potential maintenance or renovation issues?
- **Tenant Demand:** Is there strong demand for rental properties in the area?
- **Regulatory Changes:** Are there any upcoming changes in zoning laws or tax policies?

Framework for Evaluating Properties Across Different Locations and Types

1. Location Analysis

Evaluate each property's location by considering:

- **Economic Indicators:** Analyse the local economy, job growth, and demographic trends.
- **Infrastructure:** Assess the availability of transport links, schools, and other amenities.
- **Neighbourhood Characteristics:** Examine factors such as crime rates, community vibe, and future development plans.

2. Property Type Analysis

Different property types come with distinct advantages and challenges. Compare properties based on:

- **Residential vs. Commercial:** Residential properties may offer steady rental income, while commercial properties might provide higher yields but come with increased risk.
- **Single-Family vs. Multi-Family:** Single-family homes often attract long-term tenants, whereas multi-family units can offer diversified rental income but may involve more management.
- **New Builds vs. Existing Properties:** New properties may require less maintenance but could be more expensive, while existing properties might offer better value but need renovations.

3. Financial Metrics

Use financial metrics to compare investments:

- **Gross Yield:** Total annual rental income divided by the property purchase price.
- **Net Yield:** Rental income minus operating expenses divided by the property price.
- **Cash Flow Analysis:** Monthly rental income minus expenses such as mortgage repayments, property management fees, and maintenance costs.
- **ROI Calculation:** Net profit from the property divided by the total investment cost.

4. Investment Horizon and Strategy Alignment

Consider how each property fits into your overall investment strategy and timeline:

- **Short-Term vs. Long-Term:** Determine if the property aligns with your short-term income needs or long-term capital growth goals.
- **Diversification:** Assess how the property complements your existing portfolio and contributes to diversification across different asset classes or locations.

Prioritising Investments Based on Financial Returns and Personal Strategy

1. Rank Investments by ROI and Cash Flow

Rank properties based on their projected ROI and cash flow. Properties with higher returns and positive cash flow should generally be prioritised, as they offer better potential for generating income and building wealth.

2. Assess Alignment with Strategic Goals

Evaluate how well each property aligns with your investment strategy and goals:

- **Capital Growth:** If your primary goal is capital appreciation, prioritise properties in high-growth areas with potential for significant value increase.
- **Income Generation:** If you seek steady rental income, focus on properties with strong rental yields and low vacancy rates.
- **Risk Management:** Choose properties that fit your risk tolerance and investment horizon, ensuring a balanced approach to portfolio management.

3. Consider Long-Term Impact

Reflect on the long-term impact of each investment:

- **Market Conditions:** Consider how each property will perform under varying market conditions and economic scenarios.
- **Exit Strategy:** Evaluate potential exit strategies for each property, including resale value and potential for future growth.

4. Make Data-Driven Decisions

Ensure that your final decision is grounded in thorough data analysis and aligns with your investment criteria. Avoid making choices based on emotions or incomplete information.

In the world of property investment, the role of advisors and experts is crucial in navigating complex decisions and ensuring a successful investment journey. While self-education and market research are important, seeking advice from professionals such as real estate agents, financial advisors, and accountants can provide valuable insights and support. This section explores when and why to consult these experts, how to leverage their knowledge effectively, and how to build a reliable network of professionals to aid in property investments.

When and Why to Seek Advice from Professionals

1. Complexity of Property Transactions

Property investment involves multiple facets—legal, financial, and market-related—that can be challenging to navigate alone. Professionals help demystify these complexities:

- **Real Estate Agents:** Provide insights into local markets, help find properties, and negotiate deals.
- **Financial Advisors:** Offer guidance on financing options, investment strategies, and portfolio management.

- **Accountants:** Ensure tax efficiency, assist with financial record-keeping, and provide advice on maximising deductions.

2. Risk Mitigation

Investing in property carries inherent risks, including market fluctuations, legal issues, and financial uncertainties. Advisors help mitigate these risks:

- **Real Estate Agents:** Assess property values, identify potential issues, and provide market trends.
- **Financial Advisors:** Evaluate your financial situation, recommend suitable loan structures, and advise on risk management strategies.
- **Accountants:** Provide tax planning advice, ensure compliance with regulations, and help manage financial risks.

3. Strategic Decision-Making

Effective decision-making requires comprehensive knowledge and experience. Professionals contribute strategic insights:

- **Real Estate Agents:** Offer market intelligence and investment potential evaluations.
- **Financial Advisors:** Help formulate investment strategies and assess financial implications.
- **Accountants:** Provide financial forecasts, budgeting assistance, and investment analysis.

How to Leverage Expert Knowledge Without Becoming Dependent

1. Be Informed and Educated

While experts provide valuable advice, maintaining your own understanding of property investment is essential:

- **Educate Yourself:** Read books, attend seminars, and follow industry news to build foundational knowledge.
- **Ask Questions:** Engage with professionals by asking questions and seeking clarification to understand their recommendations.

2. Collaborate and Verify

Work collaboratively with advisors while verifying their advice:

- **Cross-Check Information:** Use multiple sources and seek second opinions to ensure the accuracy of the advice.
- **Build Relationships:** Establish a relationship with your advisors based on trust and transparency, ensuring they understand your investment goals.

3. Maintain Control

Retain control over your investment decisions:

- **Set Clear Goals:** Define your investment objectives and ensure that advice aligns with these goals.
- **Make Informed Choices:** Use the expert advice as a tool, not a crutch. Make final decisions based on a combination of your research and their recommendations.

Building a Reliable Network of Professionals

1. Identify Key Professionals

Create a network of professionals who can support various aspects of your property investment journey:

- **Real Estate Agents:** Choose agents with local market expertise and a track record of successful transactions.
- **Financial Advisors:** Look for advisors with experience in property investment and a deep understanding of financing options.
- **Accountants:** Select accountants who specialise in property investment and understand tax implications.

2. Evaluate and Select

When building your network, evaluate potential professionals based on:

- **Experience and Credentials:** Check qualifications, experience, and client reviews.
- **Reputation:** Seek recommendations from other investors or industry professionals.
- **Compatibility:** Ensure that their working style and approach align with your investment strategy and needs.

3. Foster Relationships

Develop strong working relationships with your network:

- **Regular Communication:** Keep in touch with your advisors and update them on your investment goals and changes.
- **Feedback and Reviews:** Provide feedback on their services and share your experiences to build mutual trust and respect.

4. Utilise Professional Networks

Leverage the networks of your advisors:

- **Referrals:** Ask your professionals for referrals to other experts, such as property managers or legal advisors, who can further support your investment journey.
- **Industry Connections:** Use their connections to gain insights, attend events, and access additional resources.

Property investment is often viewed through the lens of immediate gains and quick returns, but the most successful investors understand the importance of long-term planning. Having a vision for your property portfolio extends beyond the current market conditions and focuses on sustainable growth, financial security, and preparedness for various challenges. This section explores the significance of long-term thinking in property investment, strategies for supporting sustainable growth, and how to prepare for market downturns, economic shifts, and changing personal circumstances.

The Importance of Having a Long-Term Vision

1. Strategic Growth

A long-term vision allows for strategic planning and informed decision-making:

- **Goal Setting:** Establish clear, long-term goals for your property portfolio, such as achieving a specific portfolio size, target rental income, or capital growth.
- **Investment Horizon:** Understand that property investments typically require years to mature, and plan your acquisitions and disposals accordingly.

2. Building Wealth

Long-term planning is crucial for building substantial wealth through property:

- **Compounding Returns:** Real estate investments benefit from compounding returns over time, as rental income and property values increase.
- **Equity Accumulation:** Holding properties long-term allows for equity accumulation through mortgage repayment and property appreciation.

3. Financial Security

A long-term perspective helps in achieving financial security:

- **Retirement Planning:** Properties can provide a reliable income stream for retirement if managed and held long-term.
- **Financial Buffer:** A well-planned property portfolio acts as a financial buffer, providing stability in times of economic uncertainty.

Making Decisions that Support Sustainable Growth and Financial Security

1. Diversification

Diversifying your property investments helps in spreading risk and supporting long-term growth:

- **Property Types:** Invest in various property types (residential, commercial, industrial) to balance risk and returns.
- **Locations:** Diversify across different geographic areas to mitigate risks associated with local market fluctuations.

2. Reinvestment Strategies

Reinvesting profits and equity helps in accelerating portfolio growth:

- **Equity Release:** Use equity from existing properties to finance new acquisitions, enhancing portfolio growth.

- **Reinvestment:** Allocate rental income and sale proceeds to further investments or upgrades, compounding returns.

3. Cost Management

Effective cost management supports long-term profitability:

- **Maintenance and Repairs:** Regularly maintain properties to preserve value and avoid costly repairs.
- **Operational Costs:** Keep track of operational costs and optimise them to improve cash flow and profitability.

4. Financial Planning

Develop a comprehensive financial plan that aligns with your long-term vision:

- **Budgeting:** Create detailed budgets for property management, maintenance, and future investments.
- **Contingency Funds:** Set aside contingency funds to manage unexpected expenses and market downturns.

Preparing for Market Downturns, Economic Shifts, and Changing Personal Circumstances

1. Market Downturns

Being prepared for market downturns is essential for long-term stability:

- **Reserve Funds:** Maintain a financial cushion to cover mortgage payments and other expenses during market downturns.
- **Diversification:** Diversify investments to reduce exposure to any single market or property type.

2. Economic Shifts

Economic changes can impact property values and rental income:

- **Economic Indicators:** Monitor economic indicators such as interest rates, inflation, and employment rates to anticipate shifts.
- **Adaptability:** Be ready to adapt your investment strategy based on changing economic conditions, such as shifting focus from growth to stability.

3. Changing Personal Circumstances

Personal circumstances can affect your investment strategy and goals:

- **Life Events:** Plan for significant life events (e.g., retirement, relocation, health issues) and how they might impact your property investments.
- **Financial Changes:** Adjust your investment strategy based on changes in your financial situation, such as increased income or new expenses.

Successful property investment requires more than just making initial smart decisions; it involves ongoing evaluation and adaptation. Regularly reviewing your investment performance and refining your strategy ensures that you remain aligned with your goals, adapt to changing market conditions, and continue to optimise your portfolio's performance. This section explores how to conduct a regular review of your investment strategy, the importance of flexibility, and how case studies illustrate successful strategy pivots.

How to Regularly Review Your Investment Performance

1. Performance Metrics

To effectively review your investment performance, focus on key metrics:

- **Rental Yield:** Calculate the rental yield for each property to assess its income-generating capability.
- **Capital Growth:** Track the appreciation in property value to measure long-term growth.
- **Cash Flow:** Evaluate monthly and annual cash flow to ensure the property is covering expenses and contributing positively to your portfolio.
- **Occupancy Rates:** Monitor occupancy rates to ensure properties are attracting and retaining tenants effectively.

2. Reviewing Financial Statements

Regularly review financial statements and reports:

- **Income Statements:** Analyse income from rent versus expenses (mortgage, maintenance, management fees).
- **Balance Sheets:** Assess the value of your assets and liabilities to understand your equity position and overall financial health.
- **Cash Flow Statements:** Review cash flow statements to ensure sufficient liquidity and assess the impact of any unexpected expenses or changes.

3. Benchmarking Against Goals

Compare your current performance against your initial investment goals:

- **Goal Alignment:** Ensure that your properties are still aligned with your short-term and long-term investment objectives.
- **Adjustments:** Make necessary adjustments to meet evolving goals or new opportunities that may arise.

The Importance of Flexibility and Adapting to Changing Market Conditions

1. Market Trends

Adapt your strategy based on changing market conditions:

- **Economic Shifts:** Respond to changes in economic indicators such as interest rates, inflation, and employment rates that impact property values and rental demand.

- **Local Market Trends:** Stay informed about local market trends, such as new developments or shifts in neighbourhood desirability, that could affect your investments.

2. Portfolio Rebalancing

Regularly rebalance your portfolio to align with your updated strategy:

- **Diversification:** Adjust the mix of property types and locations to mitigate risk and capitalise on emerging opportunities.
- **Asset Allocation:** Reallocate investments based on performance and market conditions to optimise returns and manage risk.

3. Strategy Evolution

Evolve your investment strategy based on new insights and experiences:

- **Innovative Approaches:** Explore innovative investment approaches or emerging markets that may offer higher returns.
- **Personal Circumstances:** Adjust your strategy to reflect changes in personal financial goals or risk tolerance.

Case Studies of Investors Who Successfully Pivoted Their Strategies Over Time

1. Case Study 1: Diversification for Stability

An investor who initially focused solely on residential properties in a high-growth area faced market volatility and declining rental yields. By reviewing their portfolio, they decided to diversify into commercial properties and different geographic locations. This pivot provided stability and new revenue streams, enhancing overall portfolio performance.

2. Case Study 2: Adapting to Economic Changes

Another investor initially invested in high-risk, high-reward properties during a booming market. When economic conditions shifted, leading to a market downturn, they reevaluated their strategy. They pivoted to acquiring properties in stable markets with lower risk but steady rental income. This adaptation helped them weather the downturn and maintain positive cash flow.

3. Case Study 3: Leveraging Technology for Efficiency

A third investor used traditional methods for managing their properties but found inefficiencies over time. Upon reviewing their strategy, they adopted property management technology to streamline operations, enhance tenant relations, and improve financial tracking. This technological pivot resulted in more efficient management and increased profitability.

Chapter 7: Property Management Tips:

Introduction:

Property management plays a critical role in the success of any real estate investment. It goes beyond simply owning property; it involves a range of responsibilities that, when managed well, can maximise profitability, protect your assets, and minimise risks. Whether you own one property or a large portfolio, effective property management is essential to ensuring your investments perform optimally over the long term. This introduction explores why property management is so important, how it safeguards your investment, and the role property investors must play in overseeing the process, whether they choose to self-manage or hire professional services.

Why Property Management Matters

Effective property management is the backbone of any successful property investment. It is the day-to-day oversight that ensures that your assets are well-maintained, that your tenants are satisfied, and that your investment continues to generate positive returns. The importance of good management cannot be overstated, as it directly impacts both short-term cash flow and long-term asset appreciation.

Ensuring Long-Term Profitability and Asset Preservation

At the core of property management is the goal of maintaining the value of the investment. Properties, much like any physical asset, depreciate over time if not properly cared for. Regular maintenance, timely repairs, and upgrades not only help to preserve the property's value but also prevent costly, extensive repairs in the future. A well-maintained property is more likely to attract and retain quality tenants, leading to consistent rental income and fewer vacancies. Moreover, properties that are regularly updated can increase in market value, giving investors the potential for significant capital growth over time.

Property management also plays a key role in profitability. By managing expenses such as maintenance costs, property taxes, and utilities efficiently, landlords can ensure that their properties remain cash flow positive. In addition, effective management includes staying on top of rental rates to ensure that the property remains competitive in the market while maximising rental income. Setting the right rent requires a balance—too high, and you may struggle to attract tenants; too low, and you might not cover costs or realise the full potential of your investment.

Reducing Vacancies, Tenant Turnover, and Unexpected Costs

Vacancies and tenant turnover are some of the biggest threats to an investor's bottom line. The longer a property remains vacant, the more it eats into your cash flow, as you are responsible for covering the mortgage, utilities, and maintenance without any rental income. Effective property management focuses on reducing vacancies by ensuring the property is well-advertised, competitively priced, and appealing to potential tenants. Additionally, maintaining good relationships with current tenants through clear communication and prompt service can help reduce turnover, as satisfied tenants are more likely to renew their leases.

Tenant turnover not only leads to vacancies but also adds extra costs associated with finding new tenants, such as marketing the property, cleaning, and making necessary repairs or upgrades between leases. These costs can add up quickly, so minimising turnover through good property management can significantly boost profitability. By maintaining the property and addressing tenant concerns in a timely and professional manner, landlords can foster long-term tenant relationships, reducing the likelihood of vacancy.

Moreover, unexpected costs, such as emergency repairs or legal issues with tenants, can derail an investor's financial plans. A proactive management approach—regular inspections, maintaining reserve funds for repairs, and knowing when to hire professionals—helps minimise the impact of these surprises. Property management is about anticipating problems before they occur and having a plan in place to address them when they do.

The Role of the Property Investor as a Manager

As a property investor, you are faced with the decision of whether to manage the property yourself or hire a professional property manager. This decision depends on a variety of factors, including your level of experience, the size of your portfolio, the time you can dedicate to management, and your personal preferences. Regardless of the path you choose, it is essential to set clear goals and standards for how the property will be managed.

Deciding Between Self-Management and Hiring Professional Managers

Self-management can be an attractive option for investors who want to maximise control over their property and reduce costs. By managing the property yourself, you avoid paying management fees, which typically range from 5% to 10% of rental income. For hands-on investors, self-management can be a rewarding experience, offering the chance to build direct relationships with tenants and take full responsibility for the property's performance. However, it requires significant time, effort, and knowledge of landlord-tenant laws, local market conditions, and best practices in maintenance and repair.

On the other hand, hiring a professional property manager can save time and reduce the stress associated with managing properties. Property managers handle everything from tenant screening and rent collection to maintenance and legal issues. For investors with multiple properties or those who are located far from their rental property, a property manager can be invaluable. They bring expertise, experience, and established systems that help ensure smooth operations, leaving investors free to focus on other aspects of their portfolios or businesses. The trade-off, of course, is the added cost of management services, which can eat into profits, especially for investors with smaller margins.

Setting Clear Goals for Property Management Practices

Regardless of whether you choose to self-manage or hire a property manager, it is critical to set clear goals for your property management strategy. These goals should align with your broader investment objectives, whether they are focused on maximising cash flow, achieving long-term capital appreciation, or maintaining a balance between the two. Clear goals also help define the standards for managing the property, such as maintenance schedules, tenant selection criteria, rent pricing strategies, and timelines for addressing tenant concerns.

For self-managing investors, it is essential to develop a systematic approach to managing the property. This might include setting up processes for tenant screening, creating a maintenance plan, and establishing a timeline for rent reviews. If you are hiring a property manager, these goals should be communicated clearly, and regular performance reviews should be conducted to ensure that the management company is meeting your expectations.

Securing reliable tenants is critical to ensuring long-term profitability in property investment. By attracting and retaining high-quality tenants, you minimise vacancies, reduce maintenance and turnover costs, and maintain steady rental income. Below are key strategies for tenant screening, marketing, and fostering long-term relationships.

Tenant Screening Process

The tenant screening process is essential to ensure you select individuals who will not only take care of your property but also fulfil their financial obligations consistently. Here's how you can approach it effectively:

1. **Background Checks**: Conducting a thorough background check is essential for evaluating potential tenants. This includes:
    - **Credit History**: A credit report reveals an applicant's financial stability and reliability. It shows whether they have any outstanding debts, past bankruptcies, or a history of missed payments. A strong credit score is typically an indicator that the tenant will reliably pay rent on time.
    - **Rental History**: Check the tenant's past rental experiences, if any. Contacting previous landlords can give you insights into whether the tenant caused any property damage, consistently paid rent on time, or had issues with other tenants or the community.
    - **Employment History**: Verifying current employment helps you assess a tenant's ability to pay rent regularly. As a rule of thumb, tenants should have a stable income that's at least three times the monthly rent. Request proof of income through pay stubs or bank statements.
2. **Legal Guidelines for Tenant Screening**: When screening tenants, it's crucial to adhere to fair housing laws and regulations to avoid any discrimination claims. In most regions, it's illegal to discriminate based on race, colour, religion, sex, national origin, disability, or familial status. Ensure your screening process is transparent and consistent for all applicants to avoid any potential legal issues.
    - Develop a **standardised screening criteria** for all applicants. This means applying the same standards and checks to every person interested in renting the property.
    - Avoid asking personal or irrelevant questions that may be seen as discriminatory, such as queries about family planning or specific religious practices.

Marketing Your Rental Property

Effectively marketing your property is key to attracting the right tenants. A well-marketed property will appeal to quality renters, reducing vacancies and ensuring your investment property remains profitable. Here are some strategies to help you get the word out about your property:

1. **Effective Online and Offline Strategies**: The internet is one of the most powerful tools for attracting potential tenants, but traditional methods can still have an impact.
    - **Online Listings**: Property listing websites such as Zillow, Realtor.com, or domain-specific platforms in your country are great places to advertise. These platforms allow you to reach a broad audience of potential tenants who are actively searching for rentals.
    - **Local Advertising**: Consider placing ads in local newspapers, community boards, or partnering with local businesses to put up flyers. Networking with real estate agents can also help spread the word about your property.
2. **Creating Compelling Property Listings**: The key to attracting quality tenants is a well-crafted listing. Highlight the most attractive features of your property and use high-quality images.
    - **Professional Photos**: Invest in professional photography or, at the very least, take high-resolution photos during the day to make your property look bright and welcoming.
    - **Well-Written Descriptions**: Write a clear and detailed description that outlines the property's size, location, rent amount, nearby amenities, and any standout features such as a backyard, modern appliances, or recent renovations.
    - **Highlight Unique Features**: If your property offers unique selling points such as proximity to public transportation, excellent schools, or recreational spaces, be sure to emphasise them in the listing. Including a brief overview of the neighbourhood can also help potential tenants imagine living there.

Building Long-Term Tenant Relationships

Once you've secured quality tenants, retaining them is just as important to avoid the hassle and costs of finding new renters. Fostering good tenant relationships will not only help ensure they stay longer but also make managing the property easier.

1. **Clear Communication and Setting Expectations**: Establishing a clear communication channel from the beginning helps build trust and ensures tenants feel comfortable raising concerns or requesting maintenance when necessary.
    - **Lease Agreements**: Provide a comprehensive lease that outlines all rental terms, including payment schedules, late fees, and maintenance responsibilities. Make sure the tenant understands their obligations and your responsibilities as the landlord.
    - **Communication Channels**: Use modern communication tools like email, text messages, or even property management apps to streamline communication and ensure timely responses to queries or issues. Clear and open communication from day one will help prevent misunderstandings and build rapport.
    - **Responsive Maintenance**: Addressing tenant complaints, especially maintenance issues, quickly and professionally shows tenants that you value their comfort and well-being. Poor or delayed responses can result in tenant dissatisfaction, potentially leading to higher turnover rates.
2. **Offering Lease Renewal Incentives**: Keeping good tenants means offering them incentives to stay longer. Consider:
    - **Rent Freeze or Discount**: Offering a rent freeze for a lease renewal, or even a slight discount, can encourage long-term tenants to stay. For many tenants, avoiding the hassle of moving and enjoying consistent rent can be appealing.

- **Upgrade Offers**: Offer small property improvements, such as new kitchen appliances, fresh paint, or landscaping, as a reward for renewing their lease. These updates can enhance tenant satisfaction and, in the long run, increase the property's value.
3. **Maintaining Good Tenant Relations**: Beyond just fulfilling contractual obligations, building a sense of community or showing appreciation for your tenants can go a long way.
    - **Holiday or Birthday Cards**: Sending tenants holiday greetings or a small gesture on their birthdays can create goodwill and foster a positive relationship.
    - **Routine Property Check-ins**: Conduct routine property inspections (with proper notice) to ensure the property is being maintained. These check-ins can also be opportunities to ask tenants if they need any small improvements or repairs, showing them that you're invested in their comfort.

Effectively managing rent pricing and payment collection is key to maintaining a healthy cash flow for your property investment. Setting the right rental price and ensuring timely payments from tenants can significantly impact your property's profitability. This section covers how to determine optimal rent, set up efficient rent collection systems, and manage late payments.

Determining Optimal Rent

Setting the correct rental price is crucial for attracting tenants while ensuring your property remains profitable. Pricing your property too high can result in extended vacancies, while underpricing it may reduce your potential returns. Here's how to approach it:

1. **Researching Comparable Market Rates**
    - **Comparative Market Analysis (CMA)**: The most effective way to determine optimal rent is by conducting a comparative market analysis. Look at similar properties in the neighbourhood and see what other landlords are charging. Key factors to consider include:
        - **Property Size**: Ensure you compare properties with similar square footage, number of bedrooms and bathrooms, and layout.
        - **Property Type**: Compare single-family homes with other single-family homes, apartments with apartments, etc.
        - **Location**: Properties located in desirable neighbourhoods with access to public transport, schools, and shopping centres may command higher rent.
        - **Condition**: Consider whether the properties you're comparing are renovated or have features that make them more attractive to tenants.
2. **Factors That Affect Rent Price** Several factors beyond simple market comparisons influence the rent you can charge. These include:
    - **Location**: Proximity to public transport, employment centres, schools, and other amenities greatly affects rent prices. A property in a prime location can charge a premium compared to one in a less accessible or desirable area.
    - **Amenities**: Features like parking, a washer/dryer, modern appliances, or on-site fitness centres can make a property more attractive and justify a higher rental price.
    - **Market Demand**: The level of demand for rental properties in the area also plays a significant role. In high-demand areas where vacancies are low, you can charge a higher rent, while areas with higher vacancy rates may force you to lower your price to attract tenants.

- **Seasonality**: Rent prices can fluctuate depending on the time of year. In some regions, there's higher demand during specific seasons (such as summer for student housing), which can justify raising rent prices.

Once you've assessed these factors, set a competitive rent that meets market demand while maximising your return on investment.

Rent Collection Methods

Collecting rent efficiently is vital to maintaining cash flow and keeping your property financially viable. Modern tools and payment systems allow for easier rent collection while reducing the administrative burden on landlords.

1. **Establishing Efficient Payment Systems** Setting up an efficient and reliable system for rent payments will make the process easier for both you and your tenants. Here are some of the most effective options:
   - **Online Platforms**: Online payment platforms, such as PayPal, Venmo, or specialised rent collection services like Cozy, provide tenants with an easy way to pay rent electronically. These platforms also make it easier for landlords to track payments.
   - **Direct Debit**: Many landlords opt for setting up direct debit systems that allow rent to be automatically withdrawn from the tenant's bank account on a specific date each month. This ensures timely payments without the need for manual processing.
   - **Bank Transfers**: You can also arrange for tenants to make direct transfers to your bank account each month. This is less automated than direct debit, but still provides a reliable electronic payment option.
2. **Automating Rent Payments and Reminders** Automating rent payments and sending reminders to tenants can reduce the risk of late or missed payments and minimise administrative tasks. Several rent management software solutions offer these features:
   - **Automatic Rent Payments**: Enable automatic rent withdrawal from your tenant's bank account. This ensures payments are never forgotten, and it removes the need for tenants to take action every month.
   - **Payment Reminders**: Set up automatic email or text reminders a few days before rent is due. These reminders can serve as a helpful nudge, especially for tenants who may forget when rent is due.

By using these systems, landlords can create a seamless rent collection process that reduces stress and ensures regular, reliable payments.

Handling Late Payments

Late or missed rent payments can disrupt your cash flow and lead to financial issues. It's essential to have clear policies in place for handling late payments to ensure you are protected and tenants understand their obligations.

1. **Developing Clear Late Payment Policies and Fees**
   - **Late Payment Penalties**: To discourage late payments, most landlords implement a late payment fee. This fee should be specified in the rental agreement and should outline the specific amount charged for late rent. Make sure the fee complies with local laws, as some regions have restrictions on how much you can charge.

- **Grace Period**: Many rental agreements include a grace period, typically 3-5 days after the rent due date, before a late fee is applied. This gives tenants a small window to make payments without penalty while encouraging timely rent submission.
- **Payment Plans**: In some cases, tenants may experience financial difficulties and need temporary leniency. Offering a one-time payment plan or extension can help maintain a good tenant relationship, but it's important to document this agreement in writing.

2. **When and How to Issue Warnings or Start Eviction Proceedings** While eviction should always be a last resort, there may be situations where tenants repeatedly fail to pay rent or refuse to communicate. Here's how to approach the process:
    - **Issuing a Warning Notice**: Before pursuing legal action, send a formal late rent notice or warning letter to the tenant. This notice should clearly state that rent is overdue, specify any late fees incurred, and provide a deadline for payment. In many cases, this warning is enough to prompt payment.
    - **Communication**: Maintain an open line of communication with the tenant. If they are experiencing temporary financial hardship, you may be able to negotiate a solution, such as splitting the overdue rent into instalments.
    - **Eviction Process**: If the tenant fails to respond to notices and consistently fails to pay rent, you may need to start eviction proceedings. This is a legal process that varies by jurisdiction but generally includes providing the tenant with a formal eviction notice. In some cases, landlords must go to court to get an eviction order.

Ensure that all communications regarding late payments are well-documented to avoid legal complications down the line.

Effective property maintenance and timely repairs are critical aspects of property management that directly impact tenant satisfaction, the property's value, and long-term profitability. By proactively managing repairs and upkeep, you can avoid costly damages, extend the life of your investment, and ensure a high standard of living for your tenants.

Proactive Property Maintenance

Proactive property maintenance involves conducting regular inspections, preventive care, and scheduled maintenance to keep your property in optimal condition. This helps you avoid expensive repairs, retain tenants, and enhance the property's long-term value.

1. **The Importance of Regular Inspections and Preventive Care**
    - **Identifying Issues Early**: Regular inspections allow you to spot potential problems before they become serious. For example, addressing small leaks, faulty electrical systems, or minor structural issues early can prevent larger, costlier repairs down the line. It also reduces the chances of tenant complaints and legal liabilities.
    - **Extending the Property's Life**: Routine maintenance such as cleaning gutters, checking the HVAC system, and inspecting the roof helps prolong the life of key components in your property. By keeping everything in good working order, you preserve the value of the property and protect your investment.
    - **Ensuring Tenant Safety**: Tenants expect to live in a safe, well-maintained property. Proactively maintaining smoke detectors, fire extinguishers, and plumbing and electrical systems not only fulfils your legal obligations but also fosters a positive relationship with your tenants.

2. **Creating a Maintenance Schedule: Seasonal Checks and Necessary Upgrades**
   Developing a maintenance schedule is essential for staying on top of routine tasks and avoiding unexpected repair costs. Here's a general framework for creating a maintenance plan:
   - **Seasonal Checks**: Plan regular inspections based on the changing needs of your property throughout the year:
     - **Spring**: Inspect the roof for damage, clean gutters, and check windows for leaks or drafts.
     - **Summer**: Service the HVAC system, inspect plumbing for leaks, and check for pests.
     - **Fall**: Clean and inspect chimneys, check the heating system, and trim trees.
     - **Winter**: Ensure pipes are insulated, test smoke detectors, and check for drafts in windows and doors.
   - **Scheduled Maintenance**: Incorporate long-term maintenance needs such as repainting, resealing driveways, and replacing ageing appliances into your schedule. This prevents sudden large expenses and keeps your property updated.
   - **Tracking Maintenance History**: Keep a detailed log of maintenance activities, including dates, contractors used, and costs. This record helps track recurring issues and serves as a reference for budgeting and planning future repairs or upgrades.

Responding to Repair Requests

Handling repair requests from tenants in a timely and efficient manner is crucial to maintaining tenant satisfaction and preventing property damage. Having a clear system in place for managing these requests can streamline the process and ensure quick resolution.

1. **How to Handle Tenant Requests Efficiently and Quickly**
   - **Communication Channels**: Establish clear and convenient communication channels for tenants to report maintenance issues. Many landlords use online platforms or property management apps that allow tenants to submit maintenance requests directly. You can also set up a dedicated phone line or email address for this purpose.
   - **Prioritising Repairs**: Not all repair requests require immediate action, but it's important to prioritise repairs based on urgency:
     - **Emergency Repairs**: Issues that affect the health, safety, or habitability of the property, such as plumbing leaks, electrical faults, or broken heating systems, should be addressed immediately.
     - **Non-Urgent Repairs**: Less critical issues, like a broken drawer or minor paint chips, can be scheduled during regular maintenance rounds.
   - **Clear Communication with Tenants**: Keep tenants informed about the progress of their repair requests. Let them know when a contractor will be on-site, expected repair times, and any delays. This transparency fosters trust and reduces frustration.
2. **Creating an Emergency Repair Plan and Contractor Network**
   Having an emergency repair plan and a reliable network of contractors ensures you can respond to urgent issues quickly and effectively.
   - **Emergency Repair Plan**: Draft an emergency plan that outlines the steps to be taken in the event of major issues such as flooding, electrical outages, or gas leaks. Ensure both tenants and contractors know who to contact in emergencies and provide clear instructions on how to shut off utilities if necessary.

- **Building a Contractor Network**: Establish relationships with trusted, licensed contractors in various fields (plumbers, electricians, handymen, etc.). A reliable contractor network ensures you can address repairs swiftly, even in busy seasons.
  - **Negotiate Rates**: Long-term relationships with contractors often come with the benefit of discounted rates, priority service, or payment plans.
  - **Availability**: Ensure you have backup contractors in case your primary contacts are unavailable, particularly for emergencies that require immediate attention.

Cost-Effective Upgrades

Strategic renovations and upgrades can increase your property's market value, improve tenant retention, and attract higher rental income. Focusing on cost-effective improvements that offer long-term benefits ensures you maximise the return on your investment.

1. **Renovations That Enhance Property Value and Tenant Satisfaction**
   - **Kitchen and Bathroom Upgrades**: Kitchen and bathroom renovations typically offer the highest return on investment in terms of property value and tenant appeal. Simple upgrades like modern fixtures, updated countertops, and energy-efficient appliances can make a significant difference.
   - **Energy-Efficient Improvements**: Installing energy-efficient lighting, appliances, and insulation can reduce utility bills for tenants and add value to the property. Tenants are often willing to pay more for a property that offers energy savings.
   - **Cosmetic Improvements**: Fresh paint, new flooring, and updated lighting fixtures can make a property feel modern and clean without breaking the bank. These improvements are often the most cost-effective way to enhance the property's overall appeal.
   - **Outdoor Spaces**: Improving curb appeal by upgrading landscaping, repainting exteriors, or adding outdoor seating areas can make a rental property more attractive to tenants. Small investments in outdoor spaces often lead to higher tenant satisfaction and increased rental demand.
2. **Budgeting for Upgrades and Using Quality Materials for Longevity**
   Budgeting for property upgrades requires careful planning to ensure that improvements align with your financial goals. It's important to strike a balance between cost and quality to ensure that upgrades offer long-term value.
   - **Setting an Upgrade Budget**: Allocate a portion of rental income or property savings specifically for upgrades and renovations. As a rule of thumb, set aside 1% to 3% of the property's value annually for maintenance and improvements. Larger, more expensive projects (such as roof replacement or HVAC upgrades) should be planned for in advance.
   - **Prioritising Upgrades**: Not all upgrades are equally beneficial. Prioritise improvements that will have the biggest impact on tenant satisfaction and property value. For example, upgrading outdated kitchens or bathrooms typically offers better returns than cosmetic changes.
   - **Quality Materials for Longevity**: While it may be tempting to cut costs by using cheaper materials, investing in high-quality, durable materials often pays off in the long run. Quality materials reduce the need for frequent repairs and replacements, saving money and effort over time.

As a property investor and landlord, navigating legal and regulatory compliance is essential to protect your assets, maintain good relationships with tenants, and avoid costly legal disputes. By understanding and adhering to landlord-tenant laws, drafting clear lease agreements, and handling conflicts professionally, you can ensure your property management practices are both lawful and effective.

Understanding Landlord-Tenant Laws

Landlord-tenant laws vary by jurisdiction, but there are common regulations that govern the rights and responsibilities of both parties in a rental agreement. As a landlord, it's critical to understand these rules to avoid legal issues and ensure the fair treatment of tenants.

1. **Key Regulations to Follow in Property Management**
    - **Safety Standards**: Landlords are required to maintain a safe and habitable living environment for tenants. This includes complying with safety standards such as working smoke detectors, carbon monoxide alarms, secure locks, and electrical and plumbing systems that are in good repair.
    - **Health and Accessibility**: Ensuring that properties meet health codes is another legal requirement. Regular pest control, mould remediation, and sanitation measures are essential. In some cases, you may also need to comply with accessibility standards, especially if your property is classified under certain zoning regulations that require accommodations for disabled tenants.
    - **Fair Housing Laws**: In many jurisdictions, landlords must adhere to anti-discrimination laws when screening tenants. This means you cannot deny a tenant based on race, religion, gender, sexual orientation, disability, or family status. Violations of fair housing laws can result in fines, lawsuits, and damage to your reputation as a landlord.
2. **Staying Up-to-Date on Changing Laws and Zoning Requirements**
    - **Regular Updates**: Laws governing rental properties frequently change, whether it's new zoning regulations, updated safety codes, or changes to landlord-tenant laws. It's important to stay informed through regular consultations with legal advisors or property management professionals.
    - **Local Jurisdiction Awareness**: Different municipalities may have specific rules, such as rent control measures or short-term rental restrictions, that directly impact how you can manage your property. Joining local landlord associations, subscribing to legal newsletters, or attending property management seminars can help you stay current.
    - **Documenting Compliance**: Ensure you have documentation that shows your compliance with safety inspections, permits, and other legal requirements. This can be crucial in case of any disputes or legal challenges.

Drafting Lease Agreements

A well-drafted lease agreement is the foundation of any rental relationship. It should clearly outline the terms and conditions of the tenancy, the rights and responsibilities of both the landlord and tenant, and the consequences of non-compliance. A strong lease minimises confusion, reduces the likelihood of disputes, and serves as legal protection.

1. **Essential Clauses to Include**
   - **Rent and Payment Terms**: Clearly state the monthly rent amount, due date, acceptable payment methods, and any penalties for late payments. This prevents misunderstandings and ensures that both parties are aware of their financial obligations.
   - **Security Deposits**: Specify the amount of the security deposit, the conditions under which it can be withheld (e.g., property damage), and how it will be returned at the end of the lease. Include any legal requirements, such as placing the deposit in a separate account.
   - **Maintenance Responsibilities**: Clearly define which maintenance tasks the landlord and tenant are responsible for. For example, landlords typically handle structural repairs and major systems (plumbing, electrical), while tenants are responsible for basic cleanliness and reporting issues.
   - **Termination Policies**: Outline the procedures for terminating the lease, whether through non-renewal, early termination, or eviction. Be sure to include details on required notice periods and conditions for breaking the lease without penalty (e.g., military service, health reasons).
2. **Importance of Clear, Comprehensive, and Enforceable Contracts**
   - **Legal Enforceability**: The lease must be enforceable under local laws. Avoid overly complex legal jargon that can confuse tenants, but ensure the contract is thorough enough to protect your interests. Have a lawyer review your lease template to make sure it complies with state or local regulations.
   - **Clarity to Avoid Disputes**: A clear lease minimises potential misunderstandings between you and your tenants. If the lease outlines expectations in detail—such as property care, noise regulations, and visitor policies—both parties are more likely to adhere to the terms, reducing the likelihood of conflict.
   - **Regular Updates**: Periodically review your lease template to ensure it still meets legal requirements and reflects changes in your property management strategy. For instance, if new laws affect rent increases or security deposits, update your lease accordingly.

Handling Legal Disputes and Evictions

Even with a strong lease agreement, disputes may arise between landlords and tenants. Handling these issues calmly, professionally, and legally is key to protecting your interests while maintaining good tenant relationships.

1. **Best Practices for Conflict Resolution**
   - **Open Communication**: When disputes arise, communication is essential. Address tenant complaints or concerns promptly, and aim to resolve issues through discussion before they escalate. Many problems can be settled amicably without resorting to legal action if you maintain open lines of communication.
   - **Document Everything**: Always document interactions with tenants related to disputes or requests. This includes emails, texts, and phone conversations, as well as any notices you issue. If a problem progresses to legal action, having detailed records can help support your case.
   - **Mediation**: For minor conflicts that can't be resolved through direct negotiation, consider using a third-party mediator. Mediation is often a quicker, less costly

alternative to legal proceedings, and many jurisdictions offer mediation services for landlord-tenant disputes.
2. **When to Seek Legal Counsel or Use Mediation**
    - **Eviction Process**: Eviction is one of the most serious actions a landlord can take and must be handled carefully to avoid legal repercussions. Follow local eviction laws closely, which often require proper notice periods and valid reasons for eviction, such as non-payment of rent or violation of lease terms.
    - **When to Seek Legal Counsel**: In more complex disputes—such as a tenant refusing to vacate the property after eviction proceedings, or significant property damage—you should seek legal counsel. An attorney can guide you through the legal process, ensure that your actions comply with local laws, and represent your interests in court if necessary.
    - **Court Proceedings**: If a dispute escalates to court, being well-prepared is essential. Ensure that all documentation (lease agreements, communications, maintenance records) is organised and ready to present. Even in court, having a solid legal case doesn't guarantee success if the right procedures aren't followed.
3. **Dealing with Difficult Evictions**
    - **Following Legal Protocol**: Evictions must follow strict legal processes to avoid claims of wrongful eviction. This includes serving proper notice, giving the tenant time to remedy the situation, and filing eviction papers in court if necessary. Even though this process can be lengthy, bypassing legal protocols may result in financial penalties or even lawsuits.
    - **After Eviction**: Once an eviction is completed, the property may need to be cleaned, repaired, or refurbished before it can be rented again. Plan for these costs in your budgeting and determine how they will be recouped, whether through the tenant's security deposit or legal action for unpaid rent.

Effective financial management and meticulous record-keeping are critical components of successful property investment. As a property investor, managing cash flow, budgeting for expenses, and keeping accurate records help maintain the profitability of your investments while ensuring compliance with tax regulations. This section will explore key financial management practices, the importance of accurate record-keeping, and essential tax considerations for property investors.

Budgeting for Property Expenses

A well-planned budget is essential for managing the ongoing costs of property ownership. This includes not only regular expenses but also emergency repairs and unforeseen costs that may arise. By developing a comprehensive budget, property investors can avoid financial surprises and maintain consistent cash flow.

1. **Estimating Regular and Emergency Costs**
    - **Maintenance and Repairs**: Routine maintenance is necessary to keep your property in good condition and retain its value. This includes landscaping, cleaning common areas, repainting, plumbing, electrical checks, and minor repairs. Setting aside funds for both routine maintenance and emergency repairs ensures you're prepared for unexpected costs, such as a broken water heater or roof leaks.
    - **Property Taxes and Insurance**: Property taxes vary depending on location and property value, so it's crucial to research your local tax rates. Additionally, property

insurance protects against damage, theft, and liability issues. Make sure you factor in annual insurance premiums when planning your budget.
- **Management Fees**: If you hire a property manager, their fees will also need to be accounted for. Management fees typically range from 8-12% of the monthly rental income, depending on the services they provide.
- **Vacancy Costs**: In the event that your property is unoccupied for a period of time, you'll need to cover the costs of the mortgage, utilities, and maintenance without rental income. Planning for potential vacancies helps ensure that your cash flow isn't disrupted.

2. **Setting Aside Reserves and Cash Flow Planning**
    - **Emergency Fund**: A prudent property investor sets aside a contingency fund to cover unexpected costs, such as major repairs, legal fees, or tenant disputes. This reserve should ideally cover 3-6 months of operating expenses to ensure you have the financial buffer to address emergencies.
    - **Cash Flow Planning**: Positive cash flow—where your rental income exceeds your expenses—is a key objective for any property investor. Careful cash flow planning involves calculating your net operating income (NOI) and ensuring that your rental properties generate enough income to cover both fixed and variable expenses, leaving room for profit.

Accurate Record Keeping

Keeping accurate financial records is crucial not only for managing your properties effectively but also for tax reporting and legal compliance. By tracking income and expenses diligently, you can stay on top of your financial health and simplify your tax filings at the end of the year.

1. **Tools for Tracking Income and Expenses**
    - **Spreadsheets**: Many property investors start by using spreadsheets (e.g., Excel, Google Sheets) to track rental income, expenses, and cash flow. While this method is cost-effective and customizable, it can become cumbersome as your portfolio grows.
    - **Property Management Software**: Specialised property management software can streamline financial tracking by automating income and expense reporting, generating rent payment reminders, and providing real-time financial insights. Popular tools include platforms like Buildium, AppFolio, and Rentec Direct, which offer comprehensive features for managing rental properties.
    - **Mobile Apps**: Some mobile apps also provide simple financial tracking for landlords, allowing you to monitor rent payments, expenses, and tenant communication on the go. These apps can help manage smaller portfolios with less complexity.
2. **Legal Documentation and Tax Records: What to Retain and For How Long**
    - **Rent Receipts and Invoices**: Maintain detailed records of rental income, including rent receipts and invoices for any repairs or services. These documents serve as proof of income and expenses, which are critical for both tax purposes and legal compliance.
    - **Leases and Agreements**: Keep copies of all signed lease agreements, as well as any correspondence with tenants. These records help resolve disputes and prove the terms of the rental contract in case of legal challenges.
    - **Tax Documents**: Retain tax returns and supporting documentation (e.g., receipts for deductible expenses, mortgage interest statements) for at least seven years, as this is

the general timeframe for IRS audits. Additionally, any documentation related to capital improvements should be kept for as long as you own the property, as it affects the capital gains tax calculation when you sell.
- **Maintenance and Repair Logs**: Keeping detailed records of maintenance and repairs provides insight into the property's history and helps support claims for depreciation on tax filings.

Tax Considerations for Property Investors

Taxes can significantly impact your property investment returns, so understanding tax implications is essential. There are several tax benefits that property investors can leverage, including deductible expenses and strategies for minimising capital gains taxes.

1. **Deductible Expenses and Capital Gains Tax Strategies**
   - **Deductible Expenses**: Property investors can deduct various expenses associated with managing their rental properties. Common deductible expenses include mortgage interest, property management fees, repairs, property taxes, insurance, advertising, and depreciation. Keeping accurate records of these expenses is crucial for maximising your tax savings.
   - **Depreciation**: The IRS allows property owners to depreciate the value of their rental property over a period of 27.5 years. Depreciation is a non-cash deduction that can significantly reduce your taxable income, but it requires careful documentation of property improvements and asset values.
   - **Capital Gains Tax**: When you sell a rental property for a profit, you'll be liable for capital gains tax on the appreciation in value. However, there are strategies to minimise this tax, such as using a 1031 exchange, which allows you to defer paying capital gains tax if you reinvest the proceeds from the sale into another investment property.
   - **Passive Activity Losses**: If you qualify as a real estate professional, you may be able to offset other types of income with rental property losses. However, passive activity rules apply to many investors, limiting the extent to which rental losses can be deducted from ordinary income.
2. **Using a Professional Accountant for Property-Related Tax Filings**
   - **Expertise in Real Estate Tax Law**: A professional accountant with expertise in real estate can help you navigate the complexities of property-related tax filings. They can ensure that you take advantage of all available deductions and help you strategize for long-term tax efficiency, such as planning for capital gains and retirement.
   - **Tax Filing Accuracy**: Working with a professional can help reduce the likelihood of errors or omissions on your tax return, which can trigger audits or penalties. Accountants also stay up-to-date with changes in tax law, ensuring your tax strategies comply with current regulations.
   - **Maximising Tax Efficiency**: An accountant can help you structure your investments in ways that optimise tax efficiency. This includes advising on how to best leverage deductions, depreciation, and tax-deferred exchanges to minimise your overall tax liability.

Tenant satisfaction plays a crucial role in property management, directly affecting tenant retention, reducing vacancies, and maintaining a steady cash flow. Satisfied tenants are more likely to stay long-term, care for the property, and recommend it to others. As a property owner or manager, fostering good communication, providing added value, and effectively dealing with tenant issues can significantly enhance tenant satisfaction.

Fostering Good Communication

Effective communication is the foundation of a positive tenant-landlord relationship. Ensuring that tenants feel heard and valued not only improves satisfaction but also helps resolve issues quickly, preventing small problems from escalating into major concerns.

1. **Regular Updates and Quick Responses to Inquiries or Complaints**
    - **Proactive Communication**: Keeping tenants informed about important developments—such as planned maintenance, rent adjustments, or policy changes—helps them feel included and respected. Regular updates, whether through emails, newsletters, or notices, can create transparency and reduce uncertainty.
    - **Quick Response Time**: Timely responses to tenant inquiries or complaints are essential for maintaining a good relationship. Whether it's a repair request, a question about the lease, or a neighbourly dispute, addressing concerns promptly signals that you care about their well-being and are actively managing the property.
2. **Utilising Technology to Streamline Communication**
    - **Tenant Portals**: Many property management platforms offer tenant portals where tenants can easily submit maintenance requests, track payments, and communicate with property managers. These portals provide a centralised and convenient way for tenants to manage their interactions with the landlord.
    - **Apps and Messaging Services**: Mobile apps and messaging services like WhatsApp, Slack, or even text messaging allow for quick and informal communication, ensuring issues can be addressed in real time. These tools can also be used to send reminders about rent, property inspections, or community events.
    - **Automated Notifications**: Automating routine notifications, such as rent due dates or maintenance scheduling, helps tenants stay informed without the need for manual updates. This level of organisation can significantly improve tenant experience.

Providing Added Value

Offering additional amenities or services beyond the basics can differentiate your property from competitors and keep tenants happy. Going the extra mile to provide value creates a positive living experience, increasing tenant satisfaction and retention.

1. **Offering Amenities and Services that Attract and Retain Tenants**
    - **Convenient Amenities**: Depending on the property type, adding amenities such as high-speed internet, on-site laundry, or gym facilities can significantly enhance tenant satisfaction. In urban settings, proximity to public transportation, grocery stores, and entertainment venues can also be attractive selling points.
    - **Pet-Friendly Policies**: Allowing pets, where feasible, can make your property more appealing to a broader range of potential tenants. Offering services like pet-friendly common areas or dog-walking paths can also add value.
    - **Energy Efficiency**: Incorporating energy-efficient appliances, windows, and lighting not only helps the environment but also reduces tenant utility bills. Promoting these

features as part of your property's offerings can attract environmentally-conscious renters.
2. **Building Improvements, Community-Building Efforts, and Perks**
    - **Property Enhancements**: Cosmetic improvements, such as fresh paint, updated fixtures, or landscaping, can make the property more attractive without requiring significant investment. Even minor upgrades to common areas, entryways, or outdoor spaces can create a more welcoming environment.
    - **Community-Building Events**: Organising community events such as BBQs, holiday parties, or neighbourhood clean-ups fosters a sense of community among tenants. Building a positive, social atmosphere in multi-unit buildings encourages tenants to stay longer and creates goodwill.
    - **Perks for Long-Term Tenants**: Offering rewards for long-term tenants, such as discounted rent for lease renewals or small gifts during holidays, shows appreciation for their loyalty. These gestures can go a long way in retaining tenants who might otherwise look for alternative housing.

Dealing with Tenant Issues

Tenant disputes, noise complaints, and other problems are an inevitable part of property management. Handling these situations professionally and efficiently can prevent dissatisfaction from escalating and lead to better relationships with tenants.

1. **Addressing Disputes, Noise Complaints, and Neighbor Conflicts Professionally**
    - **Conflict Resolution**: Tenant disputes, whether between roommates or neighbours, can arise from a variety of issues, including noise, cleanliness, or shared spaces. Establishing a clear process for conflict resolution helps mitigate these problems. As a property manager, remaining neutral and offering mediation or solutions can help resolve conflicts amicably.
    - **Noise Complaints**: Noise issues are common in multi-unit buildings, especially in urban settings. Implementing quiet hours and enforcing them with clear lease clauses can reduce complaints. When noise problems arise, addressing them quickly with the offending tenant, and offering solutions like soundproofing, can help maintain a peaceful living environment.
    - **Neighbour Disputes**: Neighbour conflicts, ranging from parking disputes to disagreements over shared spaces, need to be handled diplomatically. Listening to both parties, mediating calmly, and finding fair solutions can prevent the situation from escalating and keep the peace among tenants.
2. **Creating a Fair and Transparent Complaint Process**
    - **Clear Complaint Channels**: Providing tenants with clear channels for filing complaints, whether through a tenant portal, email, or phone, ensures that they feel their concerns are taken seriously. It's important that tenants understand how complaints are processed, how long it typically takes to resolve them, and what outcomes they can expect.
    - **Written Policies**: Having written policies regarding noise, maintenance, and tenant conduct in the lease agreement sets clear expectations from the start. When disputes arise, you can refer to these policies to provide consistent and fair enforcement.

- **Prompt Follow-Up**: After a complaint is filed, providing updates on the status of the issue helps tenants feel heard. Even if a solution takes time, keeping the lines of communication open prevents frustration.

In today's digital age, technology has become an indispensable tool for property investors and managers. From streamlining rent collection to automating maintenance requests, property management software and tools offer immense benefits by increasing efficiency, minimising errors, and improving tenant satisfaction. However, with the rise of technology also comes the responsibility of ensuring data protection and legal compliance.

Using Property Management Software

1. **Benefits of Using Software: Rent Collection, Lease Tracking, Maintenance Logging**
   Property management software has transformed the way landlords and property managers oversee their portfolios. These tools provide comprehensive features designed to simplify daily operations, from collecting rent to managing leases and keeping maintenance records.
   - **Rent Collection**: Property management software allows for automatic rent collection through online portals. Tenants can pay rent through digital platforms, eliminating the need for manual processing and reducing the chances of late payments.
   - **Lease Tracking**: Keeping track of lease terms, renewal dates, and rental increases can be challenging, especially when managing multiple properties. Software solutions automate these processes, sending reminders for upcoming renewals and ensuring that all lease documentation is properly stored and accessible.
   - **Maintenance Logging**: A key benefit of property management software is the ability to log maintenance requests. Tenants can submit maintenance issues through a portal, and landlords can track the progress of repairs. This centralised system ensures all requests are documented, prioritised, and addressed in a timely manner, enhancing tenant satisfaction.

2. **Key Features of Property Management Tools**
   Different property management software solutions offer a variety of features that cater to the needs of landlords and property managers. The following are some key functionalities to consider when choosing a tool:
   - **Accounting and Financial Management**: Many platforms offer built-in accounting systems that help track income and expenses, generate financial reports, and prepare tax documents. This feature is especially useful for property owners managing multiple rental properties.
   - **Tenant Communication**: Software tools provide communication portals where landlords and tenants can interact regarding payments, maintenance issues, or general property-related questions. This improves transparency and helps resolve problems faster.
   - **Document Management**: Efficient document storage is crucial for leases, rental agreements, insurance, and tax forms. Property management software organises and stores documents securely, ensuring easy access when needed.
   - **Tenant Screening**: Many property management platforms offer tenant screening services, including background checks, credit history, and employment verification. This feature simplifies the tenant selection process and reduces the risk of problematic tenants.

- **Mobile Accessibility**: Cloud-based property management tools allow landlords and property managers to access data from anywhere via mobile devices, making it easier to manage properties on the go.

Automation and Efficiency Tools

1. **Leveraging Online Platforms for Advertising, Tenant Applications, and Rent Payments**
   Online platforms have revolutionised the way property owners handle tasks like tenant applications and rent payments, helping automate workflows and minimise manual intervention.
   - **Advertising Rentals**: Property management software integrates with popular property listing websites to automatically post vacant units, saving time and reaching a wider audience. High-quality listings with detailed descriptions, virtual tours, and professional photos attract potential tenants more effectively.
   - **Tenant Applications**: Many tools allow prospective tenants to apply directly online, streamlining the application process. These platforms often come with automated features to screen applicants, verify documents, and run credit checks, reducing the workload for landlords.
   - **Rent Payments**: Automating rent collection helps ensure timely payments and reduces the need for physical checks. Tenants can set up automatic payments through online portals, and landlords can schedule rent reminders. This creates a smoother, more reliable cash flow process.
2. **Improving Efficiency Through Automation**
   Automation is a key feature in modern property management technology, allowing landlords to focus on growth and strategy while routine tasks are handled by software.
   - **Automated Lease Renewals and Rent Adjustments**: The software can automatically notify tenants when leases are up for renewal and even calculate rental increases based on market trends or inflation. This minimises human error and ensures compliance with lease agreements.
   - **Maintenance Scheduling**: Scheduling regular property inspections and maintenance tasks can be automated through the software. Automatic reminders ensure that essential maintenance—such as HVAC checks or plumbing inspections—is performed on time, preventing costly repairs in the future.
   - **Expense Tracking and Financial Reports**: Automating financial tracking ensures that all income, expenses, and invoices are accurately recorded in real time. Property management tools can generate detailed financial reports for tax filings or investor updates without manual intervention.

Security and Data Protection

As property management increasingly moves into the digital space, protecting sensitive tenant and financial data becomes a top priority. Ensuring that property management software complies with legal requirements for data security and privacy is crucial.

1. **Ensuring Tenant and Financial Data Security**
   With the rise of online payments, tenant screening, and digital document storage, safeguarding sensitive information is critical. Property management tools typically include

advanced encryption methods to protect data, but landlords must ensure that these systems are robust enough to prevent breaches.
- **Data Encryption**: Property management platforms use encryption to protect financial transactions, tenant details, and sensitive documents. Ensure that your chosen software follows industry standards for encryption to safeguard data from unauthorised access.
- **Secure Access Controls**: Limit access to sensitive data by assigning different roles within the software. For example, property managers may have full access to financial records, while maintenance staff can only view work orders. Implementing role-based access controls ensures that data is accessible only to those who need it.

2. **Legal Requirements for Data Protection and Privacy**

Property managers must comply with local data protection laws, which vary by region. In many cases, this involves adhering to privacy regulations like the General Data Protection Regulation (GDPR) in the European Union or other regional privacy laws.
- **Data Retention Policies**: Different jurisdictions have specific requirements for how long tenant data must be retained after a lease ends. Property managers need to stay informed about these regulations and ensure that tenant records are securely deleted when no longer needed.
- **Tenant Consent**: Many regions require explicit consent from tenants for collecting and processing their personal data. Property managers should clearly communicate how tenant data is used and stored, ensuring compliance with privacy laws.
- **Regular Data Audits**: Conducting periodic audits of your data protection practices ensures that your property management system is secure and compliant. This includes reviewing access controls, verifying that data is properly encrypted, and ensuring compliance with privacy regulations.

Chapter 8: Scaling Your Portfolio: The 4th Property and Beyond:

Introduction:

Transitioning from owning a small property portfolio to expanding into a larger, scalable investment strategy is both an exciting and challenging journey. The leap from one or two properties to managing a growing portfolio requires a significant shift in mindset and approach. For many property investors, this transition involves moving beyond simply owning a few rental properties and beginning to think about how to build sustainable wealth, create passive income streams, and secure long-term financial security. While the initial steps into property investment may have been tentative and cautious, scaling your portfolio requires adopting a growth-oriented mindset focused on strategic expansion.

Reflecting on the Transition

In the early stages of property investment, the focus tends to be on learning the basics—understanding market dynamics, securing financing, and managing tenants. The first property often feels like a test case, a stepping stone into the world of real estate, with much of the attention centred on learning through experience. As an investor, the initial learning curve is steep, and mistakes are common. However, with each new property, investors gain confidence, experience, and a deeper understanding of how to navigate the real estate market.

After successfully acquiring and managing a small portfolio, investors often reach a turning point where they begin to think beyond just one or two properties. At this stage, the idea of scaling becomes more realistic and exciting. Investors start to realise that they have the potential to build something far greater than what they initially imagined. This shift in perspective is critical, as it marks the transition from being a small-scale property owner to becoming a more strategic, growth-focused investor.

The Importance of a Growth Mindset

Expanding a property portfolio requires adopting a growth mindset—a way of thinking that embraces challenges, sees opportunities for learning and improvement, and focuses on long-term growth rather than short-term gains. Unlike the early days of property investment, where each new purchase may feel like a significant risk, scaling your portfolio involves learning to manage risk more effectively, leveraging existing assets, and thinking strategically about future investments.

A growth mindset allows investors to see beyond the immediate hurdles and focus on the bigger picture. This mindset encourages a proactive approach to identifying new opportunities, optimising existing assets, and continuously improving investment strategies. Investors who adopt this mindset are more likely to view setbacks as learning opportunities rather than failures, which helps them stay resilient in the face of challenges.

Additionally, a growth mindset encourages continuous learning. Successful property investors understand that the market is constantly evolving, and they need to stay informed about new trends, technologies, and strategies to remain competitive. Whether it's learning about new financing options, understanding emerging markets, or improving property management practices, a growth-oriented investor is always seeking ways to improve and scale.

Key Motivations for Scaling

There are several key motivations for scaling a property portfolio, all of which centre around building long-term financial security and creating a more stable and profitable investment strategy.

1. **Building Wealth:** One of the primary motivations for expanding a property portfolio is the potential to build significant wealth over time. As the number of properties in your portfolio grows, so does the potential for capital appreciation. By investing in properties that increase in value over the long term, investors can build equity that can be leveraged for future purchases or used to fund other investments.
2. **Creating Passive Income:** With a larger portfolio comes the opportunity to generate a more substantial and consistent stream of passive income. Rental income from multiple properties can provide a reliable source of cash flow, helping investors achieve financial independence or supplement their primary income. As the portfolio grows, so does the potential for generating rental income that can cover expenses, pay down mortgages, and eventually provide a surplus that can be reinvested or saved.
3. **Long-Term Financial Security:** Scaling a property portfolio is also about creating long-term financial security. For many investors, the goal is to create a portfolio that can provide financial stability in retirement or serve as a legacy for future generations. A well-managed, diversified property portfolio can provide steady income and a valuable asset base that appreciates over time, offering peace of mind and financial security in the face of economic uncertainty or personal challenges.

Overcoming Common Fears

Despite the clear advantages of scaling a property portfolio, many investors are hesitant to take the plunge. Fear of failure, financial risk, and the complexity of managing multiple properties often hold investors back from realising their full potential. However, overcoming these fears is an essential part of the journey toward scaling and success.

1. **Fear of Financial Risk:** The fear of overextending oneself financially is one of the most common concerns for investors looking to expand their portfolio. Managing mortgages, property taxes, maintenance costs, and vacancies can feel overwhelming, especially as the number of properties grows. To overcome this fear, it's essential to build a solid financial foundation, including a detailed cash flow analysis, setting aside reserves for unexpected expenses, and maintaining a healthy loan-to-value ratio. Leveraging existing equity and exploring creative financing options can also help mitigate financial risk.
2. **Fear of Market Fluctuations:** Many investors worry about the impact of market downturns on their portfolio. While market cycles are inevitable, successful investors learn to manage risk by diversifying their investments across different locations, property types, and market conditions. Additionally, having a long-term perspective and focusing on properties with strong fundamentals—such as high rental demand, good location, and potential for capital growth—can help weather short-term fluctuations.
3. **Fear of Management Challenges:** Managing multiple properties can be time-consuming and complex, especially if the properties are spread across different locations. However, with the right systems in place—such as property management software, a reliable network of contractors, and, in some cases, professional property management services—investors can streamline operations and reduce the day-to-day burden of managing a larger portfolio.

Expanding a property portfolio beyond three properties introduces new challenges, especially in terms of financing. As your portfolio grows, so does the complexity of securing financing for additional properties, navigating stricter lender requirements, and managing multiple loans. The strategy that worked for your first two or three properties may no longer be sufficient, and investors must adopt more sophisticated financing approaches to overcome obstacles and continue growing. This chapter will explore the challenges of financing a larger portfolio, how to optimise your financing strategy, and the importance of building strong relationships with lenders and brokers.

The Complexity of Financing a Growing Portfolio

As you move beyond your first few properties, lenders may view you differently, often becoming more conservative in approving new loans. In the early stages, financing is usually more straightforward, especially for first-time buyers or investors with stable income. However, after acquiring multiple properties, lenders may consider you a higher risk because you are taking on more debt, and they may have concerns about your ability to service multiple loans, particularly during market downturns or if vacancies arise.

Key challenges include:

- **Higher Loan Scrutiny:** Lenders begin to scrutinise your overall debt levels, cash flow, and risk exposure more carefully. They may require detailed documentation of your financials and a strong track record of managing existing properties.
- **Serviceability Calculations:** Lenders assess whether your income, including rental income from your properties, can cover your existing debt obligations. This serviceability assessment becomes increasingly important as you add more loans to your portfolio.
- **Lower Loan-to-Value Ratios (LVR):** Some lenders may offer lower LVRs as your portfolio grows, meaning you may need to contribute a larger deposit for each new property. This can make it more difficult to finance additional purchases without tapping into existing equity.
- **Debt-to-Income (DTI) Ratios:** Lenders also consider your DTI ratio, which compares your total debt to your income. As your portfolio expands, maintaining a favourable DTI ratio becomes more challenging, particularly if your rental income doesn't keep pace with your borrowing.

Optimising Your Financing Strategy

To overcome these challenges, it's essential to adopt a more strategic approach to financing. Below are several key strategies to consider when financing multiple properties:

Leveraging Existing Equity

One of the most powerful tools for financing additional properties is leveraging the equity you've built in your existing portfolio. As property values appreciate over time, the difference between your loan balance and the property's market value (equity) increases. This equity can be used as a deposit for future purchases.

- **Equity Release or Refinance:** You can refinance your existing properties to unlock equity and use it as a deposit for your next property. This involves taking out a new loan based on the increased value of your properties, giving you access to additional funds while keeping your cash flow intact.

- **Cross-Collateralization:** Some investors choose to cross-collateralize, where multiple properties are used as security for a single loan. While this strategy can unlock significant equity, it also increases risk because if one property underperforms, it can affect your entire portfolio.

Structuring Loans for Growth

Proper loan structuring is critical when scaling your property portfolio. Choosing the right type of loan and structuring it appropriately can help maintain cash flow and reduce financial risk.

- **Interest-Only Loans:** Interest-only loans are often favoured by property investors, especially in the early years of property ownership, as they reduce monthly repayments and improve cash flow. This extra cash can be reinvested into the portfolio or used for renovations to increase property value and rental yields. However, it's essential to plan for the end of the interest-only period when repayments will increase.
- **Offset Accounts:** Using offset accounts can help you reduce the interest you pay on your loans while keeping funds available for future purchases. By depositing surplus cash into an offset account linked to your loan, you reduce the loan balance on which interest is calculated.
- **Split Loans:** Some investors use a combination of fixed-rate and variable-rate loans. Fixed-rate loans provide certainty around repayments, while variable-rate loans offer more flexibility and the potential to benefit from interest rate reductions. Balancing both types of loans can help manage risk and optimise cash flow.

Maintaining Cash Flow

Maintaining strong cash flow is essential when financing multiple properties. Negative cash flow can make it difficult to service existing loans and secure new financing. To keep your portfolio positively geared:

- **Choose Properties with Strong Rental Yields:** Focus on acquiring properties with high rental demand in areas with stable or growing populations. A strong rental yield ensures that rental income covers your mortgage repayments and property expenses, leaving room for profit.
- **Reduce Vacancy Rates:** Minimising vacancies by maintaining well-kept properties and building strong relationships with tenants can help protect cash flow. Properties with long-term tenants or located in high-demand areas are less likely to experience prolonged vacancies.
- **Renovate to Boost Rental Income:** Strategic renovations can increase the rental value of your properties, further boosting cash flow. Upgrades to kitchens, bathrooms, and other key areas can attract higher-paying tenants without requiring a significant investment.

Case Studies: Creative Financing Strategies for Expanding Beyond the Third Property

Let's explore two case studies of investors who used creative financing strategies to grow their portfolios beyond three properties:

Case Study 1: Equity Recycling for Rapid Expansion

Investor A owned three properties, each of which had appreciated significantly over five years. Rather than waiting to save for another deposit, the investor decided to refinance all three properties and access the built-up equity. By taking out new loans based on the increased property values, Investor A was able to unlock enough funds to purchase two additional properties without contributing any new savings. This strategy allowed for rapid expansion while maintaining healthy cash flow, as rental income from the new properties covered their mortgage repayments.

Case Study 2: Joint Ventures and Partnerships

Investor B wanted to scale beyond their third property but had difficulty securing financing due to a high DTI ratio. To overcome this, they entered into a joint venture with another investor. By pooling their resources and combining their borrowing capacity, they were able to purchase a higher-value property with strong capital growth potential. The partnership allowed both investors to share the financial burden, reduce risk, and leverage each other's expertise.

Building Strong Relationships with Lenders and Brokers

As you scale your portfolio, it becomes increasingly important to cultivate strong relationships with lenders and mortgage brokers. These professionals can provide valuable insights into the lending landscape, help you navigate complex financing options, and advocate on your behalf when applying for loans. Building a reliable network of financial partners can improve your chances of securing favourable loan terms and gaining access to financing even as your portfolio grows.

- **Choosing the Right Lender:** Different lenders have varying criteria for property investors. Some are more flexible with higher debt levels, while others may offer better terms for multiple-property owners. Working with a mortgage broker can help you identify the best lenders for your specific situation.
- **Regularly Review Loan Terms:** As your portfolio grows, it's essential to regularly review your loan terms and interest rates. Refinancing to take advantage of lower rates or better terms can improve cash flow and free up funds for future investments.
- **Building a Track Record:** Demonstrating a track record of successful property management and steady cash flow can make it easier to secure financing for additional properties. Lenders are more likely to approve loans for investors who have proven their ability to manage debt and grow a profitable portfolio.

As your property portfolio grows, diversification becomes a critical strategy for managing risk and optimising returns. While initially focusing on residential properties may offer stability and manageable risk, expanding into other property types and locations can provide a more resilient portfolio. Diversification reduces exposure to market fluctuations in any one sector and helps investors capitalise on different types of growth. This chapter will explore why diversification is crucial for a growing portfolio, the benefits of expanding into new property types, geographic diversification, and how to balance diversification with focused management.

Why Diversification is Crucial for Managing Risk in a Growing Portfolio

Diversification is a key principle in investment that applies equally to property portfolios. It involves spreading investments across different property types, locations, and market segments to minimise the impact of negative events affecting one area of your portfolio. While property markets tend to grow over time, they can be unpredictable, with periods of stagnation, decline, or rapid price inflation. A well-diversified portfolio reduces the likelihood of being overexposed to downturns in any one market or asset class.

Key benefits of diversification include:

- **Reduced Risk Exposure:** When one segment of the market is underperforming, investments in other areas may still generate strong returns, helping to balance losses.
- **Stabilised Cash Flow:** By owning properties in different categories (e.g., commercial and residential), you can create multiple streams of income, reducing your reliance on any single type of property for cash flow.
- **Access to Different Growth Cycles:** Different property types and locations often experience growth at varying times. By diversifying, you can take advantage of multiple market cycles rather than being tied to the performance of a single one.

Exploring New Property Types: Commercial Properties, Multi-Family Units, Vacation Rentals

When investors think of expanding their property portfolio, many naturally consider acquiring more residential properties. However, moving beyond this category into other property types can offer enhanced returns and diversification.

Commercial Properties

Commercial properties, such as office spaces, retail stores, and industrial warehouses, can be a lucrative addition to your portfolio. They tend to offer longer lease terms (typically five to ten years), meaning more stability in rental income compared to residential properties, where leases are usually one year. Commercial tenants are often responsible for property upkeep and maintenance under triple net leases, reducing your management responsibilities.

However, commercial properties come with their own set of risks:

- **Market Sensitivity:** Commercial properties can be more susceptible to economic downturns, especially in retail and office sectors, where businesses may struggle during recessions.
- **Higher Entry Costs:** Commercial properties typically have higher purchase prices and may require more significant upfront capital for acquisition.

Multi-Family Units

Multi-family units, such as duplexes, apartment buildings, or townhouses, allow you to acquire multiple rental units within a single property, increasing the potential for rental income and reducing the risk of vacancies. If one unit is vacant, others continue to generate income, providing greater stability compared to single-family homes.

Benefits include:

- **Economies of Scale:** Managing multiple units under one roof can be more efficient than managing several separate properties, reducing per-unit maintenance and operational costs.

- **Increased Rental Income:** With more tenants, multi-family properties generate higher gross rental income, which can significantly boost cash flow.

However, challenges include:

- **Higher Management Complexity:** Managing multiple tenants in one property requires more intensive management and can lead to frequent maintenance issues.
- **Tenant Turnover:** High turnover rates in multi-family units may create more frequent vacancies, requiring diligent tenant management.

Vacation Rentals

Vacation rentals, such as Airbnb properties or short-term holiday homes, have gained popularity as a way to generate high returns in tourist-heavy areas. Short-term rental properties can offer significant income potential, especially during peak travel seasons, often surpassing the income generated from long-term rentals.

Key advantages include:

- **Higher Rental Yields:** Vacation rentals can generate higher per-night fees than long-term rentals, especially in desirable locations.
- **Flexibility:** Owners can use the property themselves during off-peak times while earning rental income when not in use.

However, there are some downsides:

- **Seasonal Income Fluctuations:** Income from vacation rentals can be highly seasonal, making it challenging to maintain cash flow during off-seasons.
- **Intensive Management Requirements:** Frequent turnover of short-term guests requires regular cleaning, maintenance, and customer service, which may require hiring a property management company.

The Benefits of Geographic Diversification: Investing in Different Cities or Regions

Geographic diversification involves expanding your portfolio into different cities, regions, or even countries. This strategy is particularly beneficial for protecting against localised market downturns. If you have all your properties in one area and that market experiences a slump, the impact on your portfolio can be severe. Investing in different regions spreads your risk and allows you to capitalise on various growth markets.

Key benefits of geographic diversification include:

- **Minimised Regional Risk:** Property markets are influenced by local economic conditions, such as employment rates, population growth, and infrastructure development. By investing in different cities or regions, you reduce the risk of a downturn in any one location affecting your entire portfolio.
- **Capitalising on Regional Booms:** Some regions may experience rapid growth due to economic factors like a population boom, industry development, or government infrastructure

projects. By investing in different areas, you can take advantage of these growth opportunities and enjoy higher returns.
- **Access to Different Property Cycles:** Property cycles vary across regions. While one area might be in a downturn, another may be experiencing rapid growth. Geographic diversification allows you to benefit from multiple market cycles.

Challenges of geographic diversification include:

- **Increased Management Complexity:** Managing properties in different locations can be more complex and costly, especially if you need to hire local property managers.
- **Local Knowledge Requirements:** Each property market has unique factors that influence property values, rental demand, and legal requirements. Investing in unfamiliar areas requires thorough research and local expertise to avoid costly mistakes.

Balancing Diversification with Portfolio Focus and Management Capacity

While diversification is an essential strategy for reducing risk, it's equally important to balance it with your ability to manage and focus on your portfolio. Over-diversifying without the capacity to manage properties effectively can lead to operational inefficiencies, cash flow problems, and difficulty keeping track of investments.

Here are some tips for balancing diversification and focus:

- **Start Small and Build Gradually:** Instead of jumping into multiple new property types or regions at once, start by diversifying into one new type or location and build from there. This allows you to test new markets and property types while maintaining control over management.
- **Leverage Property Management Services:** As your portfolio becomes more diverse, hiring professional property management services can help you manage properties in different locations or property types without overwhelming your capacity.
- **Stay Aligned with Your Investment Goals:** While diversification is important, it's essential to stay focused on your overall investment strategy. Whether your goal is cash flow, capital growth, or a combination of both, ensure that each new property type or location aligns with your objectives.
- **Regularly Review Your Portfolio:** Continuously assess the performance of your diversified properties and ensure that they contribute to your overall strategy. If a property type or location is underperforming, be prepared to make adjustments, such as selling underperforming properties or refocusing on areas with stronger returns.

As your property portfolio grows, so too does your exposure to risk. While expanding your investment holdings offers greater potential for wealth building and financial security, it also introduces new challenges in managing and mitigating risks. Successful investors understand that an effective risk management strategy evolves with their portfolio, requiring ongoing adjustments to ensure stability and profitability. In this section, we'll explore how risk changes as you expand, the importance of liquidity and reserves, risk mitigation techniques, and how to prepare for market downturns and economic shifts.

How Risk Changes as You Expand Your Portfolio

When you own a few properties, risks tend to be more manageable. However, as your portfolio grows, the complexity and potential consequences of those risks also increase. With more properties, you have more tenants, more financial obligations, and more market exposure, which amplifies both potential gains and losses. Key areas where risks increase include:

- **Property-Specific Risks:** Owning multiple properties increases the chance that you'll encounter issues like maintenance problems, tenant disputes, or vacancies. As the number of properties grows, so does the likelihood of these events occurring simultaneously, which can strain your resources.
- **Market Exposure:** With more properties, you are exposed to a wider array of market fluctuations. If a particular location or property type experiences a downturn, it can affect a larger portion of your portfolio.
- **Cash Flow Strain:** The more properties you own, the greater the cash flow requirements for mortgages, maintenance, taxes, and other expenses. If you don't carefully manage your cash flow, one underperforming property or unexpected expense could create a ripple effect across your entire portfolio.

Adapting Your Risk Management Strategy As your portfolio grows, your risk management strategy needs to evolve. The following steps can help you adapt to new challenges:

- **Diversify your portfolio:** As you expand, consider investing in different property types (residential, commercial) or locations to spread risk. A well-diversified portfolio is less susceptible to downturns in any one market.
- **Improve tenant screening processes:** With more properties comes the need to find reliable tenants who can minimise turnover and late payments. A rigorous screening process can reduce the risk of tenant-related problems.
- **Optimise your financing:** Structuring your financing carefully is crucial for managing risk. Opt for fixed-rate loans or other low-risk financial products that reduce your exposure to rising interest rates or sudden increases in expenses.

The Importance of Maintaining Liquidity and Reserves

As your portfolio expands, maintaining liquidity becomes increasingly critical. Unexpected expenses are inevitable in property investment, whether due to market fluctuations, property maintenance, or tenant issues. Having sufficient liquidity and financial reserves ensures you can weather these challenges without compromising your investments.

Why Liquidity is Essential

Liquidity refers to how easily you can access cash or assets that can be quickly converted into cash. In property investment, liquidity is often limited, as real estate is typically a long-term, illiquid asset. However, maintaining a degree of liquidity is essential to avoid being caught in a situation where you need cash but have no way to access it quickly.

Scenarios where liquidity is critical include:

- **Unexpected Repairs:** A major repair, such as a roof replacement or plumbing issue, can cost tens of thousands of dollars. Without sufficient liquidity, such expenses can force you into costly loans or even force the sale of a property at a loss.
- **Vacancies or Tenant Default:** If a tenant leaves unexpectedly or defaults on rent, you need liquidity to cover mortgage payments and other expenses while finding a replacement tenant.
- **Market Downturns:** During economic downturns, property values and rental demand may decrease, affecting both cash flow and asset values. In such cases, liquidity helps you ride out the tough times without having to sell properties at unfavourable prices.

Building and Managing Reserves

Creating a reserve fund is one of the most effective ways to maintain liquidity. A reserve fund is an amount of money set aside specifically to handle unexpected property-related expenses. As your portfolio grows, your reserve fund should grow proportionally.

Some strategies for building and managing reserves include:

- **Percentage of Rental Income:** Set aside a percentage of rental income (e.g., 5-10%) each month to build your reserve fund. This ensures that as your rental income grows, so does your ability to handle future expenses.
- **Property-Specific Reserves:** Allocate a reserve for each property based on its specific risk factors, such as age, location, and maintenance requirements.
- **Access to Credit:** Establish a line of credit or other financing options as a backup in case your cash reserves are insufficient to cover large, unexpected expenses.

Risk Mitigation Techniques: Insurance, Property Diversification, and Tenant Vetting

Effectively mitigating risk involves utilising a combination of tools and strategies to protect your investments. The following techniques can significantly reduce the potential impact of unforeseen challenges:

Insurance Coverage

Insurance is one of the most critical tools for managing risk in real estate. As you expand your portfolio, it's essential to ensure each property is adequately covered for potential risks, such as natural disasters, fire, liability claims, and tenant-related damages.

- **Landlord Insurance:** This type of insurance covers damage to the property, loss of rental income due to tenant-related issues, and liability protection if a tenant or guest is injured on the property.
- **Property-Specific Policies:** Depending on the location and type of property, you may need specialised insurance, such as flood insurance, earthquake insurance, or commercial property insurance.

Ensure you regularly review and update your insurance policies as your portfolio grows, and work with an insurance broker to ensure you have the right coverage for each property.

Property Diversification

As mentioned earlier, diversification is a powerful tool for mitigating risk. By spreading your investments across different property types (residential, commercial, multi-family) and locations, you reduce the risk of being overly exposed to a downturn in any one market.

Benefits of diversification include:

- **Geographic Protection:** If one region experiences a market downturn, properties in other areas may continue to perform well, balancing out your overall portfolio performance.
- **Different Market Cycles:** Various property types experience growth and downturns at different times, providing a more stable portfolio across varying economic conditions.

Tenant Vetting

Reliable tenants are the cornerstone of risk management in property investment. As your portfolio grows, having effective tenant screening processes becomes even more important. Proper tenant vetting reduces the risk of missed rental payments, vacancies, and property damage.

Key steps in tenant vetting include:

- **Credit and Background Checks:** A tenant's credit score, employment history, and rental history are good indicators of their reliability.
- **Income Verification:** Ensure the tenant's income is sufficient to cover rent and other living expenses. A common rule is to require that a tenant's income is at least three times the monthly rent.
- **References:** Contact previous landlords and employers to verify the tenant's character and rental behaviour.

Planning for Market Downturns and Changing Economic Conditions

Property markets are cyclical, with periods of growth, stagnation, and decline. As your portfolio grows, it's essential to plan for these cycles and adapt your strategy to changing economic conditions.

Preparing for Market Downturns

While no one can predict exactly when a market downturn will occur, having a strategy in place ensures you can weather the storm when it happens. Some key steps for downturn preparation include:

- **Maintaining Strong Cash Flow:** Focus on properties with strong rental demand and stable cash flow, even if they don't offer the highest potential for capital appreciation. Cash flow-positive properties provide a cushion during downturns.
- **Reducing Debt Exposure:** High leverage can be risky in a declining market. Consider paying down debt or securing fixed-rate loans to protect yourself from rising interest rates or falling property values.
- **Holding for the Long Term:** Real estate is generally a long-term investment, and downturns are part of the market cycle. Holding onto your properties during downturns, if possible, allows you to avoid selling at a loss and benefit from future recoveries.

Adapting to Economic Shifts

Economic factors such as interest rates, inflation, and employment trends can significantly impact property values and rental demand. Regularly monitoring economic indicators allows you to adjust your investment strategy proactively. For example:

- **Interest Rate Changes:** Rising interest rates can make mortgage payments more expensive, reducing your cash flow. If rates are expected to rise, consider locking in fixed-rate mortgages to protect against increasing costs.
- **Inflation:** While inflation can increase property values over time, it also raises the cost of maintenance and repairs. Build inflation-adjusted estimates into your reserve planning and cash flow projections.

As your property portfolio grows, so does the complexity of managing multiple properties efficiently. What worked for one or two properties may no longer be feasible when overseeing a larger number of investments. Scaling your property management strategy is crucial for maintaining profitability, minimising stress, and ensuring consistent tenant satisfaction. In this section, we'll discuss the increasing demands of managing a growing portfolio, the decision between self-management and professional management services, the role of technology in automating tasks, and how large-scale property investors streamline operations.

The Growing Complexity of Managing Multiple Properties

Managing a few rental properties can be relatively straightforward, often involving occasional tenant interactions, routine maintenance, and rent collection. However, as you acquire more properties, the day-to-day responsibilities multiply, potentially creating challenges such as:

- **Increased Maintenance Needs:** Each additional property adds more opportunities for maintenance issues, from minor repairs to major renovations. Coordinating repairs and ensuring the properties remain in good condition becomes more demanding as the number of properties increases.
- **Tenant Turnover:** A larger portfolio means dealing with a higher frequency of tenant turnover, vacancies, and new leases. Managing lease renewals, screening new tenants, and maintaining good relationships with existing ones becomes more time-consuming.
- **Administrative Burden:** Rent collection, expense tracking, budgeting, and record-keeping become significantly more complex as you manage multiple properties. Ensuring timely payments, handling late fees, and preparing documents for tax filings can overwhelm a property owner.
- **Geographic Spread:** If your portfolio spans different neighbourhoods, cities, or even regions, the complexity of managing properties increases. You'll need to stay informed about local market conditions, regulations, and tenant demographics across multiple areas.

The key to scaling efficiently is streamlining property management processes, either by optimising your own management practices or hiring professional help.

Self-Management vs. Professional Property Management Services

One of the first decisions you'll need to make as your portfolio grows is whether to continue managing the properties yourself or hire professional property management services. Both options have their pros and cons, and the right choice depends on factors such as your time availability, expertise, and the size of your portfolio.

Self-Management

Many investors prefer to self-manage their properties, especially in the early stages of their real estate journey. Self-management offers a hands-on approach and allows for direct control over all aspects of your properties. The benefits of self-management include:

- **Cost Savings:** Self-managing can save you the cost of hiring a property management company, which typically charges 8-12% of the monthly rental income. For smaller portfolios, this can result in significant savings.
- **Greater Control:** Managing your properties allows you to personally oversee tenant relations, property upkeep, and rent collection, ensuring that everything meets your standards.
- **Increased Cash Flow:** By not paying for property management services, you can potentially increase your cash flow, improving your profit margins on each property.

However, as your portfolio grows, the downsides of self-management can become more pronounced:

- **Time-Consuming:** Managing multiple properties, especially if spread out geographically, can take up a considerable amount of time. Handling tenant issues, maintenance, and administrative tasks becomes more overwhelming as the portfolio expands.
- **Lack of Expertise:** If you are not familiar with certain aspects of property management (e.g., legal regulations, tax implications, or complex maintenance issues), mistakes can be costly.
- **Limited Scalability:** Self-managing a small portfolio might be feasible, but managing dozens of properties effectively becomes challenging without professional help or advanced systems in place.

Professional Property Management Services

Hiring a professional property management company can alleviate the burdens of self-management and provide access to expertise and resources that simplify the management process. Key advantages of professional management include:

- **Time Savings:** With a property management company handling day-to-day operations, you can focus on other aspects of your life or business. They take care of tenant relations, rent collection, maintenance, and legal issues, freeing up your time.
- **Expertise:** Property management companies are experienced in dealing with tenant disputes, maintenance emergencies, and legal compliance. Their expertise helps prevent costly mistakes and ensures that your properties are run efficiently.
- **Scalability:** Professional management is especially beneficial as your portfolio grows. Managing multiple properties across various locations becomes more feasible when you have a dedicated team handling operations.

On the downside, professional management services come with costs, which can eat into your rental income. Additionally, you may lose some direct control over decision-making and operations.

Automating Property Management Tasks Through Technology

Whether you opt for self-management or professional help, technology can play a crucial role in streamlining property management tasks, making the process more efficient and scalable. The rise of digital platforms and property management software has revolutionised the way investors handle operations, allowing for automation of many time-consuming tasks.

Rent Collection

One of the most common uses of technology in property management is automating rent collection. Property management software can handle payments, send reminders, and track late fees without manual intervention. Benefits of automated rent collection include:

- **Efficiency:** Tenants can make payments via direct debit, credit cards, or online payment platforms, ensuring faster, more reliable transactions.
- **Reduced Late Payments:** Automated reminders and penalties for late payments can help reduce the frequency of overdue rent.
- **Tracking and Reporting:** Software provides real-time reports on rent payments, making it easy to monitor cash flow and address payment issues promptly.

Popular platforms for automated rent collection include **Buildium**, **AppFolio**, and **TenantCloud**, which allow for seamless payment processing and tenant communication.

Maintenance Requests and Scheduling

Another key area where technology can improve efficiency is in handling maintenance requests. Property management software allows tenants to submit maintenance requests through an online portal, where they can describe the issue and upload photos. Benefits include:

- **Streamlined Communication:** Tenants can submit requests and receive updates on the status of their repairs, reducing the need for back-and-forth emails or phone calls.
- **Scheduling and Coordination:** Software can automatically schedule repairs with contractors and send reminders, ensuring timely maintenance.
- **Tracking Maintenance History:** The platform maintains a record of all repairs and maintenance for each property, making it easy to track recurring issues or plan preventive maintenance.

By automating maintenance tasks, you reduce the likelihood of delays or forgotten requests, improving tenant satisfaction and preserving property value.

Tenant Screening and Leasing

Technology can also streamline the tenant screening and leasing process. Automated tools allow you to screen applicants, run background checks, and even sign leases online. Benefits include:

- **Faster Screening:** Platforms like **TurboTenant** and **SmartMove** offer comprehensive background checks, including credit reports, criminal history, and eviction records, helping you make informed decisions quickly.

- **Digital Leasing:** Electronic signatures and digital leases eliminate the need for in-person meetings or physical paperwork, speeding up the leasing process.
- **Tenant Tracking:** Property management software keeps all tenant data organised, including lease agreements, payment history, and communication records, making it easy to manage multiple tenants across different properties.

Case Study: How Large-Scale Property Investors Manage Multiple Properties Efficiently

To understand how large-scale property investors streamline their operations, let's look at a case study of an investor with a portfolio of 50 rental properties spread across different regions.

Background: This investor initially managed a small portfolio of five properties but quickly expanded by purchasing multiple single-family homes, apartment complexes, and commercial properties. As the portfolio grew, managing these properties became increasingly difficult, especially with tenant turnover, maintenance issues, and rent collection.

Challenges

- The investor struggled to keep up with the administrative tasks, especially when properties were spread across different regions with varying regulations and market conditions.
- Handling tenant inquiries and maintenance requests became a full-time job, leaving little time to focus on finding new investment opportunities.
- Cash flow management became complex, with multiple rent payments coming in at different times and varying amounts.

Solution: Automation and Professional Management

- **Property Management Software:** The investor implemented **Buildium** to automate rent collection, tenant screening, and lease management. This reduced manual tasks and ensured timely rent payments, with fewer late fees or missed payments.
- **Outsourcing Maintenance:** The investor partnered with a professional maintenance service, who handled all repair requests. Maintenance requests were submitted via the property management portal, and the service provider handled scheduling and repairs. This reduced response times and improved tenant satisfaction.
- **Hiring a Property Manager:** For day-to-day operations, the investor hired a property manager to oversee tenant relations and coordinate with contractors. The property manager was responsible for addressing tenant concerns, inspecting properties, and ensuring lease renewals.

Outcome: By leveraging technology and outsourcing critical tasks, the investor was able to scale their portfolio while maintaining profitability. The investor now focuses on strategic growth opportunities rather than being bogged down by operational issues.

Acquiring new properties at the right time is critical to maximising returns in real estate investing. Market cycles, emerging trends, and economic conditions play pivotal roles in determining when to expand a portfolio. Successful investors understand that timing is everything — buying properties during the right phase of the market can lead to significant appreciation and steady cash flow, while mistiming purchases can result in diminished returns or even losses.

In this section, we'll discuss how to leverage market opportunities by understanding market cycles, identifying emerging opportunities, and maintaining flexibility in your investment strategy. A case study will also highlight how savvy investors successfully timed the market while expanding their portfolios.

Understanding Market Cycles and Timing Your Purchases to Maximise Returns

The property market moves in cycles, typically consisting of four phases: boom, downturn, stabilisation, and recovery. Understanding these phases and how they impact property prices can help investors determine the best times to acquire new properties.

1. **Boom Phase:** During the boom phase, property values increase rapidly due to high demand and strong economic growth. While it may seem like an attractive time to buy, properties are often overpriced during this phase, making it difficult to find bargains or high yields. Investors need to be cautious during a boom, as buying at the peak can expose them to greater risks when the market corrects itself.
2. **Downturn Phase:** Following a boom, the market typically enters a downturn phase, where prices start to decline due to oversupply or slowing demand. While this phase can create uncertainty, it often presents opportunities for astute investors to acquire properties at a discount. By purchasing in a declining market, investors can capitalise on lower prices and wait for market recovery, allowing for significant long-term appreciation.
3. **Stabilisation Phase:** After a downturn, the market usually stabilises, with property values plateauing and demand and supply balancing out. This phase can offer opportunities for investors to buy at reasonable prices with minimal volatility. The market's predictability during stabilisation allows investors to make decisions based on solid data rather than speculation.
4. **Recovery Phase:** As the market begins to recover from a downturn, property values start to rise again, but are still relatively affordable compared to the boom phase. Investors who buy during the early stages of recovery can benefit from appreciation while still securing properties at a lower cost. This is often considered one of the best times to expand a portfolio.

Timing is Key: To maximise returns, investors need to aim for acquisitions during the downturn or early recovery phases. This requires a strong understanding of local market conditions and economic indicators, as well as a willingness to be patient and strategic in waiting for the right moment.

How to Stay Ahead of the Competition by Spotting Emerging Opportunities

With competition in real estate often fierce, investors need to develop strategies for staying ahead of others when it comes to identifying lucrative opportunities. This involves constant vigilance and the ability to spot trends before they become mainstream.

1. **Monitoring Economic Indicators:** Keep a close watch on key economic factors like employment rates, population growth, and interest rates. Rising employment in a particular region often indicates increased demand for housing, which can drive property values higher. Similarly, areas experiencing population growth are likely to see increased demand for both rental and ownership properties.
2. **Following Infrastructure Developments:** Large infrastructure projects, such as new transportation links, schools, or commercial hubs, can significantly impact property values in

nearby areas. Investors who track these developments can acquire properties before the market fully reacts to the increased demand, gaining an edge over competitors.
3. **Analysing Market Data:** Leverage data from real estate platforms, local government reports, and industry publications to analyse trends. Identify areas where prices have not yet peaked, or where rental demand is outpacing supply. By doing so, investors can target locations that are on the verge of rapid growth.
4. **Networking with Industry Professionals:** Build relationships with real estate agents, property managers, and local experts who have their fingers on the pulse of the market. These connections can provide valuable insights into off-market deals, emerging neighbourhoods, and other investment opportunities that are not yet widely known.

Staying ahead of the competition often requires a proactive approach, where investors remain vigilant for emerging trends and act quickly to seize opportunities before the broader market catches on.

The Importance of Staying Flexible in Your Investment Strategy

Real estate investors who succeed over the long term understand the importance of maintaining flexibility in their investment strategies. Markets can change rapidly due to unforeseen economic events, shifts in demand, or regulatory changes. Investors who are adaptable and open to adjusting their approach are more likely to capitalise on opportunities and navigate challenges.

1. **Adapting to Market Conditions:** In a rapidly rising market, investors may need to shift focus from traditional cash-flow properties to areas with high capital growth potential. Conversely, in a declining market, it may be more prudent to target properties with strong rental yields to ensure steady income, even if appreciation is slower.
2. **Expanding into Different Property Types:** Flexibility may also involve diversifying across different types of real estate. For example, if residential property prices are surging and making it difficult to find good deals, investors might consider exploring commercial properties, multi-family units, or vacation rentals that offer better returns during certain market conditions.
3. **Exploring Geographic Diversity:** By expanding their investment scope beyond a single location, investors can mitigate the risks associated with market downturns in a specific region. Markets in different cities or regions may move in different cycles, offering more opportunities for growth or stability when others are stagnant.

The ability to remain flexible allows investors to adjust their strategies as needed, ensuring they can continue to find profitable opportunities, even as market conditions fluctuate.

Case Study: Investors Who Timed the Market Right When Expanding Their Portfolios

To illustrate the importance of timing the market and staying flexible, let's examine the case of two investors who successfully expanded their portfolios by timing their purchases during the market cycle.

Investor A: Buying During a Downturn

Investor A closely monitored the property market in a major city that had experienced rapid price growth during a boom phase. As prices began to decline during the downturn, many investors became hesitant, fearing further price drops. However, Investor A recognized that the downturn was an opportunity to buy quality properties at a discount.

By purchasing two properties in prime locations during the downturn, Investor A was able to secure them at 15% below their peak price. As the market began to recover, these properties appreciated significantly, and within five years, they had increased in value by 25%, generating substantial equity gains. In addition, the investor enjoyed strong rental demand, providing steady cash flow during the recovery period.

Investor B: Capitalising on an Emerging Neighborhood

Investor B focused on identifying emerging neighbourhoods before they peaked. By researching local infrastructure projects and tracking population growth in the outskirts of a rapidly growing city, Investor B pinpointed an area where prices were still low, but poised for growth.

After acquiring two properties at relatively affordable prices, the area's property values began to climb as new transportation links and retail developments were completed. Within three years, both properties had appreciated by 20%, while rental demand surged due to the influx of young professionals moving to the area for its improved accessibility and amenities.

Both investors succeeded by timing their acquisitions during key phases of the market cycle and remaining flexible in their strategies, seizing opportunities as they arose.

As your property portfolio expands, building a reliable support network becomes increasingly essential to ensure sustained growth and long-term success. Managing a single property can be straightforward, but as you acquire more properties, the complexity of financial, legal, and operational matters escalates. Having a team of professionals with expertise in areas like finance, legal compliance, property management, and accounting can ease the burden, allowing you to focus on strategic decision-making. Additionally, mentorship and peer networks offer invaluable guidance and experience-sharing to help you avoid costly mistakes.

In this section, we'll discuss the importance of creating a solid team of experts, the roles they play in supporting your property investments, and how mentorship and peer networks can be leveraged for continued growth. We will also highlight case studies where successful investors built strong teams to support their expanding portfolios.

The Importance of Building a Reliable Team of Professionals

As your portfolio grows, having a reliable team of professionals helps streamline operations, mitigate risks, and maximise returns. Each member of this support network brings a specific expertise that can address the diverse challenges of property investment.

1. **Accountants and Financial Advisors:** Financial management becomes increasingly complex as you scale your portfolio. A skilled accountant who specialises in property investment is crucial for managing cash flow, tax planning, and ensuring compliance with tax laws. They can advise on how to best structure your investments, maximise tax deductions, and avoid financial pitfalls.
Financial advisors can help you plan your long-term wealth-building strategy by assessing how each property fits into your overall portfolio and how to optimise for cash flow, growth,

and risk management. With a solid financial strategy, you can make well-informed decisions about expanding your portfolio.

2. **Brokers and Mortgage Advisors:** As you seek financing for multiple properties, a mortgage broker who understands complex financing strategies is indispensable. Brokers can help you secure the best loan terms by leveraging your existing equity and negotiating with multiple lenders. They can also advise on the best ways to structure your loans, ensuring that you maintain liquidity and flexibility while avoiding overleveraging.

   A knowledgeable mortgage advisor can provide tailored financing solutions, especially when traditional lenders may not be willing to provide loans for large portfolios. Brokers can also help you navigate refinancing options as market conditions change, allowing you to access equity from existing properties to fund new acquisitions.

3. **Property Managers:** Managing multiple properties can be time-consuming and demanding. Hiring a professional property manager ensures that your properties are well-maintained, tenants are managed, and rental income is collected efficiently. Property managers can handle day-to-day tasks like tenant screening, rent collection, maintenance requests, and repairs, freeing you up to focus on strategy and expansion.

   Additionally, property managers provide valuable local market insights, enabling you to adjust rent levels, manage vacancies, and maintain a strong tenant base. A skilled property manager can help maximise your rental returns and ensure your properties remain in good condition, preserving their long-term value.

4. **Legal Advisors:** Legal compliance is a critical aspect of property investment. As your portfolio grows, you may face more complex legal challenges, such as negotiating contracts, dealing with landlord-tenant disputes, or handling property acquisitions and sales. Having a reliable legal advisor ensures that your investment activities comply with all local regulations and that you are protected in case of legal disputes.

   Legal experts can also assist with drafting and reviewing lease agreements, ensuring that your interests are protected while minimising the risk of disputes. A proactive legal strategy can prevent costly mistakes and litigation down the line.

How Mentorship and Peer Networks Provide Valuable Insights

In addition to a professional team, mentorship and peer networks can offer valuable insights, support, and guidance as you navigate the complexities of scaling your portfolio.

1. **Mentorship:** A mentor who has experience in real estate investing can provide personalised advice based on their own successes and failures. They can help you avoid common mistakes, identify new opportunities, and offer strategic guidance as you grow your portfolio. A mentor can also help you maintain a long-term perspective, encouraging you to stay patient and focused on your goals during market fluctuations or challenges.

   Finding a mentor in the real estate community, whether through local investment groups, real estate associations, or online platforms, can accelerate your learning and development as an investor. Their experience and connections can be invaluable assets as you expand.

2. **Peer Networks:** Connecting with other real estate investors through peer networks allows for knowledge sharing and collaboration. Peer networks provide a platform to discuss strategies, share market insights, and even collaborate on deals. By learning from others' experiences, you can identify new opportunities and refine your investment approach.

   Joining local real estate investment groups, attending conferences, or participating in online forums are effective ways to build a peer network. These connections can also provide emotional support and motivation, helping you stay resilient during tough times.

Case Studies: How Successful Investors Built Teams to Support Their Growing Portfolios

1. **Case Study 1: Scaling with the Right Professionals** Investor A started with a few residential properties but found it difficult to manage the administrative, financial, and operational tasks as the portfolio expanded. Recognizing the need for a strong support team, they brought on a specialised property accountant, a reliable property manager, and a legal advisor. The accountant helped the investor structure the portfolio for optimal tax efficiency, while the property manager took over day-to-day operations, allowing the investor to focus on acquisitions.
   With this team in place, Investor A was able to double their portfolio within five years, all while maintaining a healthy cash flow and minimising operational stress. The legal advisor ensured that all contracts and agreements were airtight, helping Investor A avoid costly legal issues and disputes with tenants or contractors.
2. **Case Study 2: Leveraging Mentorship and Peer Support** Investor B was a relatively new real estate investor who had acquired a couple of properties but felt uncertain about how to scale further. They joined a local real estate investment group and found a mentor who had successfully built a large portfolio. The mentor provided guidance on securing financing for additional properties and shared strategies for negotiating better deals with lenders.
   Through peer networking, Investor B also connected with other investors who introduced them to off-market opportunities. With the advice and support from their mentor and peers, Investor B was able to grow their portfolio to six properties over the next few years. The connections made through the peer network also helped Investor B identify trusted professionals, including a mortgage broker and property manager, who were instrumental in their continued success.

Scaling a property portfolio from a few properties to a large, diversified portfolio requires careful planning, strategic decision-making, and a long-term vision. Investors must focus on setting achievable goals, structuring their portfolio for sustainable cash flow and capital growth, and leveraging key strategies such as refinancing and proper exit planning to ensure their portfolio continues to thrive.

In this section, we will explore the essential strategies for scaling a property portfolio for long-term success, including setting long-term goals, the role of strategic refinancing, how to structure your portfolio for both growth and cash flow, and the importance of having a clear exit strategy.

Setting Long-Term Goals and Creating a Roadmap for Portfolio Growth

The foundation of any successful scaling strategy is a clear set of long-term goals. Without a defined roadmap, expanding a property portfolio can become chaotic and unmanageable, leading to over-leveraging, cash flow problems, and even financial loss. A well-thought-out plan helps investors maintain focus and consistency, guiding their decision-making as their portfolio grows.

1. **Defining Your Investment Vision:** Begin by identifying what you want to achieve with your property investments. Do you want to create passive income streams, focus on capital growth,

or build a legacy for future generations? Your long-term vision will influence every decision, from the types of properties you acquire to the financing strategies you use.
2. **Setting SMART Goals:** Once your vision is clear, break it down into specific, measurable, achievable, relevant, and time-bound (SMART) goals. For example, a SMART goal could be: "Acquire 10 income-producing properties in five years, generating $100,000 in annual passive income." Each goal should include milestones that help track progress over time.
3. **Creating a Scalable Portfolio Structure:** Your roadmap should account for how you plan to finance and manage additional properties while minimising risk. This might include setting up a trust, company, or partnership structure to protect assets, reduce taxes, and ease portfolio management. Working with a financial advisor or property accountant can help you design the most efficient structure based on your long-term goals.
4. **Adapting to Market Conditions:** Property markets change over time, and your roadmap should include flexibility to adapt. If the market cools or overheats, your ability to shift strategies—whether by holding off on acquisitions or aggressively pursuing opportunities—will contribute to your success in scaling.

The Role of Strategic Refinancing in Scaling Your Portfolio

Strategic refinancing is one of the most powerful tools available to investors looking to scale their property portfolio. By refinancing existing properties, investors can unlock equity to finance new purchases, reduce their interest rates, or extend loan terms to improve cash flow.

1. **Unlocking Equity for Future Acquisitions:** Over time, as property values appreciate and loan balances decrease, properties build equity. Refinancing allows investors to tap into this equity without selling the property. By accessing the equity through a cash-out refinance, investors can use the funds as a down payment on additional properties, continuing to scale the portfolio without needing to save for each new purchase.
2. **Lowering Interest Rates:** In a low-interest-rate environment, refinancing can help lower the cost of borrowing, reducing monthly mortgage payments and improving cash flow. Improved cash flow not only provides additional financial security but also increases the investor's ability to reinvest in new properties.
3. **Debt Consolidation:** As your portfolio grows, you may have multiple loans with different interest rates, lenders, and terms. Refinancing allows you to consolidate these loans into a single, more manageable loan. This simplifies the repayment process, potentially reduces overall interest costs, and can improve your credit profile, making it easier to secure financing for future acquisitions.
4. **Timing Refinancing Strategically:** The key to successful refinancing is timing. Monitoring interest rate trends, property market conditions, and your portfolio's equity position will help determine when to refinance. It's important to work with a mortgage broker or financial advisor to assess whether refinancing will be beneficial for your long-term strategy and to ensure that refinancing costs do not outweigh the potential benefits.

Structuring Your Property Portfolio for Sustainable Cash Flow and Capital Growth

Balancing cash flow and capital growth is essential for long-term success. While capital growth provides the opportunity to build wealth over time, consistent cash flow ensures you have the liquidity needed to manage your portfolio and invest in new opportunities.

1. **Focus on Cash Flow Early:** Early in your portfolio-building journey, focus on acquiring properties with strong cash flow potential. Positive cash flow properties generate income that can cover mortgage payments, property taxes, and maintenance costs while providing surplus funds for reinvestment.
2. **Gradual Shift Toward Capital Growth:** As your portfolio stabilises and you generate consistent cash flow, you can begin to shift your focus toward capital growth properties. These properties may have lower initial yields but are located in areas with strong growth potential, such as those experiencing urban renewal, population growth, or significant infrastructure development. Over time, these properties can appreciate significantly, boosting your overall net worth.
3. **Portfolio Diversification:** A diversified portfolio helps manage risk and improve long-term stability. Diversification can involve investing in different property types (e.g., residential, commercial, multi-family) or in different geographic locations. This strategy helps protect your portfolio from regional market downturns or specific sector weaknesses.
4. **Monitoring and Adjusting the Portfolio:** As your portfolio grows, regularly review your cash flow and capital growth performance. Properties that consistently underperform in terms of cash flow or growth may need to be sold or refinanced to maintain overall portfolio health. An adaptable, balanced approach ensures your portfolio remains resilient in different market conditions.

Exit Strategies: Planning for Selling Properties, Passing Them On, or Creating a Legacy

Having an exit strategy is just as important as planning for growth. Whether you plan to sell properties, pass them on to heirs, or create a lasting legacy, a clear exit strategy will ensure your portfolio serves your long-term financial and personal goals.

1. **Selling Properties:** At some point, you may want to sell certain properties to cash in on capital gains, reduce your overall risk, or shift your portfolio focus. When planning a sale, consider market conditions, tax implications, and the timing of the sale to maximise profits. Working with a tax advisor can help minimise capital gains taxes and ensure a smooth transaction.
2. **Passing Properties to Heirs:** For investors focused on creating generational wealth, planning how to pass properties to heirs is essential. Estate planning tools such as trusts, wills, and life insurance can help ensure a smooth transfer of assets while minimising tax burdens. Early planning also allows for conversations with heirs about their roles in managing or selling properties in the future.
3. **Creating a Legacy:** If your goal is to leave a legacy beyond financial wealth, you may consider setting up charitable foundations or other structures that benefit causes you care about. Real estate holdings can be leveraged to provide ongoing funding for philanthropic efforts while still generating income for your family.
4. **Planning for Market Downturns and Personal Circumstances:** Your exit strategy should account for the possibility of market downturns or personal changes, such as retirement or health issues. Ensure you have the liquidity to manage these challenges without being forced into selling properties at inopportune times. This could involve holding a portion of your portfolio in highly liquid assets or keeping an emergency fund to cover unexpected costs.

Expanding a property portfolio offers significant opportunities for wealth creation, but it also comes with challenges. As investors scale beyond their initial properties, common mistakes can derail long-term success. Understanding the potential pitfalls and learning how to avoid them can be the difference between building a thriving portfolio and experiencing financial setbacks. In this section, we'll explore the most common mistakes investors make when scaling, strategies for avoiding over-leveraging, managing debt, recognizing the dangers of over-expansion, and learning from real-life case studies.

The Most Common Mistakes Property Investors Make When Expanding Their Portfolios

Many investors, eager to grow their portfolios, rush into acquisitions without fully considering the financial, operational, and market complexities. Below are some of the most frequent errors that property investors encounter when trying to scale:

1. **Failing to Diversify:** One of the key principles in investing is diversification. Many investors fall into the trap of acquiring similar types of properties in the same geographic area, leaving themselves vulnerable to market fluctuations. If a local economy suffers or property values drop in a specific area, an undiversified portfolio can lead to severe financial strain.
2. **Underestimating Operating Costs:** As portfolios grow, so do operating costs such as maintenance, taxes, and property management fees. Some investors fail to account for these additional expenses, leading to reduced profitability and potential cash flow issues. It's essential to have an accurate budget that includes all recurring and potential costs associated with managing multiple properties.
3. **Poor Cash Flow Management:** Cash flow is the lifeblood of property investing. A common mistake is focusing too much on capital growth and ignoring the importance of maintaining positive cash flow. Even if a property appreciates in value, poor cash flow management can lead to liquidity issues, making it difficult to cover monthly expenses or finance future acquisitions.
4. **Inadequate Due Diligence:** Investors sometimes rush into new purchases without conducting the necessary due diligence, especially when opportunities seem too good to pass up. Skimping on property inspections, failing to thoroughly research local markets, or not reviewing financials in detail can lead to costly mistakes and underperforming assets.
5. **Emotional Decision-Making:** Letting emotions drive investment decisions can be particularly dangerous when scaling. Investors may fall in love with a particular property or feel pressured to expand quickly, leading to impulsive choices that don't align with their long-term strategy. Staying data-driven and rational is critical to avoid expensive missteps.

How to Avoid Over-Leveraging and Managing Debt Effectively

One of the most dangerous pitfalls when scaling a property portfolio is over-leveraging, or taking on too much debt relative to your equity. While leverage can magnify returns, it can also amplify losses and put investors at significant financial risk if not managed carefully.

1. **Know Your Debt Limits:** Lenders may be willing to provide high levels of financing, but that doesn't mean you should take on more debt than you can comfortably manage. It's important to understand your own risk tolerance and financial limits. Avoid pushing your

loan-to-value (LTV) ratio to the maximum, as this leaves little room for market fluctuations or unexpected expenses.
2. **Maintain Strong Cash Flow:** Positive cash flow is critical for managing debt. Ensure that the rental income from your properties comfortably covers mortgage payments, maintenance costs, and other expenses. If your properties are generating solid cash flow, you'll be in a better position to manage debt and expand your portfolio sustainably.
3. **Build a Financial Cushion:** Always keep a cash reserve or emergency fund in place to cover unexpected costs, vacancies, or market downturns. This financial buffer provides peace of mind and prevents you from falling into financial difficulties if rental income drops or expenses rise temporarily.
4. **Reevaluate Financing Options Regularly:** As you scale, it's important to review your financing options periodically. This includes refinancing properties to access better interest rates, consolidating loans, or adjusting loan terms to improve cash flow. Building a relationship with a knowledgeable mortgage broker or lender can help you stay on top of financing opportunities as your portfolio grows.

Understanding the Dangers of Over-Expansion and Taking on Too Many Properties Too Quickly

While rapid growth might seem appealing, scaling too fast can lead to serious financial and operational challenges. Investors who take on too many properties in a short period often struggle with the complexities of managing a large portfolio, increased risk exposure, and mounting debt.

1. **Operational Overload:** Managing multiple properties is time-consuming and requires significant attention to detail. Over-expansion can lead to an operational overload where the investor is unable to keep up with property management tasks, tenant issues, or necessary maintenance. As a result, properties may underperform, and tenant relationships can suffer.
2. **Increased Vacancy Risk:** Acquiring multiple properties in a short period can increase the likelihood of vacancy issues if market conditions shift or if the properties are not properly marketed. Too many vacant units at once can result in severe cash flow problems, making it difficult to cover mortgage payments and other expenses.
3. **Decreased Investment Quality:** Expanding too fast often means investors are less discerning about the properties they purchase. The pressure to scale can lead to buying properties in less desirable areas, overpaying, or skipping thorough due diligence. As a result, the portfolio may grow, but the quality and performance of the properties may decline.
4. **Debt and Financing Pressures:** Rapid expansion typically requires significant debt. If market conditions change, interest rates rise, or property values drop, over-leveraged investors may find themselves unable to meet debt obligations. This can lead to forced property sales or foreclosure, damaging the portfolio's long-term viability.

Case Studies: Investors Who Scaled Too Fast and the Lessons Learned from Their Experiences

The following case studies highlight real-world examples of investors who expanded their portfolios too quickly and the important lessons that can be gleaned from their experiences.

Case Study 1: The Over-Leveraged Investor An investor, eager to grow their portfolio rapidly, purchased five properties in the span of two years using high-leverage loans. While the properties appreciated initially, a market downturn led to a drop in rental income and higher vacancy rates. With no cash reserves and high mortgage payments, the investor was unable to cover expenses, leading to the sale of multiple properties at a loss.

Lesson Learned: The key takeaway from this example is the importance of maintaining liquidity and not over-leveraging. The investor's mistake was relying too heavily on debt and failing to account for market downturns or unexpected vacancies.

Case Study 2: The Operational Overload Another investor rapidly expanded from managing two properties to managing ten within a year. With no property management experience, they struggled to keep up with tenant requests, maintenance issues, and rental marketing. As a result, the investor experienced high tenant turnover, increased vacancy rates, and falling rental income.

Lesson Learned: Scaling too quickly can lead to operational challenges that negatively impact a portfolio's performance. Proper planning and potentially hiring professional property managers can help mitigate the risks associated with rapid growth.

Final Thoughts and Key Takeaways

Throughout this book, we've explored the journey of property investment—starting from the very first purchase to the growth and management of a diverse portfolio. Along the way, we've delved into the intricacies of financing, property market dynamics, strategic scaling, and effective property management. Each chapter has provided insights into the challenges faced, the lessons learned, and the strategies that shaped the success of an expanding portfolio.

Reflecting on this journey, it becomes clear that property investment is much more than simply buying and selling properties. It's a long-term endeavour that requires careful planning, patience, and the ability to adapt to changing market conditions. As an investor, I've had to navigate hurdles such as financing limitations, fluctuating property values, and tenant management issues. Each challenge brought valuable lessons that helped refine my approach and build resilience. At the same time, the successes—like identifying high-growth areas, securing below-market-value deals, and seeing properties appreciate—reinforced the importance of due diligence and strategic decision-making.

The purpose of this final section is to highlight the most significant takeaways from the journey discussed in this book. Whether you're a new investor or looking to scale your portfolio, these key lessons and insights will provide you with practical guidance for your own property investment path. From understanding market trends to making data-driven decisions and avoiding common pitfalls, these principles are essential for achieving long-term financial growth and security in property investing.

Starting with a Solid Foundation

The first property investment is often the most significant, as it sets the stage for the entire portfolio's future growth. In my case, the initial purchase shaped my approach to subsequent investments and taught me the value of due diligence. Understanding the fundamentals—such as securing financing, thoroughly researching the market, and assessing a property's growth potential—became critical lessons that influenced every investment afterward.

A key takeaway from that first purchase was the importance of thorough market research. By analysing local property trends, rental demand, and growth projections, I was able to make an informed decision that provided both immediate rental income and long-term capital growth. Additionally, navigating the financing process as a first-time buyer highlighted the importance of securing favourable loan terms and building strong relationships with lenders. This laid a financial foundation that made it easier to fund future purchases.

Building Momentum

Once the first investment was secured, momentum began to build. Each additional property became a stepping stone to further expansion, creating equity that could be leveraged to finance the next investment. This compounding effect is one of the most powerful aspects of property investment. The first few properties not only establish your financial base but also give you valuable experience that can refine your strategy.

Mistakes made early on, such as underestimating renovation costs or overlooking important aspects of property management, also became valuable learning opportunities. These experiences helped sharpen my decision-making and prepared me for more complex investments down the line. Early successes reinforced the importance of buying below market value and focusing on high-growth areas, which became central to my overall strategy.

In summary, the lessons from those early investments were critical in building a strong foundation for long-term success. The first property taught me the importance of research, financing strategies, and attention to detail, while the next few properties helped solidify a repeatable strategy that could scale over time. These early steps, both the challenges and achievements, laid the groundwork for future portfolio growth.

Research and Market Knowledge

One of the most crucial lessons I've learned in property investment is the importance of being well-informed. Thorough research and a deep understanding of the market are what separate successful investments from costly mistakes. In every purchase I've made, researching market trends, local demographics, and the economic outlook has been the cornerstone of informed decision-making. Whether identifying the right suburb, understanding rental demand, or predicting growth potential, market knowledge plays a central role in achieving long-term success.

For example, timing the market correctly was a significant factor in several of my purchases. By understanding the property cycle—boom, slump, recovery, and stagnation—I was able to identify high-potential properties in growth phases while avoiding overpriced markets. This level of due diligence extended to every aspect of the property investment process, from assessing the structural integrity of buildings to analysing rental yields and vacancy rates in the target area. Making decisions based on data, rather than guesswork, allowed me to take calculated risks and secure properties that aligned with both my short-term cash flow needs and long-term capital growth goals.

Data-Driven Approach

Informed decision-making also means taking a data-driven approach to property investment. Tracking market trends and analysing key metrics such as rental yield, cash flow, and property appreciation rates provided me with a clear financial picture of each potential investment. This process helped me identify whether a property would generate positive cash flow and meet my return on investment goals. Leveraging property management software, online market reports, and expert insights allowed me to make more accurate projections and avoid properties that didn't align with my financial objectives.

Another critical aspect of data-driven decision-making is the ability to remain objective. Emotional attachment to a property or investment idea can cloud judgement and lead to poor choices. For instance, it's easy to fall in love with a property based on personal preferences, such as its design or location, rather than focusing on whether it makes sense as an investment. Throughout my journey, I've learned to separate personal feelings from business decisions, ensuring that each purchase is based on solid data rather than subjective factors.

By staying objective and relying on numbers, I've been able to avoid the common pitfalls of emotional decision-making. Whether it was walking away from a property that didn't meet my financial criteria or making a bold move on a seemingly undervalued market, this approach has paid off time and again. Additionally, staying informed through continuous research, tracking market conditions, and consulting with industry experts allowed me to make smarter, more confident decisions.

In summary, informed decision-making is the backbone of any successful property investment strategy. By prioritising thorough research, maintaining a data-driven approach, and avoiding emotional decisions, I was able to build a sustainable portfolio that has weathered market fluctuations and continued to grow. This disciplined approach not only minimised risk but also maximised returns, allowing me to expand my portfolio with confidence.

Setting Clear, Measurable Goals

In property investment, long-term success begins with setting clear and measurable goals. Whether you aim to achieve financial independence, build a legacy, or create a passive income stream, having specific targets in place gives you direction and purpose. Early on, I learned the importance of defining both short-term and long-term objectives, as they shaped every investment decision I made. For example, in the short term, my goal was to build a portfolio that generated positive cash flow and covered all my property-related expenses. In the long term, however, my focus shifted to building equity and creating wealth through capital growth, allowing me to secure financial freedom.

Aligning investment strategies with your personal financial goals is critical for sustainable growth. For instance, if your priority is generating immediate income, you may focus on high-yield properties that produce consistent rental returns. On the other hand, if long-term wealth accumulation is the goal, properties in high-growth areas that appreciate over time become more attractive, even if they produce less cash flow initially. These goals help define the types of properties to invest in, the locations to target, and the financing methods to use. Having these goals in place gave me the clarity and motivation to stay focused, adapt to market changes, and steadily work toward my financial objectives.

Regularly revisiting and adjusting these goals based on current financial situations, market trends, and future aspirations is equally essential. As I grew more experienced, my goals evolved from simply acquiring more properties to optimising my existing portfolio for better returns and reducing risk. This flexibility allowed me to respond to market shifts and refine my strategy as my portfolio expanded.

Strategic Scaling and Diversification

Strategic scaling is key to building a long-term, sustainable property portfolio. Expanding the portfolio thoughtfully involves balancing growth, cash flow, and risk, rather than acquiring properties haphazardly. I quickly realised that scaling too fast, without careful planning, could lead to liquidity issues and increased financial strain. To avoid this, I paced my expansion, making sure each new property complimented my overall investment strategy.

One of the key strategies I employed in scaling was using equity from existing properties. Leveraging the increased value of earlier investments allowed me to finance new purchases without tying up all of my cash reserves. This process of refinancing properties to unlock equity became a powerful tool for accelerating portfolio growth. However, I made sure to balance this with maintaining adequate cash flow, ensuring that each property was positively geared and that I had enough liquidity to cover unforeseen expenses. For long-term success, it's crucial to strike a balance between growth and financial stability, preventing over-leveraging while still using the resources at your disposal to scale.

Diversification also played an important role in mitigating risk as my portfolio grew. While my initial investments were primarily in residential properties, I diversified by exploring different property types and regions. By acquiring a mix of high-yield rental properties, long-term capital growth investments, and even commercial assets, I was able to spread risk across different markets. This strategy helped protect my portfolio from localised market downturns while allowing me to take advantage of varied opportunities in different sectors.

For example, when residential rental yields were lower in one region, my commercial property in another area continued to provide stable cash flow. Geographic diversification also allowed me to balance exposure to different market conditions, as not all regions experience growth or decline at the same time. By diversifying my portfolio, I ensured that no single market or property type dictated the overall success of my investments.

Lastly, strategic portfolio restructuring became a key element of my long-term plan. As some properties appreciated in value, I sold off underperforming or non-strategic assets to fund better opportunities. This approach allowed me to maximise returns while maintaining a well-balanced portfolio that aligned with my long-term goals. Selling a few properties to pay down debt on others helped create a stronger, more resilient portfolio with a healthier financial structure.

In conclusion, long-term planning and strategy are critical components of property investment success. By setting clear, measurable goals and pursuing a balanced, strategic approach to scaling and diversification, I was able to build a portfolio that not only grew over time but also provided consistent returns and minimised risk. This long-term vision allowed me to weather market fluctuations and steadily increase my wealth, ensuring lasting financial security.

Mitigating Risks

In property investment, effective risk management is essential for long-term success. The property market can be unpredictable, and managing property-related risks such as market volatility, tenant issues, and unexpected maintenance costs is crucial for preserving your investments. One of the most important strategies I learned early on was maintaining a financial buffer. Setting aside reserves for emergencies—whether it's a sudden repair, a vacancy, or a market downturn—ensures that you can cover unexpected expenses without jeopardising your cash flow.

Insurance is another vital component of risk management. From landlord insurance to coverage for natural disasters, having the right policies in place protects your assets from unforeseen events. Adequate insurance gives peace of mind, knowing that even in the event of a disaster or legal issue, your investment remains safeguarded.

Conservative financing is another way to mitigate risk. While leveraging equity can accelerate growth, it's important not to overextend financially. Maintaining a low loan-to-value ratio and ensuring positive cash flow for each property reduces financial strain, particularly during economic downturns or periods of higher interest rates. By staying conservative with financing, I minimise the risk of being over-leveraged, allowing me to weather market fluctuations without falling into financial hardship.

Learning from Challenges

Like any venture, property investment is not without its challenges. Over the years, I encountered several obstacles, from financing hurdles to legal disputes. In each case, the key to overcoming these challenges was resilience and adaptability. For instance, when I faced difficulties securing financing for additional properties, I explored alternative lending options and strengthened relationships with lenders. By building a strong financial profile and demonstrating a history of successful investments, I was able to navigate these hurdles and continue expanding my portfolio.

Legal issues, whether related to tenant disputes or regulatory changes, were another source of unexpected challenges. Staying informed about local laws and working with experienced legal professionals helped me navigate these issues while avoiding costly mistakes. Learning to be proactive, rather than reactive, in addressing potential problems was a lesson I took to heart, ensuring that I was always prepared for the unexpected.

Resilience in property investment often comes from the ability to adapt. The market is always changing, and smart investors know how to pivot when necessary. Whether it was adjusting my investment strategy during a market downturn or finding creative ways to manage properties more efficiently, being flexible allowed me to build a stronger, more resilient portfolio.

Building Resilience Through Smart Financial Planning

In the end, risk management is about being prepared and planning for the worst while expecting the best. Smart financial planning, from maintaining adequate reserves to ensuring your properties are well-insured, builds resilience into your portfolio. By learning from past challenges and being proactive in mitigating risks, I was able to maintain long-term stability and safeguard my investments, even in uncertain times.

These experiences taught me that risk is inevitable in property investment, but with the right strategies and mindset, it can be effectively managed and minimised.

Leveraging Equity and Financing

One of the most powerful strategies for scaling a property portfolio is leveraging equity. As your properties appreciate in value, you can tap into that increased equity to fund additional investments. Strategic refinancing allows you to unlock the equity tied up in your properties, using it as a down payment for new acquisitions. This approach enables continuous portfolio growth without needing to save large sums of cash for each purchase.

Smart loan structuring is key to maximising the benefits of refinancing. When expanding a portfolio, it's important to work with lenders who understand your goals and can offer flexible financing solutions. Interest-only loans, for example, can boost cash flow in the short term, allowing you to reinvest profits more aggressively. On the other hand, fixed-rate loans provide stability by protecting you from fluctuations in interest rates over time. Balancing these loan options based on the current market environment and your cash flow needs is essential for long-term growth.

Additionally, ensuring that you maintain a strong financial profile with a solid track record of repayments and healthy cash reserves gives you leverage when negotiating loan terms. The more reliable and profitable your investments, the easier it becomes to secure favourable financing for future deals, thus creating a cycle of sustainable growth.

Recognizing Market Opportunities

As the property market evolves, staying open and adaptable to new opportunities is crucial. Markets fluctuate, and what works well in one region or property type may not always be the best choice as conditions change. The most successful investors continuously monitor market trends and are ready to pivot their strategies when needed. This means being open to exploring new locations, property types (such as commercial or multi-family units), or emerging real estate trends, like eco-friendly housing or short-term rentals.

Timing is everything in property investment. Knowing when to buy, sell, or hold is key to capitalising on market shifts. This requires staying informed about economic conditions, government policies, and local development projects that could influence property values. Investors who are proactive and well-prepared are better positioned to act quickly when market opportunities arise, whether it's a new suburb on the rise or a downturn that presents bargain buying conditions.

Being flexible doesn't mean chasing every new trend—it's about recognizing viable opportunities that align with your investment goals and financial strategy. For instance, expanding into commercial properties may provide higher returns, but it also carries different risks and requires different management expertise. By remaining selective and doing thorough due diligence, you can grow your portfolio in a way that's both sustainable and profitable.

Staying Proactive and Prepared

To stay ahead in property investment, it's vital to maintain a proactive approach. This involves keeping an eye on market data, economic indicators, and broader real estate trends to identify potential opportunities before they become mainstream. Regularly reviewing your portfolio's performance and being willing to adjust your strategy is part of staying proactive. Whether it's restructuring your financing to free up capital, selling underperforming properties, or expanding into a new region, being ready to act when necessary can significantly enhance your portfolio's growth potential.

Networking and staying connected with industry professionals also provide invaluable insights into upcoming market trends. Real estate agents, brokers, and financial advisors often have access to early information about new developments or shifts in buyer and tenant demand. Surrounding yourself with knowledgeable professionals ensures you're always prepared to capitalise on growth opportunities as they arise.

In summary, leveraging equity, staying flexible, and maintaining a proactive mindset are key strategies for sustained portfolio growth. These approaches enable investors to navigate the complexities of the market, continuously expand their holdings, and build long-term financial security through property investment.

Mistakes to Avoid

Even seasoned property investors can fall into common traps if they aren't vigilant. One of the most frequent mistakes is **over-leveraging**—borrowing too much against your properties without sufficient cash flow to cover the increased debt. While leveraging is a powerful tool for growth, excessive borrowing can lead to financial strain, especially if market conditions change unexpectedly. Investors who over-leverage may struggle to meet loan repayments during economic downturns, leading to foreclosures or forced property sales at a loss.

Another pitfall is **under-researching** potential investments. Failing to conduct thorough due diligence—whether it's skipping market analysis, ignoring local development plans, or neglecting property inspections—can result in purchasing properties that underperform or carry hidden issues. For example, investing in a seemingly affordable neighbourhood without understanding its long-term prospects or tenant demand can lead to prolonged vacancies or stagnant property values.

Emotional buying is another common mistake, especially among new investors. Letting personal preferences influence decisions rather than relying on objective data can lead to misguided purchases. Investors might choose a property based on its aesthetic appeal or sentimental value, instead of considering factors like rental yield, location demand, or capital growth potential. Staying focused on the financials and long-term viability of an investment is critical for success.

Ensuring Long-Term Stability

One of the key strategies for avoiding these pitfalls is **resisting the temptation to rush** into decisions or expand your portfolio too quickly. The desire to scale rapidly, particularly after initial success, can lead to poor choices, such as overpaying for properties or failing to diversify investments. It's essential to strike a balance between growth and stability, ensuring that each new investment aligns with your financial goals and risk tolerance. Prioritise quality over quantity, and don't let the fear of missing out (FOMO) drive your decisions.

Additionally, maintaining a strong financial foundation through careful budgeting, adequate reserves, and conservative borrowing helps protect against setbacks. Investors who ensure their portfolio is financially resilient are better positioned to weather market downturns or unexpected challenges.

Case Studies: Lessons from Setbacks

There are many examples of investors who expanded too rapidly and encountered setbacks. For instance, some investors who aggressively leveraged their properties before the 2008 housing market crash were left overextended when property values plummeted and banks tightened lending. Without adequate cash flow or reserves, they struggled to meet their financial obligations, leading to significant losses. These situations highlight the importance of maintaining liquidity and not relying solely on continued property appreciation.

Conversely, many successful investors have recovered from mistakes by **adapting their strategies**. For example, some pivoted by selling underperforming properties, refinancing to lower interest rates, or focusing on improving cash flow rather than capital growth. These experiences emphasise the importance of learning from setbacks, remaining adaptable, and focusing on long-term stability rather than short-term gains.

In summary, avoiding common pitfalls such as over-leveraging, under-researching, and emotional buying is critical for long-term success. Taking a patient, informed, and strategic approach to property investment helps ensure sustainable growth and financial security.

Key Principles for Success

Throughout this journey of property investment, several key principles stand out as essential for long-term success. First and foremost is the importance of research and due diligence. Thoroughly understanding the market, conducting in-depth property analysis, and making data-driven decisions help minimise risk and maximise returns. Leverage has also played a critical role—learning how to use equity and financing effectively to grow a portfolio is vital for scaling investments. Additionally, strategic planning and goal-setting form the foundation for both short-term and long-term success. Knowing your financial goals and aligning them with your investment strategy allows for sustainable growth while managing risks.

Another cornerstone is risk management, ensuring that each investment is carefully balanced with liquidity, reserves, and diversification to safeguard against potential market fluctuations or unexpected expenses. Finally, flexibility and adaptability are key. The property market can shift quickly, and being prepared to pivot strategies or enter new markets is crucial for continued growth.

Mindset for New Investors

For those new to property investment, adopting the right mindset is just as important as mastering technical skills. Persistence is essential—property investing is not an overnight success story, but a long-term journey that requires dedication and patience. Patience allows investors to avoid rash decisions and wait for the right opportunities. Alongside this, continuous learning is a fundamental practice. The property market, financing, and investment strategies are constantly evolving, and staying informed is a competitive advantage.

The journey may seem overwhelming at first, but confidence grows with each successful investment. Every property bought and every strategy executed builds experience and resilience. New investors should embrace the process, knowing that mistakes are part of learning, and each challenge provides valuable lessons. With persistence and a long-term vision, even those just starting can confidently build a profitable and sustainable property portfolio.

Reflecting on the ongoing journey of property investment, it's clear that the path to success is marked by continuous learning, adaptation, and growth. As we've explored throughout this book, the property investment landscape is dynamic and ever-changing, offering both challenges and opportunities. The journey from acquiring your first property to scaling a robust portfolio is both demanding and rewarding. It requires not only strategic planning and financial acumen but also resilience and a willingness to evolve with the market.

As you move forward, remember that **taking action** is crucial. The insights and strategies shared here are just the starting point. Implementing them and making informed decisions will pave the way for your success. **Staying flexible** is equally important—markets will shift, and what works today might not be as effective tomorrow. Adaptability will help you navigate these changes and seize new opportunities as they arise.

Finally, **continuing to refine your strategies** is essential. Regularly reviewing your investments, learning from experiences, and adjusting your approach based on market trends will ensure that you remain competitive and successful. Property investment is a journey without a final destination; it's about striving for growth and improvement continuously.

By embracing these principles—taking decisive action, remaining adaptable, and consistently refining your strategies—you'll be well-positioned to achieve long-term success in property investment. The potential for growth is immense, and with the right mindset and approach, you can turn your investment goals into reality. Keep pushing forward, and may your journey be marked by prosperity and achievement.

www.ingramcontent.com/pod-product-compliance
Lightning Source LLC
Chambersburg PA
CBHW052150220526
45471CB00004B/1608